REPORT

ON THE

EXPLORATIONS

IN

GREAT TIBET AND MONGOLIA,

Made by A——k in 1879-82,

IN

CONNECTION WITH THE TRIGONOMETRICAL BRANCH, SURVEY OF INDIA,

PREPARED BY

J. B. N. HENNESSEY, ESQ., M.A., F.R.S.,

DEPUTY SURVEYOR GENERAL IN CHARGE TRIGONOMETRICAL SURVEYS.

Dehra Dun:

B. V. HUGHES.

1884.

Explorations in Great Tibet and Mongolia by A——k, 1879-82, made in connection with the Trigonometrical Branch, Survey of India.

TABLE OF CONTENTS.

	Page
Summary and Discussion	5
Note on Trade Routes and the Tea Trade	24
Translation from Diary and Notes	30
Table I. Abstract of Latitudes	85
„ II. Heights above Sea Level	91
„ III. Observations of Temperature of the Air	92
„ IV. Population, &c.	103
„ V. Abstract of Table IV	116
Vocabulary	117
Revised Sketch Map of the Explorations	Sheets Nos. 1, 2 & 3
Index to the Revised Map and a Sketch of the Jáugtháng	1 sheet
Plan of Lhása	1 „

NOTE.—The following papers on the Explorations by A——k in Great Tibet and Mongolia were printed only in proof, from time to time, as progress was made with the work. They are now published by order of the Government of India.

14th September, 1884. J. B. N. H.

ERRATA ET ADDENDA.

Summary and Discussion: Article 54: Lines 1 and 2. The statement that the watershed "lay to his left" all the way from Áta Gáng Lá to Shiár Gáng Lá is not quite exact. The distance by route between the limits named is some 250 miles, in which, for about 40 miles from Áta Gáng Lá the *real* watershed lay on the explorer's *right* hand (*i. e.* east), while for the remaining 210 miles it lay to the left (*i. e.* west). Otherwise stated, the particulars are these. Between Áta Gáng Lá and the Pass (lake), which is some 40 miles north of the former, the route lay in a depression or valley, inclined from both ends towards Rahu village; the Nagong Chu ran down the southern portion and a tributary along the northern part of this valley, so that in these 40 miles of his route, A——k had a watershed both to left (west) and right (east): the former and western watershed is however cut through at Rahu village by the Nagong Chu, which here turns westward to the Pomedh country; hence the *right* or eastern watershed is the real drainage ridge along the 40 miles of route in question, and this ridge A——k crossed at the Pass (lake) so that thereafter it lay to his left all the way to Shiár Gáng Lá.

Translation from Diary and Notes: Articles 200 and 207. The former of these articles speaks of the Chiámdo Chu; the latter of the Giáma Nu Chu; and from local information along the route, the articles state *alike* of both these rivers that they "pass by Riu Chiako", which is reported to be the name of a place of pilgrimage in Burma (upper). This *similarity* of statement regarding the two rivers may lead to the conclusion that some *definite* idea as to their southward courses is intended to be conveyed; for instance, that the rivers run on either side of Riu Chiako which is on a narrow belt of land between them. In fact however, nothing definite *is* known or intended, and hence some further explanation as follows is necessary.

Riu Chiako is reported to be a hill in Burma (upper): it is reckoned of great sanctity by the Tibetans, who occasionally visit it on pilgrimage: the journey however is greatly dreaded, especially because of the considerable heat to be endured to the south, and from one cause or another but few Tibetan pilgrims survive to return home. Along A——k's route not more than one per cent. of the people had performed the pilgrimage: these informed him, that Riu Chiako was distant some 3 months' journey along a very rugged path which quadrupeds could not traverse. All the Tibetans the explorer conversed with, including the pilgrims themselves, were ignorant of the very name "Burma," and the only name of which they appeared to retain recollection, was (naturally) that of the place of their pilgrimage—Riu Chiako: to them, their experience of the south was all covered by Riu Chiako; hence in reply to the explorer's enquiries, as to the course southward of the Chiámdo Chu, or of the Giáma Nu Chu, the answer was alike; "it runs to (or towards) Riu Chiako." Beyond this, nothing more definite is known or was intended in articles 200 and 207 of the translation.

In point of derivation, the town or large village of Chiámdo probably furnishes the river Chiámdo with its name. As regards the Giáma Nu Chu or simply Nu Chu, it runs through the Nu Chu Giu country, and in this case perhaps the locality was named after the river. Speaking of the prefix Giáma, A——k translates as, Gia = warm country, ma = downwards, or Giáma as a whole to mean, towards the warm country lower down; which *is* in keeping with the local belief that the Giáma Nu Chu (as well as the Chiámdo Chu) runs to Burma (upper).

The foregoing points having been brought to my notice, I add these remarks now after consultation with A——k.

J. B. N. HENNESSEY.

Inverniel,
DEHRA DUN,
5th December, 1884.

Explorations in Great Tibet and Mongolia, by A——k, 1879-1882 made in connection with the Trigonometrical Branch, Survey of India.

SUMMARY AND DISCUSSION.

THE exploration was designed by General J. T. Walker, C.B., R.E., Surveyor General of India and Superintendent of the Trigonometrical Survey, who dispatched the party from India on their undertaking in April 1878, and, when near the close of his own official career, welcomed its return to this country about the end of 1882: he also shortly after presented a preliminary account of the exploration to the Asiatic Society of Bengal.* The explorer and all his observations having been placed at my disposal by General Walker in view to translating, reducing, compiling and otherwise preparing the work for publication, I now submit the results, under the orders of Colonel G. C. DePrée, Surveyor General of India, in the form of the exhibits stated in the table of contents, together with this summary and discussion of them.

2. Before entering on the notes which follow, it is necessary that I should call attention to a mistake committed in the projection of the original Sketch Map (published January 1884) by which the northern portions of that publication were displaced considerably *west* in longitude, so as to necessitate issue of the *Revised* Sketch Map accompanying. There are thus two editions of the map, *i.e.*,

(I) Sketch Map published January 1884 now *superseded*.

(II) *Revised* Sketch Map now published to take the place of (I).

The mistake committed in the *superseded* map was, that the adopted magnetic variation of $2\frac{1}{2}°$ *east* was erroneously laid off as $2\frac{1}{2}°$ *west*, and it was only in course of writing these notes that this unexpected mistake was discovered. Now, as the exploration under notice extends *north* to an exceptional distance, *i.e.*, to no less than some 750 miles from origin, it will be obvious that the mistake must create a *growing* and *considerable* displacement, chiefly longitudinal, in proceeding northwards, much too large for elimination, without great inconvenience and risk of error, by reckonings made as occasion may require on the superseded map itself: hence the necessity for issuing the present *Revised* Sketch Map†, which while superseding its predecessor differs from it as said almost exclusively in longitude and only along the two branches northward, *i.e.*, from Lhása and Dárchendo; the differences are necessarily *variable* in magnitude. In all other respects, the superseded and revised maps were prepared on the same basis and principle as hereafter described; and it may be now stated once for all, that the "Map" or "Sketch Map" of A——k's explorations hereafter referred to, is always to be understood as the *revised* and not the *superseded* edition.

3. It will be seen from the Index, that the routes followed make up what may be called a triangle, of which the three points are Lhása (lat. 29° 39′, long. 91° 5½′), Chákángnamaga (lat. 37° 4′, long. 96° 30′) and Dárchendo (lat. 30° 8′, long. 102° 14′); and the sides (or flanks) may be generally described as western, eastern and southern, having a branch from Chákángnamaga north-westerly to the town of Sachu or Saitu. The route as actually followed began at Lhása, of which the position was already fixed by previous explorations, and proceeded along the western flank to Chákángnamaga, from whence it was continued to Sachu; retracing his steps to Chákángnamaga, the explorer now came down the eastern flank to Dárchendo, and then travelled along the southern flank with the intention first of crossing into British Assam from Sáma, and, when foiled in this endeavour, of closing on his origin at Lhása; but being hindered also in the latter purpose, he avoided revisiting Lhása and equally secured his object by closing on another place some 47 miles south-east of that town also previously fixed, *i.e.*, Chetáng on the river Sángpo; from thence he continued his traverse along the river for about 68 miles to Khamba-barji; but practically, the great triangle

---

* At the monthly meeting of the Society on 6th December 1882.
† It will be seen that a similar azimuthal rotation appears between Prejevalsky's two exhibits; hence his map in "Mongolia ... translated by E. D. Morgan" agrees sufficiently with the *superseded* issue of A——k's map; while the map of Prejevalsky's work in Petermanns Mitteilungen July 1883, is fairly in accord with the *revised* map of A——k's explorations. I do not mean to imply that the alteration in Prejevalsky's maps is due to mistake; in all probability it is the outcome of improved data.

of his route originates from Lhása and closes at Chetáng. The geographical co-ordinates of these points adopted in the Sketch Map are as follows:—

LHASA.

Latitude $\begin{cases} \text{Observed by Nain Sing in 1874} & \ldots \quad \ldots \quad 29\ 39\ 23 \\ \quad ,, \quad \text{by A——k in 1879, } vide \text{ Table I} & \ldots \quad 39\ 0 \end{cases}$

$$\text{Mean} \quad \ldots \quad 29\ 39\ 12$$

$$\left.\begin{array}{c}\\ \\ \end{array}\right\} \quad . \quad . \quad (\text{i})$$

Longitude, from previous explorations by Nain Sing   ...   91 5 30

CHETANG.

From previous explorations by Nain Sing, lat. 29° 15′ 0″, long. 91° 43′ 25″   . . .   (ii)

the values (i) and (ii) are those on which the great route triangle has been adjusted, as hereafter described.

4. The instrumental equipment consisted of a sextant, of some 9 inches radius, which was used, with the aid of reflections from mercury, for all latitude observations: for *distant* bearings along the route a prismatic compass was employed, a small pocket compass doing duty for minor bearings, as those of tributaries to rivers, ranges of hills and the like: of thermometers there were two of the kind especially graduated for using in boiling water and two others for air temperatures: an aneroid barometer was also provided, but it soon became erroneous and proved useless. The instruments employed were all tested both before departure and on return of the expedition, with satisfactory results. For linear measurement A——k trusted entirely to his own pace or step, which as hereafter shown is convertible into the unit of a foot or any other unit desired; and notwithstanding that in Mongolia he was looked down upon as a particularly inferior individual, because unlike the Mongols he persisted in walking instead of following the universal custom of the country which enjoins riding a horse on all possible occasions, he yet manfully strode along his travels, pleading poverty or otherwise, until at last on his return journey, along the eastern flank of his route, the Láma with whom he had taken service insisted on his riding, if only to promote flight from robbers, especially the mounted bands of the Chiámo-Goloks of whom travellers are in constant dread. Thus compelled, A——k mounted a horse, but here also he proved equal to the occasion, for he at once set to work counting the beast's paces as indicated by his stepping with the right foreleg: in this way he reckoned his distances for nearly 230 miles between Bárong Chaidam (lat. 36° 5′, long. 97° 3′) and Thuden Gomba (lat. 33° 17′, long. 96° 43′), and the results do credit alike to the explorer's ingenuity and to the horse's equability of pace.

5. It is desirable to mention certain details in connection with the observations for latitude, which were made as usual by measuring the altitude (*i.e.* double) of the sun or a star when on the meridian; the procedure more exactly stated being this. Having arrived at a suitable place for observing latitude, A——k's first care was to fix on some prominent distant terrestrial object exactly *south of his station*; this he did during daylight *with his prismatic compass*, so that knowing his (magnetic) meridian he was able to commence measuring the altitude *before* the object culminated and to note the *maximum* altitude with certainty: in fact the preliminary step of finding his meridian was absolutely necessary. Further he *invariably* compared, by eye, the azimuthal direction of the star, when culminating, with that of his meridional object, and he is confident that these two directions never disagreed sensibly: when questioned more exactly, he affirms without hesitation that the difference, if any, could not have exceeded 5° at most, and he has certainly had many years of practice and has taken thousands of bearings, so that he has an intuitive cognition of the north point *at all times* as I have practically ascertained. It will thus be seen, that his procedure in taking latitude observations, indirectly but certainly, also afforded, to some extent, conclusive evidence, that the variation of his compass (by which all his traverse bearings were taken) was never gross in amount nor did it change greatly throughout all his travels.

SUMMARY AND DISCUSSION.

6. As regards the construction of the Sketch Map, the principle of procedure will be understood from the following. Suppose a route (or traverse) beginning at a fixed station L and after passing through stations A, B, . . . K, (at each of which the latitude has been observed) to return and close on L. Then accepting some convenient approximate relation, as 2,000 paces = 1 mile, and adopting as usual for the promotion of accuracy a *larger* scale than that intended for publication, each section between latitude stations should be plotted separately by itself in the ordinary way by bearings and paces: it is these separate sectional plots which have next to be adjusted so as to form the circuit, and this adjustment should be done on another and *sufficiently large* sheet of paper (for the map) to hold *all* the sections. On this map paper draw the ordinary graticule of latitudes and longitudes to the adopted scale; also draw the particular parallels of latitude observed at A, B, . . . K, which may be understood by (a), (b), . . . (k) respectively, and plot L by its known co-ordinates. Now take the sectional plot L A, on which measure with a pair of compasses, in inches, the meridional distance or m and the longitudinal distance or l between L and A: also on the map, measure similarly the meridional distance between the parallels of L and A which call m_p, then the longitudinal distance between these two stations on the map, or l_p, will be found (sufficiently approximately for such work) from

$$l_p = \frac{l}{m} m_p \quad \ldots \ldots \ldots \ldots \ldots \ldots \ldots \ldots \text{(iii)}$$

hence lay off l_p, east or west of the meridian of L, on the parallel (a), and this will fix A on the map. Similarly proceed consecutively with the remaining sections A B, B C, &c., until arrival at K, it being borne in mind that this procedure is most suitable so long as the meridional departure between the two stations (as L and A) is not small; and this may be seen at once by supposing that A and L are on the *same* parallel, when $m_p = 0$ and the method fails. The procedure described may also be briefly stated thus: suppose that θ_a is the line from L indicating the bearing of A; then the position of A, is that point on (a) where θ_a cuts (a): thus the longitude of A depends on equability of pacing, on the accuracy of the needle including its adopted magnetic variation and the correctness of the observed latitude. In the present explorations the magnetic variation of the needle has been assumed constant throughout at $2\frac{1}{2}°$ E. as already stated.*

7. Having determined K on the map, the case now presented differs from the preceding ones, because both L and K are fixed in latitude as well as in longitude; so that, to fit in the sectional plot K L we need only make those points *on that plot* superpose the required positions *on the map*; but this would disregard errors in the position of K, besides that the circuit error would not be exhibited. For the latter purpose, we maintain on the map the required direction by the plot, and on this direction lay off the *map*-distance KL, giving a position (say) L_k instead of L: the difference between these two points is a measure of the circuit error, which may be dispersed right round the traverse if required.

8. Returning now to the Sketch Map under discussion; its skeleton route was adjusted in the manner already explained. The given fixed points were Lhása and Chetáng, as stated in para. 3. With respect to latitudes, observations were taken at 22 stations including Lhása; the value of the latter employed, being that given in (i): also including Dárchendo, where A——k being doubtful of his value from a single observation, the following was adopted instead:—

Dárchendo, from Du Halde's Atlas of China   Latitude.
"Province XI, Se-Chwen" (Jesuit Fathers, 1714) ... 30° 8′ 24″ . . (iv)

Again, Prejevalsky's route, Koko Núr to Di Chu Rab-dun, crosses A——k's traverse at Jún, where the latitude not having been observed by the latter, the value given by the former was adopted, *viz* :—

                                                   Latitude.
Jún   ...   . 36° 16′ 1″† . . (v)

---

* I am aware that Prejevalsky gives the magnetic variation at Di Chu Rab-dun as − 3° 58′·9 or say 4° E. (Mongolia, Vol. II, p. 308): this is too large for the southern portions of A——k's work, and on the whole $2\frac{1}{2}°$ E. adopted as an average appears most suitable. Schlagintweit gives the variation as 2° 48′·0 E. at Darjeeling and as 2° 30′·5 E. at Tonglo in Sikkim (Vol. I, p. 461). A——k's prismatic compass has recently been tested at Darjeeling generally, and its variation found to be about 2° 40′ E.
† *Mongolia*: Lieut.-Col. N. Prejevalsky, translated by E. D. Morgan, with Introduction by Colonel Yule, C.B., 1876. Vol. II, page 308.

EXPLORATIONS BY A——K IN GREAT TIBET AND MONGOLIA.

Lastly, in absence of observation by A——k, the following observed value was taken from previous explorations

		Latitude.	
Árcha Cho by G——M——N	... ...	30° 37′	. . . . . (vi)

Thus, apart from the known points Lhása and Chetáng, the route triangle on the Sketch Map has been adjusted on 21 latitude stations: the circuit test was made for convenience at Árcha Cho, where the point as fixed by the traverse coming round by Dárchendo (from the east) as compared with its position determined from Chetáng (west) was only about 9½ miles *south* in latitude and some 2½ miles *west* in longitude*: these results are highly creditable to A——k's accuracy and skill; the more so when it is remembered, that the entire circuit Lhása to Gobi, thence down to Dárchendo and *viâ* Sáma &c., to Chetáng is full 2,400 miles in length.

9. As regards the branch from the latitude station Sukhai to the town of Sachu; the section to Yembi latitude station was adjusted as already explained, and the average foot-value of pace thus derived was used for the continuation onwards to Sachu of only some 90 miles.

10. The longitudes of the Sketch Map in all cases depend solely on A——k's operations, and as usual are reckoned from Greenwich.

11. The skeleton route having been adjusted as described in the foregoing, the work by A——k may be compared with that by preceding explorers, as follows.

12. First from the map of Prejevalsky's work in the Mitteilungen for July 1883 and that of A——k's explorations, we obtain as follows:—

Point	PREJEVALSKY		A——K		A——K minus PREJEVALSKY	
	Lat.	Long.	Lat.	Long.	Lat.	Long.
	° ′	° ′	° ′	° ′	′	′
Crossing P†	32 12	92 5	32 10	92 12	− 2	+ 7
Jún	36 16	96 39	36 16	96 47	0	+ 8
Hoiduthára	37 19	96 18	37 21	96 27	+ 2	+ 9
Igi Chaidam	37 56	94 56	37 52	94 40	− 4	− 16
Yembi	39 3	94 2	38 58	93 28	− 5	− 34
Sachu(a)	40 8	94 30§	40 12	94 2	+ 4	− 28

. (vii)

There are also two other values for Sachu which may be mentioned here, *viz*:—

SACHU.

	Latitude.	Longitude.
By Herr L. de Loczyn‡	40° 5′	95° ′
„ the Jesuit Fathers (1711) Du Halde's Atlas of China, (b)	40 24	94 41
(c)	40 22	95 37

. . (viii)

Returning to (vii), but little need be said of the latitudes unless to point out that they agree fairly well in all cases, as was to be expected; for this element is readily determined within small limits, and the errors at different places are independent of one another. But as

---

* In the Précis of these explorations, given in the "General Report on the Operations of the Survey of India 1882-83," page 40, article 206, I stated on wrong information that the values in question were 1¼ and 1¾ miles respectively.

† This point is intended to indicate the crossing by the káfila track of the Saung Chu, or Prejevalsky's Ssan-tschu, believed to be common to the two maps.

‡ A member of Count Szechenyi's Mission from China to Tibet, communicated to me by General J. T. Walker C.B., R.E., F.R.S.

§ This value is *not* taken from the Mitteilungen, but from a letter received from General J. T. Walker, C.B., R.E., F.R.S., to whom it was communicated I believe by Herr L. de Loczyn, as the result by Prejevalsky.

(*a*). A——k estimates the height of Sachu above sea level at some 6,000 feet.

(*b*). Taken from "Fourth Sheet of Chinese Tartary" which the Editor remarks "differs widely from the First Sheet of Tibet and seems to be copied with less care."

(*c*). Taken from "The First Sheet included in the map of Tibet" on which the Editor remarks "The country has been exhibited already in the Fourth Sheet of Chinese Tartary, which seems to have been copied from an incorrect draught, or with little care."

SUMMARY AND DISCUSSION.

respects longitudes, the case is widely different: notwithstanding, the agreements are sufficiently satisfactory, and in fact are even good if we consider the limited means available, at least to A——k; and further, that the two explorations have quite independent and widely different origins, one far north and the other far south.

13. Next, following A——k's route from Jún (south-easterly) we arrive at Dárchendo (furthest east) which is the next point for comparison; the latitude adopted is that by the Jesuit Fathers (article 8. iv), but the longitude is practically quite independently fixed by A——k: here we have Gill's map* to compare with, and *all* the values to be contrasted are these:—

DARCHENDO.

	Latitude.	Longitude.	
By A——k, adopting the value of latitude by the Jesuit Fathers (see iv)	30° 8′	102° 14′	
„ Captain Gill*	30 4	102 21	. . (ix)
„ Jesuit Fathers†	30 8	101 49	

here Gill's and A——k's determinations are perfectly independent, yet they agree within only 4 miles of latitude and but 7 miles‡ of longitude, notwithstanding that A——k's values are the outcome of his traverse from Lhása up to Sukhai northwards and down to Dárchendo; in all some 1,440 miles. As to the Jesuit Fathers, their ancient determinations of longitude in Du Halde's Atlas are naturally inconsistent and unreliable to a very large extent.

14. From Dárchendo to Báthang, Gill and A——k followed the same route, and the agreement of their independent delineations, *even in details*, it will be found is very close: at Nagchukha the scale shows no difference whatever: at Báthang, the following are the numerical values comparable.

BATHANG.

	Latitude.	Longitude.	
By A——k	30° 0′	99° 33′	
„ Captain Gill	29 54	99 28	. . . . . . (x)

here the differences are only 6 miles in latitude and but 5 miles in longitude.

15. The next point of comparison is Sáma, where the two sets of perfectly independent numerical values are as follows:—

SAMA.

	Latitude.	Longitude.	
By A——k	28° 7′	97° 12′	
„ Captain Wilcox§	28 2	97 3	. . . . . . (xi)

here again the differences are only some 5 miles in latitude and 9 in longitude.

16. And in addition A——k's work is also checked in circuit as stated in article 8.

17. These verifications sufficiently prove the accuracy of A——k's operations which are excellent of their kind, and are fully equal to what may be expected from the means of surveying at his disposal and the enormous extent of his traverse.

---

* See his route map given in the Journal of the Royal Geographical Society, Vol. XLVIII of 1878.
† See Du Halde's Atlas of China "Province XI, Se-Chwen" (Jesuit Fathers, 1714).
‡ In reality 3 miles should probably be deducted from these 7 miles, leaving only 4 miles of difference, because of initial error in the old value of longitude for India.
§ "Map of the countries lying between the 21¼° and 29½° N. latitude and 90° and 98° E. longitude, shewing the sources of the Irrawadi river and the eastern branches of the Brahmaputra, comprising Assam, Muneepoor, the hilly districts of the Singphos, part of Sham and of the Chinese Provinces of Yunan and Thibet."

EXPLORATIONS BY A——K IN GREAT TIBET AND MONGOLIA.

18. Now following the explorer in his travels I take Lhása as the origin, because previous explorations have already dealt with the country south and west of that city, and proceed to summarize and discuss portions of the detailed account of travels, giving in addition some few items now elicited in course of conversation with A——k.

19. Approaching Lhása from the west along the Daibung road (see plan of Lhása), the view in advance presents Poto La to the left (or north) and Chiákpori to the right (or south) as by far the most prominent objects, raised, especially in the former case, well above the foliage, which is not too plentifully interspersed between, of moderate sized walnut, willow, apricot and other trees. Still further south the Ki Chu river flanks the city running past from east to west in a deep and moderately rapid stream, some 200 feet wide, with banks gradually sloping down to the water's edge; in fact Lhása is situated in the Ki Chu valley, which is here some 4 or 5 miles wide. The two prominent objects mentioned are on hillocks, rising some 300 feet above the Daibung road which passes between them. Chiákpori, of some three stories or floors, stands on the right-hand of the road; it includes a school for instruction in the use of medicines, of such young Dábas as evince predilection for the art, and in addition various medicines themselves are compounded on the premises from drugs imported or otherwise, and prepared, it is said, according to recipes obtained from Hindustan. Poto La further west and to the left presents an enormous pile of lofty buildings, covering a rectangle of about 400 yards in length by some 200 yards in width, surmounted at intervals by five gilded Gebis*, which sparkling in the sunlight present a dazzling and gorgeous spectacle visible for miles around. This celebrated monastery is not only the residence of the Great Lámas (Dá Lámas†) or chief priests of the Buddhists spread over Great Tibet and Mongolia, but it contains the remains of all the Dá Lámas‡ deceased for centuries past. The buildings form one solid block, rising to various heights at different places, representing sometimes so many as seven stories or floors: they contain various images which need not be alluded to here, excepting the monster image to the god Jamba. This monster image is represented as of prodigious dimensions; the figure is internally of clay, and is well gilded externally: it is seated on a platform on the ground floor, and its body, passing successively through the second and third floors, terminates in a jewelled and capped monster head above the latter floor; in all, the figure and platform are said to be 70 or 80 feet high. Now the essential feature in Tibetan worship is the performance of circuits around an image§: this is also recognised in the use of the so-called prayer wheel∥ by which the transcribed prayers are made to circumgyrate: but the circuit may obviously be made in two directions, *i.e.* with the hands of a watch, and this is the rule with far the majority who are known as Nangbas, or contrary to watch hands and this is the condition observed by a small sect of Tibetans called Baimbus. Applying the required process to the case of the monster image of Jamba, it will be seen that the pilgrim is compelled by circumstances to perform three different series of circumambulations on as many floors, at first around the god's legs, next around his chest, and lastly around his head.

20 As to the Dá Láma, never dying yet being successively buried and born¶ anew, he is installed in Poto La so veritable an infant that his mother necessarily accompanies in order to suckle him; but being debarred from the sacred premises of the Poto La on account of her sex, she is lodged in the vicinity at Shyo, and is permitted to visit her son only between the hours of 9 A.M. and 4 P.M. Whatever accomplishments he may acquire, the Dá Láma never needs to exhibit them, for he is taught to be chary of speech, and indeed necessity compels this course, since his worshippers are in thousands, and it is only to those who are wealthy or of high degree that he can afford to address even a brief sentence or two: this is always done in a deep hoarse voice acquired by training, in order to convey the idea that it

---

* Gebis are erected on the roofs of buildings which contain images for worship, and outwardly serve to indicate the presence of the latter. A Gebi is shaped like a square tent with a single pole, and in section the sloping sides first curve gracefully inwards and then widen towards the base, which varies in length up to some 30 feet, the corners of the square being ornamented each with the figure of a tiger. The frame for a Gebi is made of wood which is covered with metal plates and these are coated with gold: each structure is surmounted by a golden kalas.

† Dá Láma (Chinese) or Kiámkun-Ringboche (Tibetan): the proper name of the present incumbent is Thuden Giamcho.

‡ These are buried in coffins within the buildings of Poto La, and the sites are marked by structures called Kutungs: the holiness of a Dá Láma is estimated in proportion to the shrinkage of his body after death.

§ Not peculiar to Tibet only: such circumambulation is also required in parts of Hindustan, and in the case of the shrine at Kalinjar Fort (Bundelkhand), the pilgrim is compelled to perform circumrotation somehow, for he is obliged to go round pillars standing in water which is deep.

∥ Or Khorlo or Mani or Thugje Chemo.

¶ He may be born anywhere: the distant villages of Gada (S.W. of Dárchendo) and Lithang have each produced a Dá Láma. The spirit of the deceased Dá Láma is supposed to transmigrate into his baby successor and hence the former is said never to die.

SUMMARY AND DISCUSSION.

emanates from maturity and wisdom. Seated cross-legged on a platform some 6 feet high, he is dressed to be worshipped in the usual colors of the priesthood, *i.e.*, red and yellow, and with bare arms, as required of all Buddhist priests, and holds a rod from the end of which hang strips of silk, white, red, yellow, green and blue. The pilgrim coming in at the entrance door, advances with folded hands as if in prayer, and resting his head against the edge of the platform above him, *mentally and hastily repeats the petitions he would have granted*. These unuttered prayers the Dá Láma is understood to comprehend intuitively; he touches the pilgrim's head with the bunch of silk in token of his blessing, and the worshipper is hurried out at the exit door by attendants, only too happy if he has passed say half a minute in the vicinity of the great priest.* This is the common procedure. Persons of rank or substance are permitted to mount the platform and to perform obeisance there, receiving the required blessing by actual touch of the Dá Láma's hands; subsequently such worshipper may be allowed a seat below the platform where a few hoarse utterances of enquiry may be addressed to him by the Dá Láma, and he may also be given some food.

21. Passing onwards along the Daibung road and on approaching the Yutok Jampa, the traveller sees the two monasteries†, Chomo Ling and Tangia Ling, on his left, and on his right the residence of the two Chinese Ambáns. Before him lies the town of Lhása, and even here the dwelling houses are interspersed with religious edifices: of the latter, the most prominent on the right is the handsome temple of Jhio‡ glittering with four Gebis, while to the left is Giáng Bunmoche surmounted by its gilded spire, crescent and globe, and still further north, Rámoche, a temple capped by a single glistening Gebi. Between these objects and almost in contact with them, lies the lay city of Lhása, composed of houses two or three stories high, touching one another and crowded everywhere by Tibetans (Bodpas and Khampas far in the majority), Chinese, Nepalese, Kashmiris (including a few Mahomedans from Hindustan, chiefly from Patna) and Mongolians. Of all these nationalities, the Tibetans, or natives of the country, alone have their women with them, excepting a few instances of travelling Mongolians who may be accompanied by their wives between the arrivals and departures of káfilas. This part of Lhása, or the city proper, covers an area of less than half a square mile. The houses are built two or three stories high and mostly in blocks, around a quadrangle which is open above and is entered by a side doorway: as said, they touch one another and are crowded with occupants who live peaceably in contiguous dwellings, differences of race and customs notwithstanding: the roofs are all covered in with earth, and this is a sufficient protection against the small rainfall which comes down mostly in July and August. The city at all times contains a large number of traders with goods from various directions including Hindustan: the article most largely imported is tea, which is brought almost exclusively from China, and is always made up in the form of bricks: manufactures in Lhása itself are few and only small in amount, the curing of skins being about the most important: there is also a fragrant slow-match, called Poi, made here solely by the Dábas or priests: it emits a perfume in burning and is in common use by rich and poor alike. The water for the city is brought down from the north in two canals (see plan of Lhása) which however in their progress through the city are subdivided into many streamlets: these rills feed several shallow wells for the use of the people and eventually discharge their surplus to the south at Yutok Jampa, where, A——k adds with emphasis, the water is no longer nice.

22. Polyandrism still prevails, and though greatly decreased in Lhása (and other *cities*), it yet gives rise to a large unmarried surplus of Tibetan women, who are taken as concubines by the men of all the other nationalities, whether residents or even passing travellers§. The outcome of this order of things is, that for the time at least, practically (nearly) all men are Tibetans: they eat and drink in common, meeting in Sákhángs (hotels) or in one anothers' houses; there are about 12 Sákhángs in Lhása, and their number is on the increase; they were first introduced into the city by the Chinese, and are now so generally used, that some

---

* Every pilgrim is bound to present as an offering a piece of cloth, called Khátág, specially prepared for the purpose either of silk or of the bark of trees, varying in size from a few inches to something like a yard square. There are of course no objections to his presenting any amount of offerings in any other shape, the precious metals being considered a convenient form.

† It may be noted that nunneries or Áni Gombas, are not unknown though little seen or heard of because they are always placed in secluded localities: there is an Áni Gomba some four miles north of Lhása for the daughters of gentle folk; other nunneries open to all, are dotted widely apart all over Tibet, but there are none in Mongolia.

‡ This temple is considered of the highest order of sanctity, so much so that the primary object of the majority of pilgrims is to circumambulate Jhio, which is moreover accessible at all times to rich and poor alike.

§ The illegitimate children thus begotten, if sons, are commonly admitted into the priesthood which excludes none but the sons of butchers, blacksmiths and murderers. The descendant of a Chinaman by a Tibetan woman is called a Koko.

of them dine a couple of hundred people at one time. Thus it will be seen the Tibetans, nationalized and proper, in Lhása, form one large society and are uncommonly social and jovial: they drink a fermented liquor; in fact from the baby upwards one and all drink but are never, or very rarely indeed, drunk; nor are the priesthood exceptions, subject only to the condition that they may not drink within a Gomba, at least not openly. The social gatherings are enlivened by musical performances on the flute and a kind of guitar with bell accompaniment; to this the men and women combined dance or keep time, standing in rows on planks which act as sounding boards, and stamping in unison, now in quick now in slow measure: it is very pleasant to hear says A——k. On great occasions the Áche Lhámo are called in and the audience entertained with a theatrical performance. Finally in the summer months, when the air is mellow and the evenings lengthen, the people picnic under the trees the whole day long.

23. Notwithstanding their social tendencies, the citizens manage to pick up a comfortable living, chiefly by trade, and besides to observe the requirements which residence in the holy city imposes. Lhása, it will be seen by the plan, is encircled by a road; this is broad and well made and defines the limits within which all those must reside who wish to make *sure* of a happy state hereafter. This road is called the Ling Khor; within its circuit no blood may be shed, and so the butchers and slaughter-houses are placed without. Now the day is recognized as begun, when a loud report, as if from a cannon, issues from the vicinity of the Ambán's residence: this happens about 4 A.M. and also at 9 or 10 P.M. After the morning report, the people are to be seen in dense crowds on the Ling Khor, *all moving in one and the same direction*, and with the hands of a watch as laid down by their religion. A similar circuit is made by the devout in the evening, to say nothing of smaller circuits around Jhio (called Bár Khor) and other shrines: at least this is imperative on common folk: as to the great and wealthy, they urge that their presence would only interfere with the piety of the people, so they engage substitutes, who however are rigorously required to circumambulate for their masters. But whether done in person or by proxy, a careful reckoning is kept of the number of circuits performed; and these in occasional cases of excessive devotion are even executed by the method of successive prostrations full length on the road, each prostration beginning where the preceding one ended, called Kiáng Khor.

24. Referring here, as throughout these remarks, only to the lines of exploration under notice, the Dá Láma in his secular functions governs to Gárthok on the east and up to the Maurus or Di Chu river on the north. Omitting minor officers, he is aided by his Gialbu or Prime Minister and a council of eight, lately increased to nine; of the latter four are Dábas who wait on him in Poto La and of the five remaining, four are laymen who are helped and also looked after by the 5th, who is a Dába. There are also two Ambáns or officials from China, who are reckoned of *equal* authority, accompanied by their indispensable and important secretary called Jagpoche; as the latter writes all the dispatches to his country, his power for good or evil is reckoned as not to be overvalued: these Ambáns were originally established in Lhása with the professed object of protecting the Dá Láma, who however it is said now finds their presence embarrassing and of a nature that he could dispense with: the province they watch over, extends north to the Maurus river and Niamcho district, and eastward at least to Dárchendo: north of the Maurus-Niamcho boundary, the presiding Ambáns are those residing at Siling, or Sinning, a large Chinese town some 60 miles east of the Koko-Núr. Besides these functionaries there is an officer of the rank of Captain from Nepal: his importance however is evidently only secondary in degree, and in fact the distinction of riding in a pálki (palanquin) is an honor enjoyed only by the Dá Láma, his Gialbu and the two Ambáns; nor is it permitted to these four high potentates to travel by any other means whatever.

25. As regards trade routes to Lhása across the lines of explorations under notice, there are two from Dárchendo and one from Siling. Of those from Dárchendo, the southern is called the Junglam (or official road) and is continued beyond Lhása westward some 340 miles to Dingri: it is a made road with rough bridges and is kept in good repair, being the main line of communication between Lhása and China and the line along which the Ambáns, as well as the Chinese posts travel; it runs from Dárchendo, *via* Gárthok, Chiámdo, Lho Jong and Giámda to Lhása (and onwards as said to Dingri). The other route is called Jánglam (or northern road) and runs from Dárchendo *via* Kánzego, Kegudo, through the Hor country to Chomora (lake) and down to Lhása. The third route is to Siling and proceeds from Lhása *via* Chomora (lake), Giáro, and crossing the Dángla-homa (or Dángla *lower*) through Di Chu Rab-dun and Jún along the Koko-Núr to Siling. There is but little

SUMMARY AND DISCUSSION.

traffic between Jún and Sachu and none whatever between Bárong Chaidam and Niamcho; the latter section runs in the vicinity of the robber tribes of Chiámo Golok and Bánákhásum, and in fact it is so rarely used by travellers that the track of their footsteps can be detected only by a few expert Mongolian guides.

26. Returning to the explorer, after an unavoidably prolonged residence at Lhása he at last started, with his party of six, northwards, in company of a Káfila, which consisted of about 100 individuals. The majority of these were Mongolians, who in a few instances were accompanied by their wives; the remainder were Tibetans (or Bodpas). The Mongolians were all mounted without exception, besides that each person led a horse laden with his property: in fact Mongolians of either sex, with the command of numerous horses in their own country, are so accustomed to riding that they wonder and laugh at pedestrians: even their shepherds ride around their flocks, and in a word no Mongolian will walk on any occasion when he can contrive to ride. The Tibetans of the Káfila mostly walked, leading their laden horses. All were armed with spear, matchlock and sword, a custom so universal in Tibet as well as Mongolia that even the monasteries have adopted it of recent years. In the present case, the necessity for weapons was all the greater that Káfilas are special objects of plunder to the bands of mounted robbers who roam over large tracts of the country and appear suddenly when least expected: hence it comes about that the dominant thought which governs all procedure in a Káfila is, how to escape being plundered. To this end the present assemblage of travellers proceeded cautiously and with no needless disturbance, being preceded and followed at some 2 or 3 miles by a couple of horsemen from their party, to give warning of approaching danger; otherwise they exactly followed the advice of their Mongolian guides, to whom experience had brought much wariness as well as considerable skill in the detection and recognition of foot-prints on the ground.

27. Ordinarily, camp was struck about sunrise and the travellers proceeded on their journey, not neglecting to keep *close* order and when necessary waiting for stragglers*. A brief halt was made for tea at 10 A.M., after which the march was continued to between 2 and 4 P.M., when camp was formed for the night, the Mongolians and Tibetans occupying either flank with the horses between them; the forelegs of the latter were also generally hobbled with ironhinged fetters, rendering locomotion for the time impossible. While some set up tents, others collected the dung of beasts, generally plentiful and the sole fuel† procurable, or mixed a hasty dish of *sattu* (flour of parched corn) as a preliminary to the chief meal of the day: as to fodder, grass was always abundant and the horses fed within the limits of their tethers. In point of food, tea was prepared by thoroughly boiling powdered brick tea and adding to the strained decoction, butter‡ and salt; the tea now ready was served in small cups, chiefly wooden, one of which every individual carried day and night on his person. Sattu was consumed in the form of a paste made with water or tea. As to the principal meal of dinner, it consisted of flesh boiled in water and eaten by itself without bread, in fact flour is generally too scarce to provide bread, or to be regarded as anything but a luxury: the soup was thickened with a few pinches of flour and plenty of *Chúra* § which is abundant all over the country and is in daily use by rich and poor alike: there were no vegetables of any kind, excepting a few wild roots occasionally procurable. The business of the day being thus carried through, it was brought to a close by smoking pipes (of tobacco), of which the bowls and mouth-pieces were of metal and the stems of wood: singing or music or other needless noise was objected to, as likely to attract undesirable attention, and a guard of two Tibetans and as many Mongolians having been set, the travellers fell into well-earned sleep.

28. The bands of robbers infesting these regions may be here suitably noticed. The tribes from which large numbers adopt robbery as a profession are all of Tibetan nationality: the most numerous, powerful and best mounted bands are those from the Chiámo Golok and Bánákhásum tribes, south-west of Siling: these roam to the north in

---

* There is no special provision in a Káfila for carriage of the sick, who must needs be left behind when no longer able to ride on a horse: excepting cases of persons who can afford servants, the helpless individual is left to his fate with some food and water placed near him, and it naturally follows that as a rule he is never heard of again.

† A pair of bellows is an essential article in every Tibetan family, whether resident or travelling, for without its help the only fuel commonly obtainable, *i.e.*, dung of yáks, horses, &c., could not be ignited.

‡ There is no occasion to convert butter into ghee in a country so cold: the former is sold sewn up in leather balls of various weights up to some 30 seers.

§ *Chúra* is a most valuable article of common consumption in all Tibet and Mongolia and one of the largest products of these countries where milk of kinds is so abundant. It is made by boiling down butter-milk to a thick paste and drying the latter: in value, *Chúra* is about twice as expensive as corn flour.

EXPLORATIONS BY A——K IN GREAT TIBET AND MONGOLIA.

Mongolia and west in Tibet, but not to the east or south where cultivation more or less exists. The western robber tribes are those of the Shangshung, Nagchukha, Jáma, Áta and Yágra; these roam so far and wide apart, that A——k had often heard of their performances in the distant west, up to even the Mánsarowar lake when he was travelling in that locality. All the tribes are nomads of the kind known as Dokpas, or dwellers in *black* tents; they are all armed alike with matchlock, spear and sword, and are invariably well mounted as the risks of their lawless profession require. They regard not remonstrances from Lámás, but there is one unwritten law which they all scrupulously respect, for reasons not difficult to imagine, and that is never to plunder in their own districts. To the eastern tribes of marauders, Mongolia offers a fertile hunting field for horses, which are bred there in large numbers. It is true that the owners of these beasts carry arms like the robbers and of late years have even acquired some soldierlike qualities by being drilled, but the Mongolian is by nature timid (as well as honest) and his weapons prove to him more a source of burthen than means of self protection. Further he cannot help being vulnerable in the matter of his horses, which he can neither conceal nor protect, and which the eastern marauders accordingly drive away in herds at will. The robber tribes rear yâks, horses, goats, sheep and dogs, all of which, as well as butter-balls and bags of *Chúra*, they offer in barter with an air of much innocence and business to passing travellers; desiring in exchange tea, cloths of gay colors, jaggery and the like; but travellers are chary of familiarity with such traders, never doubting that the intention to relieve them of all they receive in exchange will fail only from lack of opportunity.

29. Following now the line of country traversed, and starting from Lhása at a height of about 12,000 feet, it is described as a succession of ascents and descents between precipitous hills, affording passages at all times restricted and in some places so narrow as to admit only a *single* line of horses: rocks abound, yet at least scanty cultivation is not absent; also, the people live in houses: this continues up to Chiomo Lhákháng, where a change of aspect commences and is fully established at Láni Lá in the Dam. The traveller has now mounted the Jángtháng, a tract so peculiar as to deserve some special notice.

30. The Jángtháng is a vast and marvellous expanse of high undulating land, of which from various causes but little is known and even this limited information is not put together, so far as I am aware. It is not pretended that many new facts can be contributed here, *if* indeed in a country of the kind many remain to be elicited, but as it is desirable that some exhibit of the Jángtháng, its occupants and specialities should be presented as a whole, I have for this purpose availed myself of the considerable information possessed by A——k which is too valuable to be neglected. I have accordingly extended the Index to the explorer's work sufficiently to the west to include the Jángtháng up to about meridian 76°, and to the north to show some portion of the country adjacent there: it is to this exhibit drawn from A——k's statements, that reference should be made in connection with what follows. The high land it will be seen is only some 100 miles broad to the west near Skárdo; it is widest on the meridian of 86° where it is some 500 miles across, and to the east it ends in an inclined width of some 350 miles, from whence it slopes further eastwards, rapidly losing its characteristics and merging into the cultivated lands of China: its length is about 1,500 miles and in area it is some 480,000 square miles or say 3½ times the area of the United Kingdom of Great Britain and Ireland. The western and southern edges are fairly well known from Skárdo to Niamcho; not so its circuit round eastwards and up to Namohoñ, nor yet its northern edge; at the same time in these respects also there is reason to conclude that the exhibit is fairly correct. The strip of Jángtháng falling in A——k's present travels lay between Láni Lá and Niamcho on the south, and was bounded on the north by the Kiún Lún* range (Añgirtákshia to Namohoñ); this however is by no means his first introduction to the Jángtháng.

31. This enormous tract of high table-land is believed to be generally some 15 or 16 thousand feet above sea level, rising to a maximum somewhere in the vicinity of the Mánsarowar lake; in a word it stands *above* the line of perpetual line of snow in Europe, and hence this expanse of land, which otherwise would be invaluable, is utterly unfit for cultivation, or, except under great restrictions, any use by man. It is said to be similar in character *throughout,* and to present a succession of easy undulations, well co-

---

* So named by Prejevalsky and also independently recognized by A——k as probably the Kiún Lún he crossed when going to Yárkand.

SUMMARY AND DISCUSSION.

vered with earth and almost free from stone: the knolls in places form into ridges which sometimes carry high and snow-clad heads, but invariably the inclines are gentle and there are no precipices: water is plentiful and in places there are even large and handsome lakes, as the Mánsarowar, Tíngri Núr, &c.; further, the whole Jángtháng is coated by a short succulent grass, which from May to August, covers the undulations with the softest of green carpets, extending far away, and visible for even 50 or 60 miles in the clear crisp atmosphere prevailing. But beyond the abundant grass, *nothing* else will grow on this high land; there is no wood or scrub of any kind for fuel; and, in a word, the products of the earth are solely suited for graminivorous animals, which run wild in enormous numbers, as the yák, goat, sheep, deer, &c.; and the weaker of these provide food for the wolf, jackal, and yi (a large wild cat) to which the carnivora are limited. It is said the grass does seed, and most probably is propagated chiefly by that means; but other seeds, as of wheat or barley, though they germinate and produce fodder for cattle, yield only *seedless* ears, and hence no food for man.

32. The northern portion of the Jángtháng, tinted green in the Index Map, is *wholly unoccupied* by man, being far too distant from lands where corn and other products necessary for human life are produced in sufficient quantities to supply its wants; it is however as said overrun by enormous herds of wild animals, chiefly graminivorous, to whom further brief allusion will be made: this uninhabited belt borders on both north and south other belts, which are dotted more or less by nomadic camps: the belt to the south (tinted yellow in the Index Map) is the continuation of the Jángtháng and is peopled by *Tibetans*, who live invariably in rectangular-shaped tents, *black* in color, made from the hair of the yák: the northern tract (tinted violet in the Index Map) is beyond and below the Jángtháng, and consists of sandy wastes not infrequently diversified by oases, which are peopled by *Mongolians* living in round, white tents made of felt. Thus, this uninhabited belt of the Jángtháng lies between the *white*-tented Mongolian nomads to the north on the sandy lands, and the black-tented Tibetan nomads to the south on the continuation of the Jángtháng; but beyond the common fact of residence in tents, similarity in feature and religion, there are wide differences between the white and black tent nomads. The Mongolian is timid, peaceable and generous, little desirous of change and anxious only to be left to his own devices: his land produces *both* corn and a variety of animals, and with these he is content and happy. Not so the Tibetan nomads, whose necessities alone tend to acquisitiveness; for unable to grow corn on their high land they must needs barter for it other articles with their southern neighbours. These black-tent nomads are called Dokpas; throughout the considerable length of their country, they resemble one another closely; they all dress and arm alike and have similar occupations and habits; and in fact clans now in the vicinity of the Mánsarowar lake (where they are less lawless than elsewhere) claim that their ancestors migrated from the Chiámo Goloks, distant some 1,000 miles to the east. The Dokpas though existing on the produce of their locomotive farms, are compelled, as said, to barter with their neighbours below the Jángtháng for articles which their own high land will not produce, but apart from this unavoidable association, they keep chiefly to their own clans, and most probably these highlanders have maintained in their semi-isolation, the primitive manners and customs of their progenitors for many centuries past. Finally, they are all more or less robbers by profession; to them might gives right, always excepting the recognised law by which the property of a fellow clansman must be respected, and hence to pursue their business in a manner lawful to them, they roam in mounted bands far and wide in search of plunder. Notwithstanding their predatory habits, it must not be omitted that they all acknowledge the Dá Láma as their spiritual head, and perform periodical pilgrimages to Lhása in order to present themselves with due reverence before their high priest. But on these, as on all other occasions, they invariably keep an eye open to business proper, and the devotional nature of an errand is not permitted to interfere with convenient opportunities for plundering their neighbours. So the Dokpa comes to be trusted by none, unless perhaps by his fellow clansmen, and by these even, only while on the highland common to *the* clan.

33. At least a few words of special notice are also due to the vast numbers of wild animals abounding mostly in the large uninhabited tract of the Jángtháng. They suffer diminution from only one cause, and that is occasional extreme severity of winter, when, deprived of grass, they die by thousands as their skeletons testify; but apart from this they lead the most peaceful of lives, multiplying and increasing in kind without hindrance; for enemies in the shape of sportsmen are practically absent, and unless disturbed by a robber troop, or by the rare passage of peaceful travellers, they have little cause for disquiet apart

from their own family events.* Indeed, the vast numbers as well as the perfect unconcern of these wild beasts, sometimes proved very embarrassing to A——k on that portion of his returning route between Namohoñ and Niamcho, where travellers but very rarely pass. Speaking chiefly of wild yâks, they were seen in such considerable herds that some three to four thousand beasts were visible at short distances and *at the same time* : handsome, black brutes, without a single speck of the white which appertains to domestication and bondage, and with long hair trailing so low as to conceal their legs, they presented to view remarkable, great, dark moving masses of animal life. Occasionally a solitary monster bull with wicked eye and questionable intentions deliberately walked up to within only 10 or 12 paces and inspected the explorers inquisitively, as if with a view to further proceedings friendly or inimical. It was impossible to regard these attentions without respect, akin to awe, for the obvious considerable physical powers of the handsome, solid looking brute, whose long hair, nearly touching the ground, gave him the appearance of enormous girth, and as if in fact he was *all* body from hump to hoof. His jet black coat glistened in the sunshine, and as his small reddish eyes seemed dancing with mischief, which the solid horns above were fully calculated to accomplish, he cocked his tail, whisking about its bushy hairy pendant, and pawing the ground vigorously, stood doubtfully regarding the travellers as to whether he should consider them friends, foes, or only curiosities: thus situated the explorers prudently steered their course as far from their visitor as circumstances permitted. A wild bull yâk, adds A——k, will probably weigh $1\frac{1}{2}$ to 2 tame ones, and his head and horns are a full load for a strong man.

34. Returning now to the Káfila which was followed to Láni Lá at the commencement of the Jángtháng, it continued its course across that high land observing every precaution against robbers. The country up to the Dáng Lá range being occupied more or less by nomads, was so far easy to traverse that the required track was sufficiently worn at intervals to admit of being found readily: but north of that range, the ground showed no track whatever, so that the Mongolian guides,† frequently at a loss in which direction to proceed, mounted neighbouring heights, in hopes of recognizing some familiar land-marks, and otherwise shaped their course from one prominence to another. It may also be noted that at the Saung Chu (lat. 32° 12′) the direct road *viá* Di Chu Rab-dun was rejected, and a more westerly course adopted as less likely to be infested by robbers: hence, on crossing the Kiún Lún (or Añgirtákshia) range the party descended on the northern side into Mongolia at Naichi. Here a complete change of aspect presented itself; the travellers now passed along an undulating valley from 1 to 3 miles wide, bounded by hills described as sandy and conglomerate in formation, a description which applies generally to all the hills seen in Mongolia.

35. The most striking feature however now prevailing was, that the surface of the land had a whitish coat, called Bácha, decidedly salt in taste, and this was seen *all* over Mongolia: this saline powder was moreover easily raised and driven about in clouds by the wind, which blows persistently and with considerable force, and the travellers painfully realized the presence of salt in the dry air by cracks in their skins where not protected by clothing. In a word, the grassy carpet and clear crisp atmosphere of the Jángtháng, was now replaced by an arid, whitish waste, while the air, generally laden with haze, sometimes became so dense in high wind that the view around hardly extended beyond a hundred paces. The salt even affected the shrubs and trees which were now met with, and this in a peculiar manner; adhering to the bark, a white coat formed around the roots and gradually spreading upwards, eventually killed the plant. At the same time oases were both numerous and extensive; indeed everywhere that water appeared on the surface there vegetation abounded luxuriantly; the grass in particular grew green and strong, rising to 2 or even 3 feet in height, and in fact it is to these instances of bountiful provision that Mongolia enjoys its ability to

---

* Having implied how very little these wild animals serve any purposes of utility (apart from the rare occasions when they may be shot for food), I am bound to notice that in one respect at least they are absolutely necessary: their dung, especially that of yáks, provides excellent and abundant fuel, without which no traveller could cook his food (almost entirely of flesh) and live to cross the Jángtháng. As a rule Tibetans never warm themselves by fires, for which therefore fuel is not used, if indeed it be available: they trust to warm clothing and feeding on flesh for conservation of their own bodily heat, and not only do they succeed thoroughly, but albeit the absence of all vegetables and even the smallest pretence of ablution, scurvy, leprosy, and in fact all skin diseases are unknown; while ailments of any kind whatever are exceeding rare. A bath would be about the most disagreeable infliction that could possibly be imposed on a Dokpa, who is known simply never to bathe; at least not voluntarily; and the reservation *is* necessary, because babies up to the age of 2 or 3 months, are, it is said, occasionally washed as a preliminary to being coated with butter. As regards the women, no lady without risking pretentions to good manners and even respectability could commit the indiscretion of washing her face; and in fact any offence of the kind would certainly justify even her friends in considering her as an exceedingly "fast" and probably not quite proper person. Though very healthy, the Dokpa ages young, losing his teeth and even eye-sight when perhaps only 40 years old: nor do they live to great ages.

† With the maps now available the Jángtháng may be crossed in any required direction with certainty by following the proper bearing as indicated by a magnetic compass: at present travellers stray very considerably, and in some instances, starting from the Lob Núr, as they imagined straight for Lhása, have been known unintentionally to arrive at the Mánsarowar Lake.

SUMMARY AND DISCUSSION.

rear the large numbers of horses, camels,* sheep, goats and other graminivorous animals for which it is celebrated. Still, notwithstanding the very considerable exceptions represented by the oases, the country as a whole (of course only so far as traversed) consists mostly of sandy wastes and is one where salt predominates and permeates so generally, that the Mongolian finds it unnecessary to take any in his tea and hardly any even with soup and flesh, while to cattle, sheep, &c., none whatever is given.

36. Passing onwards from Naichi, the Káfila proceeded along the narrow valley already mentioned, until on arrival about Golmo they debouched into the verdant and wider valley in Thaichinar. This valley has been traced from Shiáng Chaidam (east) by Thingkali and Golmo, from whence it passes on westwards south of Hazir; several rills of water run in its bed, which is moreover green with grass and foliage and presents a valuable tract for pasturage; but between it and the northern hilly ranges, there runs a dry barren belt of earthy sand, which contrasts the more prominently from its proximity to the green valley below. Dispersion of the Káfila began at Golmo, after suitable farewells and mutual offers of hospitality which occasion might hereafter permit; but beyond and above this, the company exchanged hearty congratulations on their own cunning and sagacity, by which they had evaded their enemies, the robbers, and had escaped being plundered; unfortunately, as will be seen hereafter, these congratulations proved premature to at least several of the travellers, including the explorer, who proceeded eastward to Thingkali.

37. Along the routes followed in Mongolia, the population are all nomads, always excepting the town of Sachu where the people live in permanent houses. These nomads resemble the nomads of northern Tibet in several respects, including general appearance: they are however more amiable and certainly more honest, and in fact the Mongolian (or Mongolu as he calls himself) ascribes his immunity from lightning, to his own truthfulness and respect for his neighbour's property, and points with an air of superiority to the robbers of Chiámo Golok and Bánákhásum, from whom he suffers grievously, and who, he says, *therefore* suffer frequently from thunderbolts.† The Mongolian is naturally very friendly; an individual of either sex pairs with but one mate, and even the Dába (or priest), who is also a nomad, is socially permitted to adopt a consort, albeit the law forbids him a wife. He lives largely on flesh, tea and butter, and is also not without corn of kinds; his fondness for milk is as conspicuous as in a calf, and in order to indulge this taste, he levies contributions from all animals alike, including sheep, camels, and even mares.‡ It must also be added that he is exceedingly partial to intoxicating liquors, in which every one indulges, regardless of sex or age; but though he may get drunk, he seldom quarrels, and even if incapable, so that his legs are no longer reliable, he can still sit his horse and travel in safety, as he has done from the time when he was but a baby. He can read and write in characters of his own, which differ from the Tibetan, and like his southern brethren, he owns spear, matchlock and sword with which in times of *peace* he exercises diligently; but unfortunately he is deficient in nerve; he argues, says A——k, "If I fight I *may* be killed", and so, at the first burst of the robber's war cry, he vacates his tent, almost with alacrity, and betakes himself to safer localities, until his enemy has stolen his horses and departed. A Mongolian's riches consist mostly in horses, (besides various other animals); they cost nothing to keep and little more trouble after gelding them; they are sturdy and docile and are much attached to their master who is fond of them in turn; but for all this the Mongolian cannot bring himself to fight for his horses, and it is doubtful, whether, if unable to run away, he would fight even for himself. Convinced of his foible he conceals such articles of property as he may possess in odd places, and thus in running away he has at least the satisfaction of knowing, that the tent he necessarily leaves behind is quite empty. The robber knows this too and so confines his attention to the horses solely. No Mongolian is so poor, but that he owns half a dozen horses; in a few instances there are herds of even 500 beasts. One stallion to every 20 or 30 mares is reckoned the proper proportion.

38. The explorer and the Bodpas (from Lhása) of the party pursued their course eastward to Thingkali where they camped peacefully in the neighbourhood of the nomads, who numbered some 100 tents and possessed 3 to 4 hundred horses. Here A——k and his party rested for a while and made arrangements for further progress northwards; in fact

---
* The Mongolian camel is a valuable beast of burthen in the winter months, when it has a very bushy coat of long hair; but the whole coat is shed in summer when the beast not only becomes quite sleek, but it loses all strength and energy and is practically useless.

† As a matter of fact the country of the robbers is one of mist, cloud and electricity.

‡ The mares are said to yield only but *little* milk *each* time it is drawn; the secretion however is rapidly restored, so the Mongolian repeats the milking process at *short* intervals.

the morning of their intended departure had arrived, and they were about to load their horses for the march, when as the dawn was yet breaking the robber's cry of *ullul-lullul-lu-u-u* suddenly burst on the peaceful encampment: in a word the robbers, some 200 in number, had effected a complete surprise. The Mongolians according to precedent at once scattered far and wide without making even pretence of resistance, and the robbers having seized the horses they coveted, next attacked the small party of explorers and Tibetans; there was some firing on both sides, but numbers prevailed and the robbers remained masters of the encampment, which having rifled rapidly, they departed. Eventually when the owners returned to their tents, now practically empty, they found a single dead robber, shot in the conflict, whose dress and arms enabled them to recognize, that the marauders belonged to the dreaded band of the Chiámo Goloks: in fact to the identical highland clan whom the unfortunate travellers had hitherto successfully evaded.

39. The losses he incurred here, crippled A——k and his two comrades most deplorably; notwithstanding, he collected the remnants of his effects, and bravely refusing to turn homewards, set his face towards Sachu, resolved on further exploration. But misfortune still followed him, and the facts may be briefly mentioned here. He had progressed some 330 miles towards Sachu, when one of his two comrades, who had shown aversion to further exploration and partiality for adopting Mongolia as his residence, suddenly decamped with the horses of the party as well as with nearly all the remnants of property which the robbers had failed to carry away, leaving A——k and his remaining comrade practically paupers. Under these circumstances, no one could have reproached the explorer had he now endeavoured to *retrace* his steps, but he once more rose above adversity, gallantly making his way onwards to Sachu, and it was only when detained and turned back from thence, that he at last reluctantly retrograded towards India. Even now, he chose a *new* and *far longer* route, which in the end involved his journeying over full 1,890 miles, and though penniless and dependent on charity, he continued his observations to the very end, exercising regularity, care and skill, and unconsciously evincing such unfailing courage, gallantry and sense of duty as may well be admired.

40. Proceeding northwards from Thingkali there is little of note to discuss, until reaching Yembi in the Saithang district: here there is an extensive plain well watered, covered with grass and affording excellent pasturage for large herds of animals: horses in particular are most numerous and may be counted in thousands. Yet, the climate is by no means genial, and this not so much in consequence of unusual cold, as owing to the prevalence of strong biting winds, which blow persistently and almost continuously excepting in November and December. There is little snow or rain, but distant clouds without mist are frequent: water freezes readily in the open air, excepting in July and August; and in the winter months, the successive cakes of ice formed at a spring, sometimes mount up curiously one above another in piles over 6 feet high. It is however chiefly the piercing wind which makes the climate of Saithang exceedingly severe in January and February, when all young and otherwise tender animals are removed, for protection against it, to various enclosed valleys in the hills which lie to the north. Otherwise these hills are also well known as being inhabited by a few wild human beings and some herds of wild Bactrian camels; the latter are an object of sport, and their flesh finds a ready sale at Sachu and elsewhere.

41. The most northern place visited by A——k was the town of Saitu or Sachu (Prejevalsky's Ssa tschu): it stands surrounded by small villages in the midst of an extensive and very fertile plain watered abundantly by a river, which, here flowing nearly north and south, runs close to and west of the town, where it is crossed by a strong bridge with two flat openings. Seen from the south, the town and its surrounding villages are mostly concealed amongst high trees, which are backed by distant low hills, visible in the distance so far as the usual prevailing hazy atmosphere of Mongolia permits: the most attractive feature on which the eye rests, is however the extensive and green expanse of cultivation in which Sachu stands: this verdure, so pleasant to behold in contrast to the generally arid surface of Mongolia, extends fully to Náhuli on the north-west, and in fact probably reaches to full 20 miles from the town in all directions; the land as said is highly fertile, and enjoying as it does an ample water-supply, the harvests are large and varied in kind; on them the prosperity of the place mainly depends. The city is in the shape of a quadrangle, about $1\frac{1}{2}$ miles long east and west and some $\frac{3}{4}$ mile wide: it is surrounded by a ditch some 6 feet deep and 15 wide, which encloses a solid wall about 25 feet high, with circular bastions at the corners and surmounted by a parapet pierced with embrasures at intervals: accommodation for the garrison is provided in the four angles of the surrounding wall. There are four large

SUMMARY AND DISCUSSION.

gateways, one in each side of the quadrangle, and the two roads joining opposite gateways are the main thoroughfares in the town: the bazars and dwelling houses are built mostly along these roads, which in places are covered in with straw spread on rough wooden frames: the north-west angle, at the junction of these main roads, is enclosed by a branch road, north of which stand the residence of the governor or Dáloi, the Jail, &c., &c. The four entrances are gated, but these structures are mostly out of repair and the wall enclosing the city now has several gaps in it.

42. The population of Sachu and surrounding villages is almost exclusively Chinese* who in certain respects contrast unfavorably with the Mongolians: the latter though rough and comparatively uncivilized, are honest, hospitable and generous, while the former are not merely thrifty but very exacting. Sákhángs (restaurants) are common and popular, and food including vegetables and fruit abundant and cheap†, excepting sugar which is imported. Intoxicating liquors are plentiful and drunk by one and all without exception: opium also is consumed‡, chiefly by smoking, and can be raised in the neighbourhood though not to the extent required: but notwithstanding alcohol and opium, the Chinaman is essentially peaceful and law abiding, not the less so, that punishment for even slight offences may be inflicted with such severity as to cause painful deaths. Capital punishment may not as such be ordered by the Dáloi without sanction from China: fatal results are however attained without actual decapitation, which is the recognized form of legal execution. As to houses, they are all of one floor and consist of small rooms; there is no window glass: the walls are built of blocks of clay, or what in India we should call (huge) kacha bricks, and the roofs are made up of scantlings laid *close* together with plenty of earth beaten flat above them. Fuel and straw are plentiful. The rain-fall is small, though clouds are common. A——k did not find the place cold notwithstanding its high latitude (40° 12′).

43. On the whole, Sachu cannot be compared with Lhása in point of interest, wealth or population: its people, as said, are nearly all of a single nationality—the Chinese, and its trade is mostly with the north and west, the traffic being carried in carts drawn by 2 to 5 horses. To A——k the people proved inhospitable and ungenerous, and like others who are in poverty and friendless, he was regarded here with distrust, so that the further progress northwards which he contemplated was prohibited: nor even was he able to retrace his steps towards India: eventually a Láma from Thuden Gomba, with whom he was acquainted, happened to visit Sachu, and recognizing A——k obtained leave to take him back with his party. In this company the explorer was *obliged* to ride on a horse down to Chákángnamaga, from whence the track which bifurcates eastwards (new to A——k) was followed: here he became bullock-driver to the party, and walking by these beasts was able to reckon his own paces as usual to Bárong Chaidam: for the remaining distance to Thuden Gomba, the track runs in the vicinity of the Chiámo Golok and Bánákhásum robber clans, and by way of provision for escape, if necessary, from these marauders, every individual of the party was required to ride; hence for this portion the explorer with commendable ingenuity reckoned the paces taken by the right foreleg of his steed, and the result shows that a horse steps quite as equably as a man.

44. The Jángtháng commencing at Namohoñ was left behind at Niamcho, and nothing further need be said of the country up to the latter place, as it has been discussed generally in previous remarks. Bidding grateful farewells to the Láma who had befriended him, and who was the master of Thuden Gomba, A——k continued his journey towards Dárchendo and entered on the tea-track at Kegudo, from whence, it will be seen on Sheet No. 1, the continuation of this track trends south-westerly and passing through the Hor possession strikes the line from Siling to Lhása at Chomora lake. In point of general appearance, the whole tract of country along the route *via* Dárchendo, Báthang and Gárthok to Láo village (north of Jio Gomba) is pretty nearly alike; it is rocky and of course all mountainous, but although caps of snow are visible occasionally, the hills are neither lofty nor severely precipitous; and the track runs along moderate inclines, or, as in the

---

* The people are commonly polygamists.

† Notwithstanding the fertility of the Sachu plain, the climate here, as in all Mongolia, permits of only one crop or harvest in the year.

‡ Sold for equal weight in silver. *Note.* A——k mentions the singular Chinese coin called Támimañ (or Doje or Nabchuma) a mass of silver not unlike a cocked hat in general outline and equivalent to 156 Indian rupees; hence the coin must weigh something like 4 lbs avoirdupois!

districts of Jokchen and Yulung*, over grassy undulations; generally the road or passage is ample in width, but in a few instances, as along the left bank of the Di Chu, beasts of burthen can pass only in single file. There are patches of cultivation at intervals; grass and water are plentiful, and even wood (in addition to yâk-dung) may be obtained occasionally for fuel: moreover the track is not liable to attacks from robbers, except occasionally in Jokchen and Yulung near which the Jángtháng† borders on the north-east. Herds of yâks and jophos carrying tea were met several times, for as stated, the explorers were now on the Jánglam or northern tea route between Dárchendo and Lhása, and occasionally traders returning from Kegudo were also seen, carrying deer-horns, woollen fabrics, skins of wild beasts, pods of musk and the like, which they had obtained in barter for tea. But beyond these occurrences, there is little to note of the journey, or of changes in aspect of the country, excepting the beds of the great rivers between Dárchendo and Láo, where the Nag Chu, the Di Chu and the Chiámdo Chu run in wide valleys, well studded with large trees and underwood.

45. Arrived at Dárchendo A——k was once more in a town and amidst comparative civilization, circumstances which however rather aggravated the consequences of his poverty, so that in his distress, and hearing of the Jesuit Fathers who reside there, he determined to appeal to them for help: this was generously rendered both in advice as to his future progress and money, so that A——k was enabled to proceed onwards with a somewhat lighter heart. But little need be said of Dárchendo, which is well known as the emporium for all the Chinese tea from the gardens to the east; it is from this place that the two tea routes to Lhása diverge: one following the Jánglam or northern route and the other the Junglam or southern and official road, as stated elsewhere. Dárchendo is described as in a narrow valley, surrounded by snow-capped hills, of which the loftiest are probably those to the north. It may be added here that the whole tract of country passed through from Thuden Gomba to Láo yields but *one* harvest annually.

46. It will be seen that from Dárchendo A——k travelled along the official road; he however had occasion to leave this road at Gárthok, proceeding south-westerly to Sáma (as will be presently explained) so that it was not until his arrival at Lho Jong that he again joined the Junglam, which, between the places named, runs up north to Chiámdo and then down again south. From Láo village southwards, the country changes in various ways; the hills are very rocky, rugged and precipitous, and with exceedingly narrow valleys; cultivation is plentiful to the extent of ground available, and not only are the crops abundant but the climate admits of *two* harvests in the year: where *all* these circumstances obtain, the country is called the Rong, and as respects the route followed, they were experienced up to Áta Gáng Lá; but it is understood that the Rong lay below (south of) A——k's route by only some 20 to 30 miles the whole way to Chetáng; the province of Potodh being just north of and that of Pomedh in the Rong: thus, so far as the route followed is concerned, from Láo to Áta Gáng Lá *viâ* Sáma, it lay throughout in the Rong, yet it is in this portion of his journey that A——k saw the heaviest snow-clad and presumably the highest mountains.

47. Proceeding south from Láo village, the lofty peaks‡ of Khákárpo, perhaps 20,000 feet high, attracted attention; A——k concludes that the range on which they stand is cut through a little south of them by the Chiámdo Chu, because Khákárpo being a place of pilgrimage, pilgrims from Lhamdun pass *round* it to the south and rejoin the road at Dáyul Gomba: it was also locally affirmed, by a few persons who had evidently travelled southwards and visited certain shrines in Burma, that the Chiámdo Chu, and also the Giáma Nu Chu ran into that country: this evidence and the topography from Lepper's map suggest the conjecture that the Giáma Nu Chu falls into the Salwin, but on this point and all others in localities *not adjoining* his route, A——k of course cannot speak from personal knowledge.§

48. From the Koli Lá (perhaps 14,000 feet high) the Rirapphási peaks (estimated at some 20,000 feet in height) became visible; these are plainly connected with the Neching

---

* These are the two most famous yâk breeding districts on this line; other equally favorable localities occur in the Hor country.

† The robbers being all horsemen can only operate on the Jángtháng or adjoining open and undulating lands.

‡ A distinction may be noticed between the snow hills of the Jángtháng and those of the Rong. In the Jángtháng the snow cap is a round bluff and is immediately followed below by the coat of grass which covers the undulating ground and extends continuously down to the ordinary levels of the high land. In the Rong the peaks are precipitous and pointed; the snow line is followed by a belt of a mile or so of grass, succeeded by brushwood which grows stronger and higher in descending and eventuates in lofty and large timber trees.

§ The Nag Chu and Di Chu were locally considered as rivers running into China.

SUMMARY AND DISCUSSION.

Gángra range, which was crossed at Tila Lá, height 16,100 feet. The explorer was now in the horse-shoe-shaped basin of the Zayul Chu, one of the feeders of the Brahmaputra, and travelled down the bed of that river to Sáma, with the lofty Neching Gángra range on the north and its lower continuation south, both ranges being *visible* at intervals: he has no doubt that the peaks of the Neching Gángra are the loftiest he saw, and by estimation A——k places their height at some 25,000 feet.

49. Up to Sáma, A——k had travelled in the glad expectation that he could pass straight across the Mishmi (or Náhoñg) country, and in fact only some 30 miles now divided him from British Territory; but he soon found to his great disappointment, that those few miles presented a barrier impenetrable not only to himself, but to the people of Zayul themselves: in a word none of the latter dare venture to cross into Assam through any of the neighbouring tribes. Beginning in the latitude of Áta Gáng Lá, the Lhoyulis (or Lhobas) stop the way: from thence along the south-west border the Mishmis refuse passage: while across the range, south-east of Zayul, the Zayulis have no communication whatever: thus Zayul is absolutely shut in on east, south and west. That the Mishmis and Lhoyulis mean what they say, is proved by their killing every one from Zayul who ventures much beyond the border villages; on the other hand the Mishmis freely enter into Zayul for purposes of barter. The reasons for this one-sided arrangement are however not difficult to see, for at present the Mishmis and Lhoyulis are the middle men, in point of British produce, between Assam and Zayul; a monopoly in trade which would wholly disappear if the Zayulis could venture across into Assam. Apart however from inability to satisfy their curiosity as travellers, the people of Zayul have some reasons to be content with the arrangement, for the articles they barter in return are valued chiefly by their neighbours, who are content to accept salt and any animals whatever with *large horns* in exchange; in fact, content or otherwise, the Zayulis—peaceable and even timid—are unable to penetrate the tribal barriers, and so must needs admit their neighbours to barter or deprive themselves of all imports.

50. These circumstances however were of little consolation to the explorer, who after his long journey was now bitterly disappointed at finding the few remaining miles to British Territory absolutely barred, by barbarians who would certainly kill him like all other intruders, if he ventured into their country; and yet, as will be seen subsequently, but for this very disappointment which compelled him to perform a circuitous route around the Sángpo* he would not have solved one of the most interesting geographical problems of modern times. Reluctantly turning his steps from home, A——k gallantly faced northerly once more, and at the Áta Gáng Lá crossed over from the Roug: here he came across the only glaciers in his journey, and these at the pass *united*, so as to slope contrary ways; the height of 14,690 feet which he determined was probably some 2,000 feet below the glacial ridge.

51. With the Roug left behind, the explorer was once more in country similar to that already described, such as he had passed through before reaching Láo village and yielding only one harvest annually: these features with but little variation continued along the remainder of the exploration. At Lho Jong he rejoined the Junglam (southern road) and again met bands of traders between Lhása and Dárchendo: leaving the road at Chomoráwa Giachug, he turned southerly to Chetáng and eventually closed his work at Khamba-barji, having some 4 or 5 miles before crossed the Junglam, now leading from Lhása *viâ* Giangze and Shigatze to Dingri.

52. Returning now to the geographical problems which A——k has helped to solve, broadly stated, one relates to the Irrawaddy and the other to the Brahmaputra. I do not purpose to enter needlessly into all the various conjectural hypotheses hitherto advanced (naturally on the limited evidence available) but to include these generally and only so far as necessary, and to dwell on the evidence which A——k has now secured.

53. I first dispose of the question as to the north-western watershed of the Irrawaddy. It will be seen from Sheets Nos. 1 and 2 that the Zayul district is peculiar, in that it is locked in right round by a high and continuous watershed, which is cut through only at one place, *i.e.*, by the Zayul Chu in about lat. 28° and long. 97° 5′: the district is made

---

* Sángpo merely means "a large river" and is equally applicable to *all* large rivers. The proper name of the river, south of Lhasa, called Sángpo on Sheet No. 1, is Cháng Chu or Nári Chu.

up of two valleys; in the eastern runs the Zayul Chu proper, rising at Tíla Lá; the western is the bed of the Rong Thod Chu, rising at Áta Gáng Lá; the two streams unite near Shíkha and then cut through the range, which in absence of other designation may be called the Rong Thod-Mishmi range.* Now points on these ranges and mostly the ranges themselves, were actually seen and visually followed out by A——k, and his verbal account in addition leaves no doubt, that apart from minor defects, which only an actual topographical survey could elicit, his delineation is in the main correct. On this evidence it now stands determined that the watershed of the Irrawaddy is the Zayul-Khanung range. This also makes it almost impossible for the Sángpo† to run down the Mishmi country, and carrying the Zayul Chu‡ with it to discharge into the Irrawaddy, as has sometimes been imagined. A——k ascertained by local enquiry, that a small stream (not a large one) does run down part of the Mishmi country and joins the Zayul Chu on its way to India, i.e. to the Brahmaputra; but in reply to further enquiry, as to whether this small stream could be the Lhása river (i.e. the Sángpo) the people ridiculed the idea.

54. Now following the explorer from Áta Gáng Lá onwards, it will be seen in Sheet No. 1, that the watershed lay to his left, i.e. south, all the way up to Shiár (i.e. east) Gáng Lá where he crossed it, so that it now fell on his right up to Nub (i.e. west) Gáng Lá: in fact the district of Arig (like Zayul) is ringed by a watershed, which is pierced only at one place, and that at Aládo Giachug by the Daksong Chu. It is needless for my present purpose to follow the watershed further west, for I have already arrived *west* of Gya-la-Sindong, (the place down to which the Sángpo has been traced) and the question immediately in hand is, whether the Sángpo runs *east* from Gya-la-Sindong. I have shown in Art. 53 that the Sángpo does not cut through the watersheds up northwards from the Zayul-Khanung range to Áta Gáng Lá, and in this article, attention has been called to the continuation of this watershed which runs round Gya-la-Sindong to east and north from Áta Gáng Lá. Further A——k positively affirms, that this watershed was nowhere cut through by any river whatever; least of all by a river so large as the Sángpo; and I am confident that this statement is quite reliable. Thus taking Gya-la-Sindong as a centre, the Sángpo has no exit all the way round north and east, nor along the Rong Thod-Pomedh range or the range at the head of the Mishmi valley; i.e., it has no exit right round Gya-la-Sindong from north down to a point (call it X) somewhere in latitude $28\frac{3}{4}°$ and longitude $95\frac{1}{2}°$.

55. Having stated this much, I come to the geographical problem that has hitherto awaited an answer. The Sángpo rises near the Mánsarowar lake, and from thence it has been traced, practically continuously for some 850 miles, to Gya-la-Sindong, where exploration downwards is barred by savages§: what is the further course of this river? As already shown it has no exit anywhere north or east‖, down to the point here called X; hence unless it disappears in the bowels of the earth it *must* feed the Brahmaputra. The tributaries here of the latter and their discharges¶, are as follows:—

Discharge of	Cubic feet per second.	Proportional part.
Dihang	55,500	1
Lohit + Tenga	33,800	0·6
Dibang + Sesiri	27,200	0·5
Subansiri	16,900	0·3

Also of the Sángpo we are told by A——k, that at Chetáng the stream was some 400 feet wide; subsequently we know that it received the Daksong Chu, which, even at Aládo Giachug before receiving the Kongbo Giámda Chu, was (the explorer adds) *not* fordable: as to depth of the Sángpo at Chetáng, this is described as "very deep"; no measurements were made, but a depth of 25 or 30 feet A——k thinks certainly existed; moreover the water deepened rapidly from the banks; and in point of velocity a man walking fast on the shore could not keep up with a boat floating down the stream; under these circumstances the discharge per

---

* From want of other names, I here call the ranges round Zayul district by names compounded of the two districts which each divides; thus Rong Thod-Mishmi between the Rong Thod valley and the Mishmi country; similarly I adopt Rong Thod-Pomedh and the range south-east of Zayul valley I call Zayul-Khanung.
† I continue calling it so only to suit previous discussions.
‡ In this case, how should the Lohit river be fed; discharge 33,800 cubic feet with that of Tenga river?
§ The unexplored portion of the Sángpo between Gya-la-Sindong and British Territory is hardly 150 miles long.
‖ It will be seen in Sheet No. 1 that a track runs across the Pomedh country, from Nankhazod (in Nagong, north of Áta Gáng Lá) to Giámda (in Kongbo), passing some 20 miles north of the bend in the Sángpo above Gya-la-Sindong: this track is frequently used by pilgrims to Lhása, many of whom were questioned by A——k and stated that the track *does not cross* the Sángpo; thus affording confirmation of the fact, that this river has no exit eastwards at least north of Nankhazod.
¶ Determined by the late Captain H. J. Harman, R.E., and given on Sheet No. 1.

SUMMARY AND DISCUSSION.

second was probably full 40,000 cubic feet at Chetáng, and this was more likely to be increased than decreased in progress to British territory.

56. Now since the Sángpo discharges into the Brahmaputra west of X, we have to select a recipient from the 4 tributaries mentioned in article 55. I put the (Lohit + Tenga) out of consideration, because to reach it the Sángpo must so to speak run through the Dihang and (Dibang + Sesiri), and of the remaining 3, the Dihang alone is of the estimated volume of the Sángpo, the other 2 being only ½ or ⅓rd the required volume. Hence the conclusion I arrive at is, that the Sángpo and Dihang are identical; and in fact, if this is not the case, there appears no answer to the question how comes the large discharge of 55,500 cubic feet to be created in the Dihang? Believing that geographers will coincide in the identity above indicated, I conclude my remarks by pointing out that the solution thus afforded by A——k gives additional value to his remarkable explorations.

57. I can notice the tables attached, only briefly.

Table I gives the *individual* values of latitude, and so affords evidence of the accuracy attained by the observer.

Table II exhibits the heights determined, all from boiling-point observations of a thermometer in the usual way. The aneroid barometer unfortunately got out of order and the observations taken with it being useless are not given.

Table III gives air temperatures, affording points for discussion which however I am unable to enter into at present. It is likely to prove useful for reference.

Table IV. I have here collected A——k's estimates, for each *place*, of the facts given; which relate to the strip of country say 2 miles wide, on either side and along his route.

Table V is an abstract of Table IV for each *district*: the last column gives the estimated population per square mile along the strip of 4 miles in width: excluding the uninhabited portions of the Jángtháng, the total length is 2,470 miles, which for a strip of 4 miles wide gives an area of 9,880 square miles, and hence for a population of 127,883 souls, the average per square mile is 12·9 souls: this however *includes* the principal towns: but otherwise, south of the Jángtháng generally, the population is estimated by A——k to be about the same as along his routes, so that for the whole of this area generally, 10 souls per square mile would probably not be too high an estimate.

The Vocabulary will be found useful.

58. The country south of the Jángtháng, it will be seen, is watered by the Ja Chu, the Di Chu, the Chiámdo Chu and the Giáma Nu Chu; all large streams, of which the Di Chu is the largest: in point of fact however the people make no use of the rivers for irrigation; nor are the streams suited for navigation even down to a considerable distance below A——k's southern route. I am unable, from want of time, further to discuss particulars, which will be found in the Account of the Explorations.

J. B. N. HENNESSEY,

Mussooree,
25th June, 1884.

Deputy Surveyor General,

In charge Trigonometrical Surveys.

Addendum to the preceding Summary and Discussion of Explorations by A——k in Great Tibet and Mongolia 1879-82.

NOTE ON TRADE ROUTES AND THE TEA TRADE.

The explorations by A——k in 1879-82 suggest considerations, regarding certain trade routes in Tibet and subjects connected with the same, which appear of sufficient importance to be noted here, in view of their proving useful for promoting trade between Tibet and India and also in other respects. I therefore put together here the following facts elicited in conversation with A——k, remarking once for all, that regarding Tibet as made up of two portions, generally east and west of the meridian of Lhása, the portion here particularly contemplated is that recently visited by the explorer, *i.e.*, the *eastern* portion.

2. I begin by mentioning the Chinese tea gardens east of Dárchendo; these supply the whole of the tea consumed in eastern Tibet, besides furnishing enormous quantities to Lhása for local use and for despatch westward and southward, including Bhutan. Beyond the obvious fact that these gardens must be very extensive, and that they are said to commence some 140 miles east of Dárchendo, nothing more can be added here; except a few words as to the preparation of the rectangular blocks or bricks, in which form all the tea for Tibet is prepared in these gardens. Assuming that the green leaf has as usual been manufactured into the ordinary tea in dry leaves, a certain proportion of the quantity to be converted into bricks is boiled in water over a fierce fire and for a considerable period; this yields an intensely strong tea-juice or concentrated extract, which moreover has the required property of being very adhesive: the remaining portion of the leaf-tea is next worked into a stiff pudding with the tea-juice, and forced into rectangular moulds, from whence the blocks taken out are now in the shape of long, solid bricks. These bricks dry in the shade or store-rooms, and are fit for transport a few weeks after preparation. A tea-brick is called Dum or Barka.

3. The next step is packing: this is done in packets of four barkas, which are placed lengthwise in a line and abutting one another; some leaf-tea is strewed around and the whole enclosed in yellow paper; this yellow package of four barkas, called a khotu, is now slipped into a wicker-work, hollow, rectangular tube, made for the purpose, and secured there; after which it is ready to be carried to Dárchendo.

4. The tea carriers may be described as a very nationality of porters, of whom men and women alike are able to carry great weights and over very difficult paths, and even children acquit themselves creditably in the same way. Porterage has been their occupation for generations, and in fact they are the *only* porters in eastern Tibet: the ordinary natives (Bodpas and Khambas) are but indifferent weight carriers, while the nomad or Dokpa of the Jángtháng is of but little use once off his horse. So the transporting of tea from the gardens to Dárchendo is performed entirely by the Giáma Rongbas, who inhabit the intervening tract of country (perhaps some 100 miles square and called Giáma Rong). This tract is mountainous and precipitous, and all the tea traffic is carried along a mere footpath, which is tortuous, of needless length and runs up and down steep inclines, so that it is quite unfit for beasts of burthen; notwithstanding, the Giáma Rongba, man or woman, will sometimes carry up to even 3 maunds per individual all the way to Dárchendo, performing say 7 miles daily or the journey in some 20 odd days. As already said, the whole of the tea consumed in eastern Tibet, and also that despatched onwards from Lhása is supplied by these gardens: this *must* be a considerable total weight, and as all of it is carried on the backs of the Giáma Rongbas, it follows, that these people must be correspondingly numerous. The tea is delivered at Dárchendo at the risk of the tea-planters, who take payment in coin: the purchaser at this place removes the wicker-work packing, and the khotu is then sewn up in leather; it is now fit to be transported on yáks, jomos, mules or horses alike. These animals all carry wooden pack-saddles, from which the khotus are swung on opposite sides by leathern straps: the yák carries only four khotus or from 1 to $1\frac{1}{2}$ maunds, and travels under 10 miles daily: the jomo or mule carries eight khotus or about double the weight of the yák and travels say 15 miles per day.

5. The tea purchases at Dárchendo are made with one of two objects; *i.e.*, for transport direct to the great emporium at Lhása, or for sale in large quantities to tea-dealers

NOTE ON TRADE ROUTES AND THE TEA TRADE.

along the two trade routes between the two towns; in the former case payment at Lhása is made in coin, but in the latter the coin is largely supplemented by barter: the tea-dealers in turn retail to small tradesmen mostly in barter, and between these and the people barter necessarily prevails. So that, notwithstanding that silver currency to a certain extent does obtain, *the* currency of the people is *brick-tea*. This fact at once proves the universality of the use of tea in the country (Tibet), a fact none the less striking, that the unit of exchange, *i.e.*, a brick of tea, is not national but foreign. Even the lawless Dokpa, or black-tent nomad, will accept payment in brick-tea for any thing he possesses, and in a word any person in eastern Tibet, if not drinking his native malt liquor, drinks tea every day and all day; he scorns at a water drinker and will take none of that element himself: as a common usage a strong decoction of tea is always ready to hand in most households, so that, diluting this with hot water, a Tibetan can obtain the required draught at short notice. Conjectures on the subject are unavoidably of limited weight, but at a guess, A——k thinks that a married couple with 2 or 3 children, *if economical*, will consume about a seer of tea monthly.

6. Several kinds of tea are sold at Dárchendo: the principal kinds are these; the prices being stated in Indian money and at Dárchendo, and the weights by estimation in Indian seers:—

Rigárkárpo weighs about 3 seers per brick, price some 3 Rs. per brick.
Sarti Chuba   „   2½   „   12 As.   „
Chuba   „   2½   „   8 As.   „
Giátpa   „   2   „   ⅓rd Re.   „

besides, there is the Jángjápari leaf-tea in about ½ seer packets at 4 or 5 As.: of all these the Rigárkárpo is considered the best: the Giátpa is made up of refuse including twigs and has the least strength or flavor. The Chuba is probably most generally consumed. Decoction of the tea seed is also appreciated, especially at large entertainments, not only for its good qualities but because it is quickly prepared.

7. This brings me to the two trade routes from Dárchendo to Lhása, on one of which at least tea is practically, if not quite absolutely, the only article of traffic: the route mostly for tea is the northern route and is called the Jánglam; it passes by Kegudo, through the Hor country (of which nothing can be said), by Chomora (lake) and so down *viá* the Dam to Lhása. The southern route is called the Junglam or government road along which the officials and the post travel between China and Lhása; it runs through Gárthok, Chiámdo, Lho Jong, and so to Lhása. Of these the Jánglam conveys far the larger traffic: the Junglam is used by traders who are mostly *resident* on this line, as the Choñgpoñs (or governors) of Lithang, Báthang, &c.

8. Following first the Jánglam, it passes through cold tracts, and largely over the Jángtháng, that marvellous expanse of high land, dwelt on at some length in my Summary and Discussion of A——k's explorations*: here the yák and his less timid descendant the jomo (besides some mules, &c.) breed and multiply almost innumerably, hardly needing more care than does the abundant grass growing around them; so that, after deducting a certain number for affording sustenance in flesh and milk to their owners, there still remains an enormous surplus of these beasts, representing an almost unlimited amount of carrying power, which runs to waste. Some small portion of this waste has been utilized by the tea-trader in diverting his route northwards over the Jángtháng, and this demand is willingly met by the cattle owner who requires nothing more in return than a minute fraction of the tea which his beasts carry: time is of little consequence to all concerned; the drivers saunter along with their beasts, which graze as they travel, and once on the soft plain of the Jángtháng, the former absolves himself of all needless attention to his cattle, which for 2 or 3 days consecutively are never unladen, proceeding on their course feeding all day, lying down at nights under their loads and rising with them next morning to saunter on again: under these circumstances it is easy to see that the cost of carriage is almost nominal. The cattle breeding grounds are in the Jokchen and Yulung districts and the whole tract from Kegudo across the Hor country *viá* Chomora down to the Dam, only some 75 miles north of Lhása: the two districts first named carry from Dárchendo to Kegudo, where the beasts are changed for others, which are succeeded by fresh batches at some place (not known) in the Hor

---

* See also Index Map.

country, and thereafter at will from Chomora downwards. Thus the trader proceeds according to his object, *i.e.*, direct to Lhása, or, marching as he does down the centre of the nomad *i.e.*, camps in the Jángtháng, disposes of his commodity by replenishing the tea stocks *en route*. The distances along this line are as follows:—

	Miles.
Dárchendo to Kegudo	440
Kegudo to Chomora (lake)	290
Chomora to Dam Chuchan	85
Dam Chuchan to Lhása	75
Total	890

9. The second trade route runs along the Junglam or Government road from Dárchendo to Lhása, *i.e.*, through Lithang, Báthang, Gárthok, Chiámdo, Lho Jong, Giámda &c : here yâks and jomos are absent, and in fact would die from the rise in the temperature, and the carrying is done by horses and mules, which moreover are not obtainable *on hire* but are the property of the traders themselves; the route also runs through comparatively civilized tracts, where, if the people can afford to buy more tea, the expenses of the trader are also greater: the traffic is said to be considerable and large herds of laden beasts are to be met, but it is not confined to tea, and, taken all together, the inference is that the tea carried by this route is more to replenish stock on the road than to supply the emporium at Lhása, where competition of the Junglam with the Jánglam and cheaper route appears impossible. In respect to distances by this route we have

	Miles.
Dárchendo to Gárthok	250
Gárthok to Chiámdo	180
Chiámdo to Lho Jong	110
Lho Jong to Giámda	255
Giámda to Lhása	140
Total	935

10. It will be seen from the foregoing, that carriage by the Jánglam road must needs be cheaper than by the Junglam, because of the enormous carrying power on the Jánglam, not only available, but even running to utter waste; at the same time, as the Jánglam runs far north, the use of the Junglam as a tea route must be a necessity, to feed the demand in southern tracts. Thus, in considering the competition at Lhása, of tea from the gardens east of Dárchendo and from India, it is the cheaper carriage by the Jánglam we have to take into account : this cost is obviously so small that it may almost be left out of reckoning; nor am I in a position to estimate it with much accuracy. For a rough approximation, the cost may be found thus. A driver is usually required to look after some 40 yâks, whose united loads may be set down at 60 maunds. The yâks would stand useless if not carrying tea, and working or idle they feed themselves; so that practically they cost the owner *nothing*, and this is the view he takes of the matter himself. The driver lives on the produce of the Jángtháng itself where he travels, and where flesh, milk and butter are exceedingly cheap; corn flour is a luxury to him, but even allowing him half a pound of this daily, with some tea, and remembering that he dresses in the skins of the beasts around him, 2 to 3 Rs. per

---

NOTE.—In addition to the Dárchendo tea, which alone is used in Tibet, I might however mention the Siling tea (east of the Koko-Núr): it is also in the brick form but much harder and can be powdered only by hard pounding: the Tibetans declare it is wanting in color and strength and will have none of it; yet the Mongolians use it exclusively by preference: so much for difference of taste, which in these instances *must* have been acquired by habit. The distances of the route Lhása to Siling are as follows:—

	Miles.
Lhása to Giáro	203
Giáro to Di Chu Rab-dun	212
Di Chu Rab-dun to Jún	195
Jún to Koko-Núr	185
Koko-Núr to Siling	120
Total	915

The traffic along this route is small and is generally limited to a couple of káfilas either way in the year, but no Siling tea is imported into Tibet by káfilas or otherwise. By an odd arrangement this route is closed to the Chinese.

NOTE ON TRADE ROUTES AND THE TEA TRADE.

mensem *must* be more than necessary for his keep. Now if the whole 900 miles may be travelled in 3 months, and we allow 6 months for a journey *including return*, the latter period is represented by at most $3 \times 6 = 18$ Rs., on account of the driver, for 60 maunds; or say 3 maunds per rupee; and if to provide for wear and tear of saddles and leathern thongs, &c., &c., we even treble the amount, the result is that carriage from Dárchendo to Lhása costs 1 rupee per maund for the 890 miles, or under $\frac{1}{4}$ pie per maund per mile. The charge per mile for 1 maund by railway in India varies from $\frac{1}{2}$ to 2 pie per mile.

11. As to the population (west of Dárchendo and south of 36° latitude) in *all* Tibet and Bhutan, which consumes the Dárchendo tea, that is a question to which no reliable reply can be given without more information than is at present available; in fact it is difficult to say how far east, west and south this tea *is used*, wholly or in part. But under certain assumptions it is practicable to find the areas required with moderate correctness, and from thence to argue to results for what they may be worth. The areas I proceed to find are (1) those of the nomadic portion of the Jángtháng (tinted yellow on the Index Map), and (2) of the strip south of it, which beginning at Tadam is itself bounded to the south at first by the British frontier and thereafter (including Bhutan) by the Tibet southern boundary (conjectural) back to Dárchendo.

Area of	Square Miles.
Nomadic portion of Jángtháng (tinted yellow on the Index Map)	234,000
Strip south of yellow tint down to British frontier and then (including Bhutan) following out the bar-cross-bar line (supposed Tibetan frontier) up to Dárchendo. ...	229,000
Total area ...	463,000

This total area excludes the Giáma Rong, and no doubt other large tracts to the east, with which this note has no concern; also Nepal &c.; but it includes Bhutan: and it is highly probable that this total area is *less* than that area *west* of Dárchendo where *the* tea is consumed. Now the average population along the routes followed by A——k is about 13 per square mile as shown in Table V of Summary; but for the total area now under consideration, so far as I can ascertain and estimate, on the average 5 souls per square mile would probably be an *under estimate*; adopting this number,

Total population for total area $= 463,000 \times 5 = 2,315,000$ souls.

Again if we assume 5 souls to a family of the lower orders, and, as said in article 5, that an economical household of the kind will consume only 1 seer of tea per mensem,

We have, total annual consumption of tea in the total area

$$= \frac{2,315,000 \times 1 \times 12}{5} = 5,556,000 \text{ seers} = 140,000 \text{ maunds nearly.}$$

Or, as people like to think of tea in pound measure, the foregoing indicates that the consumption of tea in the area discussed is most probably *more than eleven and a half millions of pounds annually*, a result so considerable, that India would sensibly benefit by sharing in it to the extent of even a moderate fraction.

12. Coming now to the point; the question for consideration is competition between Indian and Dárchendo tea in Tibet. There is no other opening into Tibet for Indian teas nearly as favorable as that to Lhása, so I assume that the question resolves itself into comparative cost of the two kinds of tea *at Lhása*[*]; and it is certain that an emporium of the kind is an essential factor in the matter. But before briefly alluding to the cost of carriage of Indian teas, I first return to Art. 10, where it is shown that cost of carriage from Dárchendo to Lhása cannot exceed 1 Rupee a maund. Were there no other features remaining in that route to consider, I do not see that the subject of cost of carriage would be worth further

---

[*] I make no doubt that this question has received consideration at far more competent hands than mine, and the same may also be said on several other kindred points, which I therefore touch on but very briefly. The subject however is of such great importance, that I do not exclude certain items here, which may (or may not) have already been discussed to better purpose.

discussion, because India could not possibly compete with the Jángtháng in this respect; and I repeat, my remarks refer only to cost of *carriage*, not to cost of manufacture, on which I do not venture to say a word. The feature remaining, is the difficulty the Dárchendo tea has to encounter between that place and the gardens: here, as said, the road is very bad, and probably it will be left so for many years; the tea is all carried by human beings (the Giáma Rongbas) and the journey takes some 20 days: a man will carry say 10 khotus; a woman about 8 khotus; so the two may be said to carry 18 khotus or 2¼ maunds per individual on the average. I cannot elicit directly what the cost would be expressed in Indian money[*]: I can only learn that payment is made mostly in tea (which is a fact for consideration) to the porters, who are poor as a class and easily satisfied; still a couple are said to consume the equivalent of some 6 Rs. monthly on food alone: if this be so, and the trip and return journey be set down at say 35 days, the charge *per individual* is probably not less (including say 2 Rs. saving) than $(3/8 + 2)$ = say 6 Rs. for the month and five days; this for 2¼ maunds gives some 2 Rs. 11 As. the maund; or to avoid too low an estimate, call the charge even 4 Rs. per maund from the gardens (generally) to Dárchendo: next, adding 1 Re. from the latter place to Lhása, there results 5 Rs. per maund as cost of carriage from the Chinese gardens to Lhása. This, if correct, would be *the* charge, than which carriage from the Indian gardens to Lhása must be *less*[†], in order that these gardens should compete with advantage.

13. Now as to the Indian gardens, a great deal is necessary before they can compete in carriage, the first and most important consideration being the best line of communication with Lhása; this should obviously pass many miles east of Darjeeling and be facilitated by rails of some kind as far north as practicable; beasts of burthen would answer for the remainder: but I repeat, the line must I think run considerably east of Darjeeling, it must be helped to the utmost extent by rails, and for the remainder carriage by human agency must be entirely eliminated. What comes of carriage by man in contrast to cattle-carriage may be illustrated by the following rates which I am told now obtain from Darjeeling to Lhása

	per maund Rs.	A.
Darjeeling to Phári, say 90 miles by road; carriage by men at Rs. 5/8 for 1½ maunds … … … =	3	11
Phári to Lhása, say 217 miles by road; carried by cattle at Rs. 1/8 for 1¾ maunds … … … =	0	14
Total, Darjeeling to Lhása … =	4	9

which gives, carriage *per mile* per maund

| By men | … | … | … | … | … | 7·87 pies |
| ,, cattle | … | … | … | … | … | 0·77 ,, |

i.e., man-carriage is more than 10 times as expensive *there* as cattle-carriage. Further, the carriage from the Chinese gardens *viâ* Dárchendo to Lhása (some 1030 miles) being estimated at Rs. 5 per maund, the carriage from Darjeeling to Lhása (say 310 miles) is as above Rs. 4/9, or but 7 As. less, leaving the latter small amount only as a set-off against the carriage from the Indian gardens to Darjeeling. These illustrations are perhaps worth exhibiting, at the same time I do not mean that the route for Indian teas to Lhása was ever contemplated to run *viâ* Darjeeling.

14. A few words too at a venture may be added on Indian tea. There are many hundreds of acres under cultivation in the valley (Dehra Dún) below this place, but so far as

---

[*] If not already known, no doubt full particulars could be obtained from the Jesuit Fathers resident at Dárchendo; but conversion from payment in tea to Indian money is beset by several difficulties which may lead to erroneous conclusions: the conversion is not a mere matter of arithmetic.

[†] Unless indeed the Indian tea-planter can *manufacture* for less than the Chinese? As respects the Chinese, I cannot separate the 2 items involved (apart from carriage from the gardens to Dárchendo), *i.e.*, (1) cost of manufacture all told, (2) profit to tea-planter (who it will be remembered delivers at Dárchendo); but calling the 2 items added together "total value" then we can make a guess at this, per pound as follows. Take the Chuba tea, said to be most commonly in use, (article 6): the price at Dárchendo for 5 seers is Re. 1, and hence for 90 seers (a porter's load) the price is Rs. 18: deduct 4 Rs. (article 12) to porter, and there remain 14 Rs. for the 90 seers, which give at the rate of 1 An. 3 pie per *pound* for the said total value. Or if we include porterage with the said total value, then 90 seers yield Rs. 18, which give 1 An. 7 pie per *pound*. If this be true, India must exercise rare ingenuity and economy to compete successfully in Tibet.

NOTE ON TRADE ROUTES AND THE TEA TRADE.

I am aware no one there *at least* has ever attempted to imitate the Chinese brick tea; and yet if India is to compete with Tibet, there can be no manner of doubt she must do so with the self same article Tibet is accustomed to, *i.e.*, tea in *bricks*. Moreover, it is easy to see, that the hard compact brick is a box in itself, and offers resistance to degeneration from atmospheric causes by means both effective and economical. Nothing but failure can result from trying to force leaf-tea on people, who, like the semi-civilized Tibetans, are accustomed to tea in brick; and in a word it is difficult to imagine any form so portable and exactly suited to the circumstances, in Tibet as well as elsewhere, than tea in brick.

15. But besides the subject dealt with in the foregoing, there is another if possible of even greater importance, which is almost wholly neglected. I allude to trade in the soft, costly wool called Pashm, or shawl-wool. Whatever else the Jángtháng may fail to grow, there can be no doubt that hundreds, or even thousands of maunds of pashm are necessarily produced there every year and *wasted*. Pashm *can* grow only in cold countries, and otherwise the conditions prevailing in the Jángtháng are exactly suited to its production by means of the herds of all kinds of innumerable animals bred there; but Tibetans neither know its value nor how to collect it; and in fact the industry has yet to be taught them, as has already been done in a few localities, including Máusarowar lake, which feed Kashmir. The conclusion is obvious: if Indian tea could be exchanged for Pashm, if not for coin, the advantages accruing to both Tibet and this country would be very considerable indeed.

J. B. N. HENNESSEY,

Deputy Surveyor General,

In charge Trigonometrical Surveys.

Mussooree,
27th June, 1884.

Explorations in Great Tibet and Mongolia, by A——k, 1879-82, made in connection with the Trigonometrical Branch, Survey of India.

TRANSLATIONS FROM DIARY AND NOTES.

NOTE.—*The bearings hereafter given are all reckoned from the true north; to obtain them, all the original magnetic bearings have been increased by 2½° for variation of needle.*

I left Darjeeling on the 24th April 1878, accompanied by my faithful companion L——c and another servant M——g engaged for the exploration, and reached the right bank of the Teesta river at night-fall. The next day I arrived at Kalingbug, a small bazár of 15 or 20 shops, where a market is held every Sunday; and we halted for three days in order to collect supplies for the journey. On the 29th April we arrived at Poidung village, on the 30th at Rinag, and on the 1st May at Chujáchen village; a heavy fall of rain detained us here for a day. On the 3rd May we reached Lingdam, on the 4th Pangdam and on the 5th Gani, all three being customary halting places. On the 6th we crossed the Jaleb mountain and arrived at Náthang, also a halting place. Snow now began to fall and detained us for three days. On the 10th May, we arrived at Kubug, a halting place, where grass is abundant, and where the Tibetan boundary is reached. The villagers of Rinchen Gáng migrate here for the months of October, November and December to pasture their flocks and yáks. On the 12th May, crossing the Kubug Lá or Bodh Lá pass, which was covered with snow to a depth of three feet, we arrived at Langta, a halting place. Here firewood (from a kind of fir tree) and grass are abundant.

2. The 13th May brought us to Rinchen Gáng (invaluable rock), a village of 30 houses. Towards the west and up an ascent of about 500 paces there is a Gomba in which some 10 or 12 Dábas and a Láma reside. They occupy themselves solely in reading religious books and repeating hymns aloud. This village lies in the Domo patti; all the villages of this patti are situated on the banks of the Domo Chu river, which flows from the north to Lho or Bhutan. They are sparsely inhabited as the soil is poor and yields but little corn, so that only one crop is raised annually. Ne, dau, turnip and potato are grown. We remained here two days to collect supplies and re-pack our merchandize.

3. Leaving Rinchen Gáng for Galing Kha on the 16th May, after travelling for some 3 miles, we reached Chumbil on the Domo Chu river, the residence during the summer season of the Gialbu (Rája) of Dainjung or Sikkim. It is a large, paka, square, three storied palace, surrounded by a wall of rubble stone, having two large gates, one to the north and the other to the south. There are some 40 houses close to and south of the palace. Thence the road crosses a wooden bridge about 40 paces in length, close to Chumbil; and 3 miles further it brought us to the junction of two streams, one coming from the N.W. and the other from the N.E., which uniting flow southwards under the name of the Domo Chu river. Following the left bank of the N.E. stream we reached Galing Kha village containing 40 houses. On the right bank of the same stream, opposite to Galing Kha and close to Rupu Kha village, there is a Gomba called Dong Kar. The last named village is the most northern of the Domo patti. Dág Kárpo, a halting place, was reached on the 17th May. The route from Kubug to this place is very narrow and rugged.

4. On the 18th we reached Phári Jong, a fort on the top of a small solitary hill about 1,200 paces in circumference at base. The fort is some 200 feet above the surrounding plain, and has steps leading up to it on the east. It has no tower or enclosing wall. The country round is level for about 4 miles but not cultivated. There are some 200 houses to the S.E. of the fort. Wood for fuel is not procurable, but its place is supplied by dried dung of the domesticated yák. The Jemo-Lha Ri (female god peak), otherwise Chumalári Hill Station of the Great Trigonometrical Survey, is visible from the surrounding plain. About 12 miles to the west are 12 Chuchans the waters of which are reputed to possess different healing properties, so that they are said to cure 12 different diseases. The people of this neighbourhood very seldom seek medical treatment, but when ill they are content to bathe for a week or so in the springs.

TRANSLATIONS FROM DIARY AND NOTES.

5. Two Jong Pons (a Tibetan expression which literally means the fort-master), the farmers of the taxes under the Lhása Government, bear rule here for periods of three years. Their duty is to guard the road and levy taxes, equal to one-tenth the value on any merchandize which passes, and to decide cases of a civil and criminal nature. M——g having fallen ill detained us here for three months.

6. Leaving Phári on the 16th August we halted at Chu Gia. Thence crossing a small mountain we passed the night of the 17th at Dhuna, a village of 10 houses, and on the 18th reached Kála, a village of 60 houses. Here we met with cultivation. Some 18 miles from Dhuna and to the right of the road lies the Rám Cho lake, the water of which begins to freeze about the middle of October, and a month later it is so hard frozen that none flows out; a thaw usually sets in about the beginning of February. Near Kála and to the west is another lake called Kála Cho. The villagers of Kála spend a good deal of time in fishing. They wade out into the lake, which is not deep, for a long distance and catch numbers of large fish in nets dragged by four men. The fish are dried in the sun and so prepared for the market. On the 19th we halted at Samáda, a village of 10 houses with some cultivation about it. The route from Dág Kárpo to Samáda is wide, smooth and level. On the 20th we arrived at Tángo, having passed a small hot spring on the road.

7. The 21st August saw us at Giángche, a small town on the right bank of the Pena Náng Chu river. The town is situated about two small hills which lie east and west and are united by a saddle; the western hill is further connected with the chain of mountains to the north. On the eastern hill, which is about 600 feet above the surrounding plain, is a large fort similar in construction to that at Phári; and on the western hill a Gomba inhabited by 500 Dábas. In this Gomba there is a Chiorten,* called Pángon Chiorten, which is considered by the Tibetans a most holy place. Besides the fort and temple there are about 1,000 dwelling houses on three sides of the double hill. Woollen cloth called Nhambu is manufactured. There is a large market, and traders from Nepal and China reside here. We remained for six days to exchange our articles of merchandize. The road from Samáda to Giángche is rugged and stony.

8. On the 28th Upsi village was reached where there is a large Giakhang or Chinese stage-house; and on the 29th we halted at Ralung village which also possesses a Chinese stage-house. The road from Giángche to this place is smooth, wide and level. On the 30th the road crossed the Ralung Lá or Kharo Lá pass by an easy ascent and brought us to Jára, a Chinese stage-house. To the north of the last named pass lies a very high peak, near the base of which is a small glacier. On the 31st we reached Nangárche Jong stage-house, close to the Yámdok Cho lake. This lake was the largest I had met with. It is like a horse-shoe in form and almost encircles a small hill on which is a large temple dedicated to Dorje Phámo. A number of villages are said to be situated on the hill. The lake contains a great number of fish, not larger than a span, which are sold in Lhása. They are caught by angling through holes in the ice.

9. On the 1st September, travelling along the northern shore of the Yámdok Cho lake, we reached Pete Jong stage-house, and on the 2nd, crossing the Khamba Lá pass, arrived at Khamba-barji stage-house. The pass is on the boundary of the Cháng and Ú divisions of the Ú Cháng province. On the 3rd, a mile distant from the last halting place, we struck the right bank of the Cháng Chu (Brahmaputra) river which we crossed at Chiák-jamchori (iron bridge at the rocky bank) by a bridge and arrived at Chushul Jong stage-house. The bridge is formed of two iron chains, one on each side: from the chains thick ropes are suspended to the depth of four yards: by these ropes planks, three feet long and one foot broad, are supported lengthwise so as only to admit of one person crossing at a time. The chains are stretched very tight† and are fastened round huge blocks of wood buried beneath immense piles of stone: the length of the bridge is about 100 paces. On the 4th Natháng on the right bank of the Ki Chu river, was reached: the river is about 80 paces wide. On the 5th September 1878 we arrived at Lhása. Here we replenished our stock of merchandize.

---

* Chiorten is a colored building of varying height, rising in rectangular blocks, each diminishing in size. On the centre of the top-most block there is a carved wooden tapering cone, on the summit of which is a golden crescent and ball. The central portion is hollow and in course of building, images, religious books and other objects of veneration are placed within.

† Nevertheless there is a sensible curve: when we crossed, the surface of the water below the centre of the bridge was about 50 feet, while at the two ends it was much more.

EXPLORATIONS BY A——K IN GREAT TIBET AND MONGOLIA.

10. After spending some time in Lhása, waiting for a caravan to start for Mongolia, I heard that one was about to leave. I went at once to the Gar Pon or Sardár of the caravan and enquired the date of its departure, but could obtain no definite answer beyond this, that the caravan might start about the month of February. I pressed him to fix the date but failed. "My long experience has taught me", he said, "that when the date is "fixed, the robbers' spies who are here, communicate it to their masters, and then the caravans "never arrive safely at their destination." In November he sent for the other traders and myself and begged us to excuse him from going to Mongolia on account of his being under a heavy debt of 500 tamímas or kurs (1 kurs = 156 rupees of Anglo-Indian coin) which he must liquidate before leaving the city. This was very discouraging as we had no other experienced man to lead us. At last we agreed to subscribe and pay his debt. After four months further delay he gave up the idea of conducting the caravan, and I had no alternative but to wait for another. In August one arrived from Mongolia; and as half of this Káfila was to return immediately, I went to the leader and requested him to take me with him; he consented and we left Lhása on the 17th September 1879.

11. During my stay at Lhása I employed myself in learning the Mongolian language. Moreover during June and July of 1879 I took a series of air thermometer observations.

12. Lhása city, about 6 miles in circumference, is situated in a tolerably level plain surrounded by mountains. It is on the right bank of the Ki Chu river. In the centre of the city stands a very high, square temple called Jhio, the roof of which is covered with golden plates. The images in it are numerous, but the most important of them are of Jhio Sakia Muni, and of Palden-Lhámo or the goddess Káli of India. The former is said to have travelled to Tibet from India where he is called Shákya Muni. The idols are richly inlaid with gold and precious stones, and have various ornaments round their necks. Near the temple are situated the court-house, the police station and the treasury; the temple and the three buildings are surrounded by a street 30 feet broad, on either side of which are shops kept by Tibetan, Chinese, Nepalese, Kashmiri and Azimabad (Patna) merchants. Bhánágshio, Tumsikáng and Rámoche are the streets where foreign traders (new arrivals) generally find quarters, and Wángdusiga is an open square where a large market is held every morning for the sale of all kinds of articles.

13. At the western extremity of the city and on a small hill is a medical school called Chiákpori, having some 300 Dába students. There is no fixed period of study, but as soon as they become efficient they obtain appointments, either at the recommendation of the head teacher or by their own exertions. The school is also the repository of many kinds of medicines for the use of high officials. To the north of the school and at the base of a mountain is a large palace, the residence of the present Gialbu or Rája. To the north-east of this palace is a large and strong fort, built on a low isolated hill with winding steps leading to it from the north and east, and named Poto La or Chai, the residence of Kiámkun-Ringboche or the Láma—the chief spiritual and secular adviser in Tibet. He is supposed never to die, but his soul transmigrates into another body. When he dies, his body is placed in a coffin and after some days is buried, and a hollow monument of metal plated with gold is raised over the spot; this monument is called a Kutung and resembles a small Chiorten in shape.

14. The new Láma is said to appear within a year from the date of the last Láma's death. His birth is recognised by the contemporary miracles* at or about his birth-place. His parents inform the nearest chief official, who, after holding a strict enquiry into the matter, brings it to the notice of the Gialbu who then represents the Lhása Government. Then the private attendants of the late Láma immediately repair to the house, in order to test the veracity of the report by signs which they profess to know. When the birth of the Láma has been fully established by this corroborative evidence, some of the chief officials go to his birth-place in order to remove him and his parent to some Gomba or temple near the city, where they are lodged till the auspicious hour arrives for his being brought with great honor to Poto La fort. As soon as he is of age, civil and ecclesiastical affairs are entrusted to him. When miracles are reported to have taken place at the birth of more than one child, election is made by casting lots.

---

* Among the strange events may be mentioned the following:—The blossoming, in the immediate vicinity of the birth-place, of fruit trees some months before their usual season; the casting of two or more young by animals which as a rule do not cast so many at a birth; and the sudden recovery from fatal illnesses of persons coming in contact with the new born child.

TRANSLATIONS FROM DIARY AND NOTES.

15. To the north of the city stands a large Chiorten, called Giáng Bunmoche, erected in honor of a Tibetan hero who is said to have killed 100,000 of his enemies (Chinese) on the spot. Close to it is a temple called Rámoche Jhio, a sacred place of worship.

16. During the first month* of the Tibetan year all the gods and goddesses are supposed to be present in Lhása, and a large gathering of Tibetans takes place. Some of them come in order to pay homage to the idols, and others simply as spectators. All the Dábas and their head Lámas from the Sára, Daibung† and Ganden (Galdan) Gombas go there in order to unite in prayers for the future welfare of the country; their expenses during the month are borne by the State. During this period the city is governed by the Lámas of the Daibung Gomba, whose will becomes the supreme law for the time being: they inflict arbitrary punishments for trifling offences. Such of the richer classes of inhabitants as may have in any way incurred their displeasure leave the city and live in the suburbs. The poorer classes who are always dirty and never change their clothes, now sweep and whitewash their houses through fear of being punished by the Lámas for their uncleanliness. So long as these Lámas govern Lhása, they are feasted at the public expense or by the richer people and are entertained with sports. On the 2nd day of the new year (say the middle of February) all the inhabitants gather together to witness a feat performed by two men‡, each of whom in turn mounts on a wooden saddle and slides down a strong rope fastened from the fort walls to a post buried about 9 feet in the ground. Fifteen days after this the great festival of Chionga Chiopa is celebrated.

17. Another festival is held during the next month and continues for 10 days; it is called Chongju Saiwang. During this festival a Tibetan of a certain tribe is summoned by the Láma; his face is colored half black and half white and a leather coat is put on him; and he is immediately turned out of the city, and ordered to go to Chetáng, viâ Samaye, where he resides for the year. At Samaye he is obliged to remain for seven days, and to sleep at nights in a solitary room (in the Gomba) called the Gate of Death, which is filled with skins of huge serpents and wild animals, images of Rákshhas, &c., all calculated to excite feelings of terror in the individual. During his seven days' stay he exercises despotic authority in Samaye, and the same during the first seven days of his stay in Chetáng. The Láma and the people give him much alms because he is believed to sacrifice himself for the welfare of the country. It is said that in former times the man who performed this duty died at Chetáng in the course of the year, from the effect of the *mantras* (prayers) repeated by the Lámas and Dábas after his departure; but now he survives and returns to act his part the following year.

18. The Government consists of one grand Láma, one Gialbu who is also a Láma, four secretaries and five counsellors. The Láma is the chief ruler in Tibet and is consulted in cases of emergency; he is the last resort of appeal, and his decision is invariably unquestioned. The Gialbu is his prime minister, and next to him in rank, and is elected from among the head Lámas of one of the four Lings (divisions) named Kontia Ling, Chomo Ling, Tangia Ling and Chajo Ling. His soul is also supposed to transmigrate into another body.

19. Two other important officers, called Ambáns, who are representatives of the Chinese Government, are stationed here; they are appointed for a term of three years.

20. Whenever any dispute arises between two parties of foreigners of the same nationality, who domicile there, it is decided by the chief man among them; but when the parties are of different nationalities, inquiries are conducted by the Tibetan rulers who decide the case, and if necessary assign punishment, and deliver the offenders to their respective headman for the execution of the sentence. Robbery is frequent in the city as thieves are assisted in the disposal of stolen property by the Nepalese merchants.

21. The number of males in Tibet is very small in proportion to the other sex. It is considered a religious duty for parents to offer their firstborn male child to be brought up as a Dába, and frequently the younger male children also enter this order of their own free will. When they grow up they are not allowed to marry, nor to cohabit with women.

---

* The month begins about our mid-February.
† These are gombas about 3 miles W. and 25 miles E. of Lhása: the latter is reckoned the most ancient of the monasteries belonging to the Gilukpa sect of the Nangba sect of Buddhists.
‡ These men are always chosen from a village in the vicinity of Shigáchi.

22. The manners and customs of the Tibetans are nearly the same as those of other hill tribes. The practice of polyandry is common, four or five brothers having one wife. As a reason for the practice I was told that when there is only one woman in a family all the members lived peaceably together, while in the other case they are obliged to separate. The marriage ceremony is conducted without much formality. Three forms of marriage are recognised by them; first, when a girl is of age, she elects her consort without consulting her parents or near relations; secondly, when the parents of a girl select a husband for her, they then retain the couple in their house; thirdly, when a man selects a wife for himself he takes her to his own house. The women are free and independent, and are very serviceable and painstaking: maid servants are numerous and can be obtained on nominal pay.

23. Three dialects are spoken in Tibet. Kham Kai or the Kham dialect of the inhabitants of the province so-called to the east of Lhása; Bodh Kai of the people of the Ú Cháng province; and Doag Kai of the nomads of Nari Khorsum. Of these three, the second, which is spoken in and around Lhása, is polished and is the language in which most of their sacred and other books are written.

24. The principal articles of diet are:—*Sattu* (parched grain ground into flour) and Nepal and Bhutan rice, fish, goat's flesh and other animal* food commonly used by man, tea, and beer made from barley or *ne* and fermented by the addition of some kind of spice; this is known all over Tibet under the name *chhang*. The latter is kept in closed earthen vessels† for some days and is either drunk in that state or a kind of spirit is distilled from it.

25. The climate of Lhása is very healthy and no contagious disease is ever known to prevail. Small-pox once raged there some 40 years ago when numbers of the people died; the inhabitants are very much afraid of it, believing it to be incurable. Inoculation, as a preventive, is unknown, and even if recommended by foreigners is not adopted.

26. One crop only is raised in Tibet; this is sown in April and reaped in September. The chief articles of produce are: wheat, *ne* (a kind of barley), the Indian and Chinese pea, *taichun* (a kind of pulse), *pekang* (a kind of mustard) and *dau* (a kind of grain). The edible roots are the potato, turnip, radish, &c.

27. Buddhism is the religion of the country; there are two sects, one named Nangba and the other Chiba or Baimbu. The former is distinguished by its members circumambulating temples keeping them on their right side, whilst the latter walk round in the opposite direction; this is one of their religious ceremonies. The Nangba sect has subdivisions named Ningma, Sakia, Gúba and Gilukpa. Corpses of *all* but Lámas are taken to the top of a mountain named Dhoto which is set apart conveniently in the vicinity of villages and towns; here they are cut in pieces and thrown to kites and crows by the relatives and friends of the deceased, and this act is held in much esteem by those performing it.

28. The nobility is an hereditary one. The following are the chief families: Sandu Photáng, During, Seta, Bhandi Shia, Raga Shia, Lhalu, Yutok and Poti Kháñsa. A noble is called Dunkur.

29. On the 17th September 1879, we left Lhása and started for Mongolia. The caravan included 105 souls, 60 of whom were Mongolians of both sexes and the rest Tibetans, including my party of six. Three-quarters of a mile from the Rámoche Jhio temple in Lhása is a garden named Dabchilinga and the same distance further and on the left of the road is a small fort built for the Chinese soldiers, to the east of which is a parade ground named Dabchi, where the Tibetan troops twice a year display their military skill before the Ambán. A mile eastward from Dabchi is Chiángro village (10 houses). At the distance of a mile from the fort and bearing $337\frac{1}{2}°$ is a temple called Sára Gomba, containing 5,500 Dúbas for whom food is provided by the Lhása Government. Two miles further the road crosses a small stream, which issues from the Phembu Gong pass, and flowing to the south falls into the Ki Chu river; 50 paces to the east is Parisiga, a hamlet of 5 houses, and on a spur of

---

* Not omitting that of hog, oxen and yák.

† These are earthen vessels which have undergone a special preparation by having the bark of certain shrubs previously steeped therein in order to render them air-tight: and as it costs some trouble to make a really air-tight vessel, it is much valued by the owner.

the Phembu Gong mountain, about 500 paces to the west, is a temple, called Kecháng Gomba. Three-quarters of a mile further the same stream is re-crossed. Huñgusíga village, four houses, is 50 paces to the east, and a Romkháng or cemetery, where the Mahomedans of Lhása bury their dead, is 50 paces to the west. Some 450 paces to the west of the cemetery is Khutho Gomba on a spur of the Phembu Gong mountain. About $1\frac{1}{2}$ miles further and to the left of our route is Gákánáka Cheñkháng, a temple dedicated to one of the passionate and vindictive gods. A nála running from the west joins the stream (which flows along the road) about $1\frac{1}{2}$ miles north of the temple. Continuing our journey for about $1\frac{1}{2}$ miles we reached Lingbu Jong, a ruined fort, where we stopped for the night. The road is very good for 4 miles, the remaining part of it is stony and rugged but having an easy gradient. Forage is abundant.

30. The next day, after a difficult ascent of about 2 miles by a rough and stony road, we reached the Phembu Gong pass. The range bearing this name runs from the east. Boiling point observations were taken here (height 16,320 feet). No trees were visible but a small kind of grass covered the whole range; from the pass the descent is precipitous for about $2\frac{1}{2}$ miles to a stream which crosses the road towards the left. About $5\frac{3}{4}$ miles further down, we reached Baya, a small village; the stream re-crosses the road towards the right about a mile below the village and flowing for about 2 miles at a bearing of $67\frac{1}{2}°$, joins the Phembu Chu stream. About $1\frac{1}{8}$ miles from the village we found two temples, one called Langta Gomba, containing 50 Dábas, about 500 paces to the east, and the other Nálenda Gomba, containing 100 Dábas, a mile to the west. About 3 miles from Baya village the road crosses the Phembu Chu stream, $1\frac{1}{2}$ feet deep and 15 paces broad, flowing from the west; this stream, about 20 miles to the south-east, joins the Ki Chu river: near the junction is a temple called Digung inhabited by about 250 Dábas. A mile to the north-east of the place where the Phembu Chu stream was crossed, another stream issuing from the Chak or Chiág pass to the north, falls into that stream: 3 miles beyond the stream, is Debungsíga or Naimár, a village of 20 houses where we halted for the night; it lies in the Phembu Patti. This locality is well cultivated and the produce finds a ready sale at Lhása. The fields are watered by irrigation cuts led down from the Phembu Chu and other smaller streams.

31. Leaving Debungsíga on the 19th and proceeding for about $2\frac{1}{2}$ miles along the right bank of the stream from the north, we arrived at a village. About three-quarters of a mile from the village and bearing $86\frac{1}{2}°$ is a fort called Lundub Jong with 50 houses around it. Two Jong Pons, Tibetan officers, who reside in this fort, have charge of the Phembu Patti, extending from the Phembu Gong to Chak passes. $1\frac{3}{4}$ miles further, at a distance of three-quarters of a mile from the road and bearing $82\frac{1}{2}°$, there is a gomba containing 50 cells. Three miles higher up is a small village to the west and $1\frac{1}{2}$ miles further another small stream flowing from the east falls into the nála which issuing from the Chak pass runs parallel to the road to the right: $1\frac{1}{2}$ miles onward it crosses the road to the left. Half a mile further up, a small stream from the west falls into the nála, now running parallel to it on the left. After an ascent of $2\frac{3}{4}$ miles, the last half mile of which is steep, we arrived at Chak pass, where boiling point observations were taken (height 15,840 feet). The Chak range runs from the west. After an easy descent of $\frac{3}{4}$ of a mile, a stream issues from the left and flows towards the north and $1\frac{3}{4}$ miles further on crossed our route towards the east; three-quarters of a mile further it joins another stream from the west, and the united stream empties itself into the Tálung Chu river. About $4\frac{3}{4}$ miles from the pass is an encamping ground, where we halted for the night. A mile to the west of this place is a large gomba called Tálung Gomba or Jáng Tálung, the residence of the well-known Láma of Tibet, named Má Ringboche, and of about 300 Dábas. Grass and fuel are abundant: the road is stony.

32. On the 20th, about 300 paces from the encamping ground, we crossed to the left bank of the Tálung Chu, 3 feet deep and 35 paces wide, which flowing to the north-east joins the Ki Chu river. About 6 miles from our last halting place, is Phondu Jong fort, having 50 houses to the south. It is situated at the confluence of the Rong Chu and Migi Chángpo rivers, and the Tálung. The first is a large river about 40 paces broad. It is formed by two tributaries, one coming from the Dam district, called the Dam Chu, and another from the Láni Lá, which meet about 3 miles from the fort. The second river, which is about $3\frac{3}{4}$ feet deep and 65 paces wide, issues from the Nin-Chen-thangla range, and after flowing through Shangshung district and then along a portion of the boundary of Reting it reaches the junction; these two with the Tálung Chu form the

well-known Ki Chu river. Near the fort and a little above the junction is an iron* bridge 40 yards long similar to that at Chiákjamchori. During the rainy season boats are used for crossing the river †: boiling point observations were taken near the fort (height 13,340 feet). 6¾ miles further up we reached Chamchúnang, a deserted village on the right bank of the Migi Chángpo river, where observations for latitude and of the boiling point were taken (latitude 30° 16′ 30″, height 13,230 feet). Grass and firewood are found here; the latter of the *padam* (a kind of fir) tree. The road is rugged and narrow up to Phondu Jong, the remainder wide, smooth and level. The Tálung district extends from the Chak pass to Phondu Jong fort. The tract of land, which lies to the left of the Migi Chángpo river to the south-east of the road and between the Phondu Jong fort and Chámchunang, is called the Phondu district.

33. On the 21st, two miles further up we arrived at Chiomo Lhákháng (50 houses) with a small temple of the same name: it is at the junction of a stream with the Migi Chángpo river. On the right bank of the Migi Chángpo, distant 5 miles and bearing 72½°, there is a large monastery called Reting Gomba where 200 Dábas reside: this was the last place on the route where I saw cultivation. 4½ miles further along the right bank of the stream a small nála from the west falls into it; and 2½ miles further up another nála, bearing 302½°, empties itself into the same: 3 miles further still is the Márnio Lá pass, where boiling point observations were taken (height 14,960 feet). This pass has an easy ascent and a very gentle descent; it forms the northern boundary of the Reting district, which extends to Chiomo Lhákháng southwards. About ½ a mile from the pass is Láni Tarjum, a halting place, where we passed the night. At this place there are some 50 tents occupied by members of the nomad tribe, which is under the control of a Tarjum Pa (a head-man appointed by the Lhása Government to each Tarjum) whose duty it is to have horses and yáks in attendance for the Lhása officials. These people receive no wages for their services, but are allotted tracts of land, on payment of some annual taxes, large enough to graze their cattle during the whole year, and they always keep them within the prescribed limits. They are held strictly responsible for all accidents and for the safe transit of all goods within their limits. Their tents are made of the long, coarse, black wool of yáks. At the time of our arrival there was a fall of snow about a foot deep, and fuel and and fodder were difficult to obtain.

34. Leaving Láni Tarjum on the 22nd we reached the Láni Lá pass by an easy ascent of 2¼ miles. Boiling point observations were taken at the pass, (height 15,750 feet). The Láni Lá range comes from the east, and far off in that direction are some high peaks covered with perpetual snow. A stream issues 2½ miles from the pass and after flowing to the north for about 4½ miles is joined by another stream from the west. A mile further is a Dam Chuchan (a hot spring of the Dam district), in which the inhabitants of the neighbourhood bathe at least twice a year. There are three square kacha tanks‡ 21 feet long and 2 feet deep which are always full of water; in these the bathers remain immersed up to their necks until the perspiration runs from their foreheads, when they leave the tank, and lie down wrapped up warmly for some minutes; after this they drink some beer and take food. About 1¼ miles from the spring is a halting place called Yár Khorchen, where there are three small kacha houses, two for the shelter of travellers and one for a Khorchen (a large Khor or Khorlo§) in the Dam valley which lies north-east and south-west. The valley is about 15 miles long and 5 miles broad, and is watered by a small stream called the Dam Chu, about 2 feet deep and 20 paces broad, a tributary of the Rong Chu river. Three miles to the west of the halting place is a paka house belonging to the Chigeb (ruler or Lambardár) of the Dam valley. There are some 200 tents of nomads, whose occupation is the grazing of cattle consisting of ponies, yáks, goats, and sheep; some of them are traders, who bring *bul* (a kind of soda) and salt from the Tengri Núr lake and exchange them for corn and cloth at Lhása. In addition their own valley furnishes several other commodities for

---

* Wrongly marked on map as *rope* bridge.

† The boats are made of hides stretched on a wooden frame work; the hides most valued for this purpose are those of the wild yák, and next those of the domesticated yák.

‡ The temperature of these was roughly estimated at about 120°.

§ A Khorlo is a revolving, drum-like cylinder, made of paper covered with red parchment, on which is written the sacred formula in large golden or red characters. The paper also has the same formula many times repeated printed on it (by engraved characters on wood). Khorlos are of various sizes: the smaller are covered with silver, copper or brass plates, and are constantly held in the hand. The paper is folded round a reed, through which passes an iron pin. A thong is fastened to the lower end of pin of large Khorlos and is used for revolving them. It is believed by the people that constantly keeping the Khorlo in motion purifies them from sin.

TRANSLATIONS FROM DIARY AND NOTES.

exchange; for instance, yâks, goats, sheep, ponies*, butter, &c. The nomads are Tibetans, very stout and warlike; they are not subject to the Lhása Government, but acknowledge the authority of the Ambán. The valley is noted for its pasturage. The head Láma has 300 mares stabled here under the charge of a Chi Pon (a master of the stable); they are milked every day during summer, and a kind of fermented liquor is prepared, after the Tibetan process of distillation, for the use of the head Láma; it is the only liquor which he is allowed to take. About two days' journey from the valley is the Namcho or Tengri Núr lake, and some 10 days' journey to the north of the lake are wild people scattered over the hilly regions. We halted two days at Yár Khorchen, where observations for latitude and boiling point were taken (lat. 30° 30′ 55″, height 14,460 feet).

35. Leaving the halting place on the 25th September 1879, and crossing four streams coming from the east, at 2, 4, 5¾ and 6½ miles respectively, from Yár Khorchen, we reached the Chiokche Lá pass after a march of 9½ miles. The four streams flow to the S. W. and uniting form the Dam Chu river. The pass has a gentle ascent and a similar descent on the other side. A mile before the pass is reached there are eight small, unprotected Chiortens. The pass forms the northern boundary of the Dam district. 4¾ miles further we crossed the Lhai Chu river, 2 feet deep and 30 paces wide, coming from the north-west; it issues from the Nin-Chen-thangla range and flowing to the south-east falls into the Migi Chángpo river. A road runs up the Lhai Chu river and thence across the Nin-Chen-thangla pass to the Tengri Núr lake. At a distance of about 23 miles, bearing 116¼°, is Potámolam, one of the high peaks covered with perpetual snow. The road was good throughout this stage. We stopped for the night on the left bank of the Lhai Chu river.

36. On the 26th we had a long march of 24 miles: at 2 miles from our halting place we crossed one of the principal sources of the Migi Chángpo, 2½ feet deep and 50 paces wide, coming from the north. Further on we forded 5 streams coming from the east, 8, 9, 12¾, 16¼ and 17½ miles respectively from our last halting place. These streams join a river from the Shangshung Lá pass, which flowing to the south is joined by the Lhai Chu. The road which was good lay through a valley between two spurs running to the south, which are connected by an easy low pass called Shangshung Lá, distant 23 miles from the last station. About 12¾ miles distant from the pass and bearing 232° is a high snowy peak, called Samden Kháñsa. We camped for the night on a level piece of ground covered with grass about three-quarters of a mile beyond the pass: during the march we passed some nomad tents at intervals.

37. On the 27th we marched 19¼ miles along a level and wide road, and reached the left bank of a stream coming from the south-east where we encamped: on this march, after 7¼ miles we came to the Yu Chu stream flowing from the east and joining another stream which issues from a square lake about a mile broad, and situated about 3 miles to the west of the road. The united stream flows northwards and is called the Nag Chu: the lake is said to be in a large, level valley about 32 miles long and 8 miles broad; about 4 miles from the right bank of the Yu Chu stream is the Yu Lá pass, with an easy ascent over a spur of the range to the east. Two snowy peaks are visible from it, one at a distance of about 37 miles, bearing 304½° and another about 40 miles bearing 322½°.

38. On the 28th, after marching 5¾ miles up an easy ascent, we crossed the Kárchen Lá pass over a spur from the range to the east. This pass forms the northern limit of the Shangshung district, which is said to contain 500 tents of nomad tribes. 14¼ miles from the pass we crossed to the left bank of the Nag Chu river, 2¾ feet deep and 40 paces wide, and reached a Máne Khorchen (a house containing a large Khor or Khorlo) where we passed the night. From this place a direct road branches to Sining or Siling, a large city of the Chinese Empire situated about   miles to the   of the Koko-Núr Lake. We chose the circuitous road by Shiabden Gomba, where we hoped to replenish our stock of provisions which was running short.

39. On the 29th, about 5 miles beyond Máne Khorchen, we crossed a stream from the left, which two and a half miles further down falls into the Nag Chu river. This river is said to water the Hor district to the N.E. Three-quarters of a mile further is Shiabden Gomba in which dwell 100 Dábas; it is surrounded by some 150 houses and tents: there is

---

* The country is found too cold for asses, and hence neither asses nor mules are found in these parts, although in the immediate neighbourhood of Lhása they are both in abundance, some of the mules being very tall (about 14 hands) and valued at some 700 or 800 Rs.

a large house for the Jong Pons. 1¼ miles to the south is a group of hot springs within an area about half a mile in circumference. The thermometer gave a temperature of 140° for one of the springs. Shiabden Gomba is in the Nagchukha district. Grass is abundant. The district contains some 3,000 tents of nomads. Some of the tribes are much addicted to robbery which they commit far off to the west. The climate is cold. Observations for latitude and for height by boiling point were taken (lat. 31° 28′ 27″, height 14,930 feet). Supplies are procurable. Tibetan silver coin is current in all these districts: there are no gold or copper coins. The silver coin is of two kinds; one known as Chánja Paulung is an old coin, it has no alloy in it and weighs a quarter of a tola: the later coins, distinguished by the names of the rulers who coined them, have alloy in them and weigh half a tola. Both kinds of coin have the same value which is equivalent to six annas of Indian money: they bear the common name of Tanka. For small change coins are cut up into pieces. The Indian rupee is also current. We spent three nights at Shiabden Gomba.

40. On the 2nd October we crossed a spur about 5 miles from the temple, and 3½ miles further reached the Thaigár Lá pass by an easy ascent. After passing the spur we recrossed the stream we had passed just before reaching Shiabden Gomba. Two miles north of the pass is a lake, named Chomora, 2 miles long and 1½ broad, and around it were a number of nomad encampments. Eastwards of the lake, a road runs to Dárchendo, a great tea mart. We camped for the night a short distance beyond the pass.

41. On the 3rd, after marching 3½ miles, we reached the direct road from Máne Khorchen. Here we heard that a gang of mounted robbers from the Jáma district, about 300 in number, was returning by this road laden with booty obtained from the Tengri Núr district. It consisted of 100 hill ponies, 300 yáks and 5,000 goats and sheep. To escape an attack we diverged again towards the north-west, and after marching about 2 miles reached the place where the ponies belonging to the Mongolian caravan, with which I was travelling, had been left behind for pasturage when going down to Lhása, and we waited there till the gang passed. At 4 P. M. we started and proceeding north-east for about 2½ miles again struck the direct road, and 2¼ miles further halted at the base of a mountain. About 40 miles distant and bearing 98¼° is Sutodampárabge, a snowy peak.

42. On the 4th, about 5 miles from the last halting place we crossed a stream 1½ feet deep and 12 paces wide flowing down from the north-west, and 5¼ miles further we reached the Tájang Lá pass by an easy ascent: the range runs at a bearing of 117½°. This pass is on the boundary between the districts of Nagchukha and Jáma: the latter is said to contain 1,500 tents. The district is governed by two Ambáns who reside at Sining. Having descended 1½ miles from the pass we reached a stream flowing to the north, and proceeding along its bank for 8 miles crossed another stream, 1½ feet deep and 12 paces wide, falling into it from the west. Half a mile further we reached Khamlung encamping ground where there were about 50 tents, and here we remained for the night. Latitude and boiling point observations were taken here (lat. 31° 57′ 44″, height 15,050 feet).

43. On the 5th, after an easy ascent of a mile, we crossed the Khamlung Lá range, bearing 122½° for a short distance from the pass so called and then turning to the north-east. To the north of the range lies the Áta district, containing 500 tents. A stream flows from the range to the north and about 6¼ miles from the pass is joined by another stream from the west 1½ feet deep and 15 paces wide. The united stream after flowing 2¾ miles along the road turns to the east. To the left of the pass and 4½ miles distant is an encamping ground where we saw about 60 tents; and about 5 miles further is a small lake to the west of the road. 3¾ miles from the lake is the boundary between the Áta and Yágra districts. Half a mile beyond the boundary a road branches off to the north-east to Siling *viâ* Di Chu Rab-dun and Jún. This road, though direct, is not safe, owing to its being much infested by robbers: we therefore kept to the same northern route which is seldom used by travellers. 2 miles to the east is a lake about 8 miles in circumference. At the distance of 2¼ miles from the boundary and on the left bank of the Saung Chu stream, 1¾ feet deep and 25 paces wide, coming from the north-west, is an encamping ground called Giáro, in the Yágra district. Here we remained for the night and I took boiling point observations (height 14,540 feet).

44. On the 6th, after travelling about 8 miles, we arrived at the bank of the Yágra Chu stream, which issues from the Dáng Lá range and flowing to the south falls into the Saung Chu stream. The road from the Dam district to this place is good and wide, but

TRANSLATIONS FROM DIARY AND NOTES.

further up it is rugged and stony, and passes through a narrow valley between two long spurs of the Dáng Lá range. 9½ miles from the bank of the stream another small stream from the north-west joins the Yágra Chu. 3½ miles further we reached Yágratodh encamping ground where there were some 80 tents occupied by nomads. We stopped for a night at Yágratodh; and I took boiling point observations (height 14,950 feet).

45. On the 7th October 1879, crossing the Yágra Chu stream to the left bank and having proceeded about 3,800 paces, we saw three snowy peaks to the left at distances of 4, 4½ and 6 miles, bearing 312°, 329¼° and 339° respectively, and one to the right at a distance of 8 miles, bearing 72½°: three miles further we re-crossed the same stream. About 1½ miles further on, a stream from the east joins the Yágra Chu, and 1½ miles thence another stream from the north-west falls into it. 2 miles beyond we passed a snowy peak close to our right and 4¾ miles further reached the junction of a stream from the north-east with the one along which we were travelling. Two snowy peaks were visible from this place at distances of 10 and 16 miles and bearing 62¼° and 50½° respectively. Having crossed the main stream and proceeded ½ a mile further we came to a stream from the north-west which falls into the former and 2 miles beyond we arrived at an encamping ground where we halted. Snow fell during the night.

46. On the 8th, half a mile from our halting place, we crossed a small stream from the north-west which joins the Yágra Chu. About 8 miles further on two peaks were visible, one distant 4 miles and bearing 326¾° and the other 23 miles and bearing 41½°. A mile further is the Dáng Lá pass: it was covered with two feet of snow, which fell during the preceding night. Dáng Lá is a long range of mountains running from the west and possessing several snowy peaks and spurs. It is the northern boundary of the Yágra district which contains 1,000 tents. About 100 miles to the west of the pass is the Amdo district which is sparsely inhabited by nomads; beyond it to the north and west the only inhabitants are a rude and ignorant race: they clothe themselves in skins of animals and dwell in small tents also made of skins. Some of them possess guns*, (obtained from Tibetans by bartering hides) which are used for killing wild animals whose flesh they roast and eat. They decline to eat vegetable food, even when offered them, as they say it makes them ill. The inhabitants of the country between the Dam and Yágra districts chiefly live on meat and *sattu* (flour of parched grain). No tree grows in these districts. Dry dung of both the wild and domesticated yâks is used for fuel. Grass is abundant. The country to the north of the pass is uninhabited even by nomads. Boiling point observations were taken at the pass (height 16,380 feet). 1¾ miles of an easy descent from the pass brought us to a stream which rises in the Dáng Lá range and flowing for 6½ miles along the route, joins the Lugrab Chu river which is 2 feet deep and 35 paces wide and comes from the west. The united stream after flowing about 14 miles along the right of our road, turns to the east. From the left bank of the river the track runs through an open country. Grass and fuel (dry dung of wild yâks) is found in abundance all along the route. Proceeding for 3¾ miles, by a wide, level road along the left bank of the river, we reached Khetinsirig, a halting place, from whence two high snowy peaks are visible, one bearing 274° and distant 14¼ miles and another bearing 276½° and distant 12½ miles. Wild animals are numerous here; for instance, *dong* (the wild yâk), *cho* (a deer), *goa* (a species of antelope resembling the chamois), *na* (a wild goat), *nhen* (a wild rocky mountain sheep), *chiánku* (a wolf), *háze* (a kind of fox), *yi* (a wild cat), *kiáng* (a wild ass), *chipi*† (a marmot), *rigong* (a rabbit), *ábra* (a rat without a tail), *demo* (the brown bear): of this last, one species called *mide* has feet resembling those of a man, and is very savage; it often walks erect and attacks any human being it sees. During the night three feet of snow fell. We had much reason to fear robbers and we therefore formed ourselves into groups, each consisting of 10 men, to guard the caravan at night.

47. On the 9th, we left the halting place and proceeding 6 miles we met five mounted robbers. On being questioned they said that they were residents of the Yágra district. They followed us for two marches intending to carry off our beasts of burden, but were unsuccessful, as we gave them no opportunity. About 15 miles from the last halting place we saw a lake about 7 miles in circumference, nearly 2 miles to the right. 5½ miles further we crossed a pass by an easy ascent, and descending thence at an easy

---

* They can manufacture their own ammunition.

† During winter it does not come out of its den and is believed by the Tibetans to sleep. It yields a large quantity of fat which is used as an ointment for gout, &c.

gradient for 2¼ miles, we reached Yakin-hapchiga, a halting place, where we rested for the night. A stream 1½ feet deep and 12 paces wide bearing 300°, emanating from the pass, crossed our route from the left. It flowed along our next day's road some 12 miles, re-crossing it in two places, and then turned to the north-east.

48. On the 10th October 1879, 14¼ miles from our last halting place, we saw two snowy peaks, bearing 300¼° and 297½° and distant 11½ and 12 miles respectively. There are two more high snowy peaks to the right, bearing 36½° and 35½°, distant 24 miles each. 3¾ miles further up a stream, bearing 212½°, crossed the road and flowing to the right for 4 miles joined the stream from the south. 7 miles onward there is a halting place called Átag-hapchiga (height 15,080 feet) where we passed the night.

49. On the 11th, after marching 4¼ miles, we crossed a small stream from the west. 2¾ miles further we crossed a pass with a slight ascent. 17 miles beyond the pass there is an encamping ground, called Maurusen Khua (the bank of the Maurus)—the river is otherwise named the Di Chu or Thoktho—close to a small fresh-water lake. We halted here a night. There was no trace of a road beyond Átag-hapchiga; and we were guided by some Mongolians in our caravan who recognised the route by the aid of certain hill peaks. Observations for latitude and of the boiling point were taken here (latitude 33° 48′ 25″, height 14,230 feet).

50. On the 12th, having gone about 2½ miles, we saw two snowy peaks near each other, bearing 323½°, and about 16 miles distant: 2½ miles further, we arrived at the right bank of the Maurus river. It is supposed to issue from the Tengri Núr lake and to water Chinese territory. It flows here in 7 channels each about 40 paces wide, the entire breadth of the river including the islands being 800 paces: the greatest depth was 3 feet. The banks of the channels are boggy. One of the horses sank up to its belly but we succeeded in extricating it.

51. A stream running from the north-west joins the Maurus 2 miles to the south-west of the route. Small bushes*, called by the Tibetans Taru, about a foot high, were found growing along the banks of the river. The river here forms the boundary between the Chinese and the Tibetan dominions. Boiling point observations were taken on the left bank of the river (height 14,660 feet). 4¼ miles further is a pass having a slight ascent. 5 miles beyond the pass we observed a snowy peak distant 37 miles and bearing 110°. About 13 miles from the pass is a halting place, called Bukhmangne, a little below the top of another pass of little height. From the left bank of the river to Bukhmangne we had no fresh water; wherever water was found it was brackish, and a small stream which crossed the road had also the same taste. We stopped at the pass for the night. The general character of the pass and the neighbouring plains, is that they are bare of trees, although covered with grass and verdure. Dry dung of the wild yák is used for fuel.

52. On the 13th, after proceeding 10 miles we crossed a large river called Uláng-miris, Namchuthai Ulangmiris or Chu Mar†, which flowing to the east, joins the Maurus river, and the united stream meets the Ma Chu at the Di Chu Rab-dun ferry. It here separates into 10 small channels averaging about 35 paces in width. The entire bed including the islands is 1,200 paces broad and the river was nowhere more than 3½ feet deep. Boiling point observations were taken on the left bank of the river (height 14,640 feet). 5 miles from that place is Kágchinar encamping ground. Here we found several pools of fresh sweet water. Our road to-day which was good lay along a wide plain between two ranges of mountains distant some 10 miles on either side.

53. On the 14th, 10¼ miles from the encamping ground we came to a Cha Chu (salt water stream) from the north-west and flowing to the south-east. 5¾ miles further up, we crossed another Cha Chu 1 foot deep and 20 paces wide flowing from the left, which issues from the Dungbura range. From hence a snowy peak is visible at a distance of 17 miles, bearing 126½°. Re-crossing the same stream 4¼ miles further on, we reached Dungbura‡ Chádámo§, an encamping ground. A foot of snow fell here. The road was good as in the last stage.

---

* These bushes are thorny and bear a small yellowish round fruit. This has an acid taste and is made into a kind of pickle.

† Ulangmiris, Chu Mar and Ma Chu all have the same signification, viz., *red river*. There is another river bearing these names, see para. 59.

‡ *Dung* means a shell and *bura* blowing. This place is so called as it is said that when one of the Grand Lámas went to see the Emperor of China the gods came down to welcome him here and blew the shell.

§ Chádámo in the Mogolian means 'this side', Nádámo, 'the other side'.

TRANSLATIONS FROM DIARY AND NOTES.

54. On the 15th October 1879, 5¼ miles from the encamping ground, we crossed a stream from the north coming from the Dungbura range which joins the Cha Chu. The joint stream below the encamping ground was brackish, but from that place up stream it tasted fresh. 6¼ miles further we observed a high peak of the Dungbura range, distant 5 miles, bearing 239½°. 1¾ miles further still is the Dungbura Khuthul (pass) which has an easy ascent. The general direction of the long range bearing this name is from east to west. 1¼ miles from the pass, a stream emanating from the range flowed along our route. 7 miles from the pass is an encamping ground called Dungbura Nádámo, where we stopped for two nights on account of a fall of snow. Some traces of a road were visible to-day but it was stony and narrow.

55. On the 17th, having marched ½ a mile we came to a stream from the north which falls into that issuing from the Dungbura range. 4½ miles further, we crossed to the left bank of the stream which was 1½ feet deep and 30 paces wide. ½ a mile further, a stream from the south joins the latter. After proceeding 5 miles, we found the stream which flowed along our route took a bearing of 82½°. 4½ miles beyond a brackish stream crossed our road towards the east. 4 miles further still, we came to several pools of fresh water. We stopped here for the night. Our day's march was almost entirely over snow.

56. Next day we struck eastwards for 3 miles to regain the right route which we had missed after passing the brackish stream, owing to its being hidden beneath snow. After three-fourths of a mile we crossed a low easy pass and some 8 miles beyond forded a stream coming from the north. 10 miles further, we arrived at the base of the Khokhosili range, and halted for the night on the bank of a stream coming from the north.

57. On the 19th, following up the stream for 5 miles, we crossed the Khokhosili Khuthul pass which has an easy ascent. 11 miles from the pass we reached the Khokhosili encamping ground on the right bank of a stream, 1½ feet deep and 15 paces wide, along which the route lay for the last 6 miles. The general direction of the range is from east to west. Observations for latitude and of the boiling point were taken here (lat. 35° 10′ 37″, height 13,430 feet). Snow fell and we were obliged to remain here for two nights. Our beasts of burden suffered badly from the snow, and were unfit to proceed with the caravan in the morning. As there was no fear of being molested by robbers we were left behind to follow when we could. Of three ponies which had fallen ill one died, but the other two recovered.

58. On the 21st, after proceeding about 7 miles, the stream along which we were marching turned to a bearing of 82½°. 1½ miles further we crossed a low pass and descending gradually for 1½ miles, we reached a small half-frozen lake of fresh water. We easily tracked the caravan by the marks of the horses' hoofs on the snow. We passed the night on the shore of the lake.

59. On the 22nd, after travelling for about 2¾ miles, we came to a small lake, where we met with a Mongolian caravan going to Lhása. It was composed of 150 souls (men and women), 80 camels and 100 ponies. When asked if they had seen our caravan, they at first answered in the negative, but afterwards acknowledged having observed, far off along the opposite bank of the Ma Chu river, a long line of what they supposed to be wild animals but which they now agreed must have been the caravan. Caravans as a rule, are very considerate towards each other: they never fail to aid any person or persons whom they find separated from or deserted by their caravan. They treated us very kindly and unsolicited offered us a large quantity of provisions of which we took only five seers of sattu. At noon we reached the right bank of the Ma Chu or Chu Mar river, which is about 4¼ miles from the lake. We searched up and down along the bank for a ferry; but unfortunately we found none and were obliged to cut a way for ourselves, about a foot broad, through the ice from one bank to the other. We did this, because the half frozen river was not hard enough to bear either baggage animal or man, and the bed being boggy it was necessary that the crossing should be rendered as easy as possible. We however lost a pony and a mule which stuck in the bog and which we could not extricate. My attendant L——c lost his toe while crossing the river, and this gave him great pain and made our future progress very slow. Night came on by the time we had crossed; in the darkness we could find no fuel and were forced to go to sleep without any food. To recruit ourselves we halted on the following day. Boiling point observations were taken on both banks: (right bank height 14,040 feet); (left bank height 14,050 feet). The entire breadth of the river is about 700 paces, it is 2 feet deep and

is here divided into 5 channels: it is said to flow into the Chinese empire. Three snowy peaks are visible from the right bank of the river at distances of 36, 38½ and 32 miles and bearing 311¼°, 318½° and 356° respectively.

60. On the 24th October 1879, after marching a mile we crossed the Añgirtákshia stream, 2 feet deep and 15 paces wide, which issues from the range of that name, and flowing to the right joins the Ma Chu river. 10¾ miles from the stream is Mugzisolma, a halting place, on the bank of a stream which flowing from the north here changes its course towards the east. Here we found tracks of our caravan, and rested for the night. We had only dry horse-dung for fuel which is inferior to yák-dung.

61. On the 25th, 6¾ miles from our last halting place, we again crossed the Añgirtákshia stream, and following up its right bank for 3½ miles, we arrived at the place where a stream from the north joins it. 3¼ miles further we reached the Añgirtákshia encamping ground. Observations for latitude and the boiling point were taken here (lat. 35° 33′ 35″, height 13,690 feet). From the Dam district to this place grass and dry yák-dung were abundant; wild animals were numerous. The route generally speaking was good.

62. On the 26th, a mile from our encamping ground we came to a stream from a bearing of 32½° which joins the Añgirtákshia stream. 2½ miles further on, another stream from the west joins it. After proceeding for 4 miles, we ascertained that the stream had its source about 2 miles to the west. A steep ascent of 1½ miles then brought us to the Añgirtákshia Khuthul pass. The Añgirtákshia*, a long range, lies east and west. It is probably the same range as is called Kiún Lún and here and there had peaks covered with snow. At a distance of 12 miles from the pass, and bearing 88°, is a high snowy peak of the range. A stiff descent of 1¼ miles brought us to a stream along which the route lay for 4 miles, when the stream turned off at a bearing of 82½°. We halted near this turn. Snow fell this afternoon. Scarcity of grass, on account of snow, caused the death of two of our animals. This day we had a rugged, stony and narrow road with several ascents and descents.

63. On the 27th, after proceeding 1¼ miles we crossed a stream from the west, which flowing to the east joins the stream from the south. Further on, by a steep ascent of a mile, we reached the Naichi Khuthul pass. Naichi is a small range which shoots off from the long range of Añgirtákshia. From thence we had an easy descent of 8 miles to the base of the pass, where nomads (Mongolians) encamp for a portion of the year to pasture their flocks and herds. This place, called Amthun, is at the junction of the Naichi Gol river from the west and a stream from the Naichi Khuthul pass. We met with great difficulties to-day during the course of our journey. Our beasts of burden had decreased in number and a portion of the baggage was left at the last stage for which the poor beasts had to trudge back. With much trouble we reached the pass. There we were obliged to leave half of the baggage under care of two men and to remove the other half. Having arrived at Amthun we returned to the pass to bring down our baggage, and fortunately found the same Mongolian caravan which we had met on its way to Lhása. It appeared that the caravan had returned from the Khokhosili encamping ground, as it could not proceed to Lhása on account of snow. We stopped at Amthun for a night. This is the first stage where we found firewood (obtained from a thorny tree about six feet high). Here grass was abundant. From Lhása up to this place our direction had in general been northerly but henceforward we proceeded eastward.

64. On the 28th, after proceeding 6¼ miles we reached Naichi, a nomad camp of 10 tents. From Yágra to Naichi the country is quite uninhabited. Mongolian tents are made in a curious manner. When a tent is pitched it bears a resemblance to a dome, round at base. The wooden framework, which when set up presents a lattice-like appearance, is, for the sake of convenience in packing and carriage, divided into five, seven, or nine pieces, according to the size of the tent. Each piece when it is rolled up looks like a bundle of sticks. The top piece has an opening for the smoke to pass out. The frame is covered with a kind of coarse woollen cloth, called *Chhingba* or *Phingba* bound round with a long rope which keeps it tight. They do not divide the tent into compartments. It has only one opening for ingress and egress which is closed by a kind of rough door made of planks fastened together by wooden pins. They cook inside. All males,

---

* This range is so called on account of a grass which grows in abundance here, which is used in medicine and is also burnt as an incense before idols.

TRANSLATIONS FROM DIARY AND NOTES.

females and children live together. A tent about 12 yards in circumference can be made for Rs. 12.

65. The general direction of the Naichi valley, which is a sub-division of the Thaichinar district, is from west to east. The level portion is about 50 miles long and with an average breadth of 3 miles. It is bounded on every side by low mountains, on which no snow was visible, and even when it does fall it quickly melts away. The valley is intersected lengthways by the Naichi Gol river, which receives only a few tributaries from the mountains, but is mostly fed by numerous springs of fresh water along its banks. The ground is generally smooth being only furrowed here and there by the beds of dry mountain torrents. The valley is covered with rich pasturage which affords sustenance to large herds of ponies, sheep (with thick tails), camels (Bactrian) and goats. At the eastern end of the valley the river widens to thrice its previous breadth. This valley is occupied by nomads who dwell in tents, 10 in number, each containing about six souls. They shift their camp from place to place along the whole valley for convenience of pasturage. Their diet chiefly consists of milk and boiled flesh. Grain forms only an inconsiderable portion of their food and is imported from the Khorlu district about 100 miles to the N. These people, like the rest of the Mongolians, are hospitable. They milk their mares; this when rendered acid by the addition of sour milk is called *cheka* and a kind of spirit distilled from it is called *arki*. The Mongolians are well-built and stout but timid. Their marriage customs are very simple. A man courts his intended bride for two years after which the parents of the pair construct a new tent for them, and provide a feast for their community. After feasting and dancing the marriage ceremony is considered to be completed. Yâks are rare here. We stopped at Naichi for five days. We here overtook our own caravan, but it started before we were ready to accompany it. The Mongolian caravan intended to remain here till the snow cleared off. Observations for latitude and of the boiling point were taken at camp (lat. 35° 52′ 20″, height 12,010 feet).

66. We here replenished our stock of provisions, purchased more beasts of burden, and on the 3rd November 1879 resumed our journey. Proceeding 8½ miles down the stream we stopped for the night. At distances of 4 and 6 miles, and bearing 334° and 31½° respectively were two peaks to the left of our halting place.

67. On the 4th, after marching for 7 miles, we crossed to the left bank of the Naichi Gol river, which is 40 paces wide and 2 feet deep and has a rapid current. Here, a dry bed of a stream from the south joins it. 2½ miles further on we reached Tháglaga, an encamping place of the nomads within a wide level plain, where we halted for the night. These encamping places are distinguished by circular raised platforms over which the tents are pitched and on which fires are lighted in iron grates. Fuel and grass were abundant.

68. Next day, marching along the left bank of the river, we crossed a dry bed of a stream, a mile distant from the last halting place, which issuing from the northern mountains joins the river. 7¼ miles further on, a stream from the south joins it. To the right is a peak at a distance of 5½ miles and bearing 164°. 1½ miles onward a dry bed of a stream from the north joins the river. We stopped here for the night. Grass and fuel were abundant.

69. On the 6th, marching 9¼ miles along the left bank of the river, we reached Shiárthoge, an encamping place. Here, two streams—one (dry) from the north and the other from the south—join the river. Boiling point observations were taken (height 10,370 feet). Grass and fuel were abundant.

70. On the 7th, we followed the river for 1¼ miles, when it turned to a bearing of 114½°, for a distance of 3 miles to wind round a spur after which it flows to the north-east. A stream from the south (probably the same stream which issued from the Añgirtákshia range and flowing for 4 miles turned to a bearing of 82½°) joins the river opposite to the foot of the spur. 2¾ miles from the last nomad encamping place is a pass, called Khokhotham, over this low spur but which has a steep ascent. 2¼ miles further on, we arrived again at the left bank of the river. A quarter of a mile onward we crossed it and reached Saikhanthoge, a nomad encamping place. The river is 70 paces wide and 3½ feet deep; its current was rapid and it was very difficult to ford. This is the last encamping place of the nomads of the valley. We stopped here for the night as there was no grass for our beasts at a convenient distance onward. From Saikhanthoge we again turned to the north.

EXPLORATIONS BY A——K IN GREAT TIBET AND MONGOLIA.

71. On the 8th November 1879, our route, which now lay at a distance from the river, after 2½ miles crossed a stream from the east, which flowing to our left for 1½ miles joined the Naichi Gol river. 16¼ miles further, we reached Gile, an encamping ground, where we halted, having passed *en route* three dry beds of streams at distances of 5½, 12¼ and 15 miles respectively from the right bank of the stream. Fire-wood was found but no grass.

72. On the 9th, after marching for 4¼ miles along the right bank of the river, we reached a place half a mile to the east of the junction of two dry beds of streams with the river, one coming from the east and the other from the west. Up to the junction our route lay through a valley, but further on it passed over an open sandy plain. The river from Saikhanthoge, up to the junction, flows in a deep channel, and as the lateral valleys are almost all dry there is no grass along this portion of the route. A plant about 3 feet in height, and on the leaves of which the poor beasts had to satisfy themselves, only grows here and there. Proceeding 5 miles from the junction we crossed a dry bed of a stream coming from the east, which joins the river half a mile to the west. 3¾ miles further on, we observed the top of a spur bearing 225° and distant 7 miles. Of the two chains of mountains between which our route lay as far as the junction, one from thence turns to the west and to the north of which a large tract of desert lies, and the other runs to the east. 4 miles onward we camped for the night on the right bank of the Naichi Gol river. Our beasts fared worse than in the last stage because even the plant, the leaves of which had supplied fodder, now failed.

73. On the 10th, after travelling 6½ miles we entered a tract where grass and fuel were abundant. 5 miles from thence is a nomad camp, called Golmo, situated in a densely wooded forest, 6 miles broad and about 100 miles long. The forest trees, named by Mongolians *humbu*, *harmo* and *chhak*, are about 6 or 7 feet high. The second bears a kind of black or red fruit, in flavour like the raisin, which is gathered in November for future use and for merchandise. Tall grass occupied nearly the whole forest. Some 50 tents are scattered here and there. Nomads, generally speaking, are very stout, and their lips have a yellowish color. Their wealth consists in live-stock, such as sheep (the species which has a thick tail), goats, camels (Bactrian), ponies and Mongolian kine. The last are like the hill cows of India; but are covered with somewhat longer hair in general of a greyish color. The principal articles of diet are boiled flesh, milk, butter and sattu, the last is brought from Khorlu. Brick tea is in general use in Mongolia. The climate is mild and very salubrious. During the rainy season the soil is moist, and a kind of white saline incrustation is said to spread over the trunks of trees from which after a time they die. In that season insects, such as gnats, &c., are very troublesome. From the point where we entered this grassy tract our route changed to an easterly direction. The Naichi Gol river flowing to the north for 40 miles through a desert is said to empty itself into a lake, called Hára Núr, which is about 60 miles in circumference and has no outlet. The water of the lake is brackish. About 100 miles to the north-west is Hazir, the residence of the Jhása (chief) of the Thaichinar district. Hazir contains 500 tents, and some of the residents are said to be very wealthy, having as many as 500 ponies and 5,000 goats and sheep. Nomads of the Thaichinar district are met with up to about 150 miles to the west of Golmo; but from thence is a dreary uninhabited plain which extends 150 miles. The Tánthus (men with white turbans), probably the inhabitants of the east of Khotan, are said to live on the other side of the plain. They sometimes cross it in their hunting excursions and take shelter in the tents of the nomads. Some six years ago seven mounted Tánthus are said to have taken shelter in the tents. After some days, when they had obtained full information respecting the moveable property, they, one night, butchered the occupants and absconded with their property. Since then the Mongolian nomads have ceased to live on the border of the uninhabited plain. Mongolian women, generally speaking, wear no ornaments. Their dress is a kind of long, loose garment which hangs to the ankles. The clothes of men and women are made of woollen cloths and skins of the wild animals. Women generally occupy themselves in making clothes for their husbands and children. The men trade with Lhása and China. Their manner of salutation is peculiar. They repeat the words "Amur Bhaino" (safe and sound) and stretch out their open hands when they salute an equal or a stranger. When they salute a man of rank or a king they first put their right hand on their foreheads and then repeat "Amur Bhaino" and stretch their hands as before. We found the nomads very hospitable. No sooner does a caravan approach than they immediately crowd around it and civilly ask the following questions "Is your health good?" and "Is your journey safe?" Further, they invite the members of the caravan to lodge with them. They present their guests with tea, butter, milk, meat and a kind of fresh cake fried in oil which is brought all the way from China. We stopped

TRANSLATIONS FROM DIARY AND NOTES.

at Golmo for 10 days. Observations for latitude and of the boiling point were taken (lat. 36° 25′ 18″, height 8,790 feet). A glass of my sextant had become loose and caused me much anxiety.

74. On the 21st November 1879, we left the nomad camp and proceeding for 7½ miles crossed a small stream from the south. We observed two peaks to the right of the route at distances of 15½ miles each, bearing 202½° and 162°. 5 miles further we reached Hurthothále, a nomad camp of 20 tents. Here we visited a ruined enclosure of mud walls of ancient date. It is said that it was erected by nomads as a safeguard against the incursions of the marauders from the east. We passed a night here. Our route had lain through the heavy jungle before mentioned. Grass and fuel were abundant.

75. On the 22nd, after marching 6¾ miles, we reached a place, whence a peak was observed, bearing 162½° and distant 17½ miles. 5¾ miles further is a stream coming from the south which flowing for some miles to the north loses itself in the desert. On the banks of the stream lies a nomad camp of 50 tents, called Thugthe. From Thugthe a route branches off northward to Choñju. 4½ miles further we arrived at Thágthe, a nomad camp of 50 tents. Water is obtained from wells as there is no spring or stream within several miles of the camp; in these wells the water is found very near the surface of the ground. We were detained here for two days, as two of our ponies had gone astray.

76. Leaving this camp on the 25th, we reached Dála, a nomad camp of 4 tents 4¼ miles distant, where there is a spring of fresh water. After travelling 10 miles further we arrived at Chúgu, a nomad camp on the bank of a stream which flowing to the north loses itself in the desert. A spring of fresh water was found on the route about 11¼ miles from our last halting place. We stopped at Chúgu for the night.

77. Next day having marched 12 miles we reached Dhánáhotho, a nomad camp of 2 tents. We saw no springs of water along this portion of the route; but from nomad encampments visible here and there at a distance from the road, I conclude there must have been water in the vicinity.

78. On the 27th, 4¾ miles from our last camp, we crossed a stream from the south. Further on, we noticed *en route* several springs of fresh water. 6¼ miles from the stream we crossed a low sand ridge running S.W. and N.E. and terminating in the latter direction about a mile from the route. 5¾ miles from thence is a brackish stream which flows to the north-east. Salt is found incrusted on the banks of the stream. This kind of salt is in general use in the country; I heard of no rock or mineral salt being found anywhere. 3¼ miles further we arrived at Thingkali, near the junction of a stream coming from the south-east with the Bai Gol river, where there were 100 tents and 10 kacha houses. There are a few fields: one crop of barley is raised annually. Observations for latitude and of the boiling point were taken here (lat. 36° 24′ 25″, height 7,720 feet). The Bai Gol river running from the east after watering the Thingkali plain flows to the north, where it is lost in the desert. We here overtook our old caravan which had left us at Naichi. Those members of the caravan who were Mongolians and residents of adjacent places took leave of us and went to their homes: only the Tibetans who were to accompany us remained. We decided to stop here for a few days in order to rest our animals and to replenish the stock of *sattu* which had run short. We did not observe any water-mills in Mongolia; but noticed small hand-mills, made of light red sand-stone brought from Hoiduthára in the Khorlu district. Two days after our arrival, some of our Káfila friends and ourselves went out shooting, as we had heard that the wild animals in the mountains to the south, distant half a day's journey, were unequalled in fatness and flavour, and that their skins were valuable. We hunted here for four days and succeeded in shooting some animals (wild yáks and wild asses). On the fifth day we returned from our trip and intended to start next morning the 5th December. Unfortunately just as were preparing to depart we were attacked by a band of some 200 mounted robbers of the Chiámogolok tribe, who had come to rob the residents of Thingkali, and finding us encamped there fell upon us also. Seeing no means of escape we had recourse to arms. We were quite unprepared; but we hastily equipped ourselves and with the assistance of some of the residents resolved to make a defence. At first a desultory firing from a distance commenced from both sides; but the robbers soon left off firing and rushed on us with swords and spears. One of them was shot dead; but as they pressed on and we did not find ourselves strong enough to encounter them in a hand to hand fight, we gave way and ran with our arms and instruments. They

fell upon our property and took whatever they found worth having, and departed. They succeeded in carrying away 300 ponies belonging to our caravan and the residents. We were robbed of most of our property as in what was left behind in the confusion and hurry we found only two of our loads containing petty articles of merchandize. After the robbers had departed the nomads from the adjoining encampments having collected together for pursuit, we joined them and followed in the track of the robbers till the evening: and although we did not succeed in coming up with them we returned next day with whatever they could not carry in their flight and had left on the road. This consisted of 50 ponies, mostly lame or otherwise unfit to keep up with them, and some property which they found too heavy or unprofitable. The caravan now dispersed. The Mongolians had as before stated already taken their departure, and of the Tibetans some seeing themselves unable to continue their journey returned to Naichi to join the caravan going to Lhása, and some remained at Thingkali waiting for some other opportunity to return. We were obliged to discharge our Tibetan servants as their services were no longer required. The general direction of our route from Golmo to Thingkali was from west to east. At the latter place we observed a peak, bearing 167° and distant 12 miles.

79. Having hired three bullocks on which to load what remained of our property, we left Thingkali for Khorlu on the 13th December 1879. Some of our Thingkali friends accompanied us to barter flesh, leather cords, and butter for grain. Retracing our steps for about a mile to gain the right road we proceeded for 6 miles and stopped at Hárori, a nomad camp of 2 tents. We halted here the next day also on account of the owner of the bullocks not having arrived as promised.

80. On the 15th December, proceeding for a mile along the left bank of the Bai Gol river, we crossed to the right bank at a place where it was 4 feet deep and 20 paces wide. Half a mile from the right bank and to the north-west, we saw a kacha walled enclosure, built by Mongolian nomads to store their surplus property. 3¾ miles from the last stage we observed 4 peaks, bearing 116°, 143°, 338° and 348°, and distant 41, 31½, 49 and 41 miles respectively. The horizon towards the north was generally hazy and the range had been at such a distance from the route as to allow of no observations to peaks on it. 13 miles further on, we reached Dabásuthu, a nomad camp of 4 tents, where we stopped for the night. To-day's route was level and sandy.

81. On the 16th, having gone a mile we crossed a stream from the south. Proceeding about 7 miles further we reached Harahusun, an encamping ground on the right bank of a branch of the Bai Gol river, 2 feet deep and 10 paces wide, which flowing north-west loses itself in the desert. The forest which commenced near Golmo ends here. There were a variety of small birds in it; and a bird like the golden pheasant, which I had noticed nowhere else, was here very numerous. We stopped here for two nights to allow our bullocks to graze as we were informed that there was no grass throughout the next stage.

82. On the 18th, 4½ miles from our encamping ground we forded a stream from the south-east. 2¾ miles further we forded another from the south-east, and about three quarters of a mile still further we crossed a third stream from the same direction: the water of all these three streams was brackish, that of the two latter particularly so. These two flow in deep channels and their beds and banks were incrusted with salt: there is no fresh water for miles. In winter travellers obtain it from the upper layer of ice on their frozen surfaces; but in other seasons they have to bring a supply of it from Harahusun. After flowing north-westward for some miles these streams lose themselves in the desert. 2¾ miles from the last brackish stream we crossed a pass with an easy ascent, and two miles further halted for the night. We found no grass and no water, but firewood was abundant. The chain of mountains we crossed to-day runs north of the Thaichinar district from east to west, and is there of a sandy formation: it looked higher in the middle than at its eastern and western extremities. It separates the Thaichinar and Khorlu districts.

83. On the 19th, proceeding for about 3 miles we passed over a dry bed of a stream coming from the north-west, and 4 miles further crossed a low ridge which running to the north for 15 miles joins a long range of mountains nearly parallel to the chain mentioned above. 14¾ miles further we reached Chákángnamaga, an encamping ground at the southern corner of a lake, called Thosu-Núr, about 12 miles long and 8 miles across where it is broadest. Its water is brackish and impregnated with sulphur. Close to the camp is a hot spring the water of which flows into the lake. Water for drinking and cooking

TRANSLATIONS FROM DIARY AND NOTES.

purposes is obtained from the upper layer of ice from the surface of the lake. This camp is at the junction of the roads from the Thaichinar and Jún districts and which proceed by the western and eastern shores of this lake respectively to Hoiduthára and Gobi in the Khorlu district. This latter district is the granary of the nomads of Thaichinar and Jún. The encamping ground abounds with firewood from dwarfed trees, but grass is scarce. We halted here a night. From Harabusun to this place the path is good, but during the rainy season it becomes muddy and difficult near the salt-water streams before mentioned.

84. On the 20th December 1879, traversing the western shore of the lake for 12 miles we arrived at the right bank of a stream, 3 feet deep and 25 paces wide, named Khorlu Gol, which emanating from the Khorlu-Núr lake empties itself into the Thosu-Núr lake. The latter is said to have no outlet and is surrounded by a low sandy ridge. 1¾ miles up the stream the route diverged from it, and 5¼ miles onward we arrived at Sukhai, the winter residence of the Hoiduthára men, where about 100 tents were dotted about. The nomads remain here for four months in winter, pasturing their camels on the leaves of the dwarfed trees with which this plain, which is about 12 miles broad and 50 miles long, abounds, while they send their herds of ponies, goats, and sheep, to pasture on the rich grass and verdure of the mountains to the north of Hoiduthára. About 4 miles to the east is the Khorlu-Núr lake, 10 miles long and 9 miles broad, which is fed by a stream and a river; the former coming from the north-west waters the barley fields at Horga and Hoiduthára which produce large quantities of grain, and the latter from the far-distant east has Gobi on its right bank close to the lake. Gobi is a large nomad camp of 100 tents, and has some 10 subterraneous store-houses for grain, which are replenished from the annual produce of patches of cultivation round the camp. Fields after being once cultivated are allowed to lie fallow for the next three or four years that the soil, which is not manured, may recover its fertility. Before sowing the seed, the soil is turned up with a plough drawn by oxen, or with a kind of small pickaxe. Only one crop of barley and *ne* is raised in the year: other grains do not thrive here, the climate being too rigorous. Gobi is about 17 miles distant from Sukhai which is on the opposite side of the lake. It is the seat of the Besi (chief). The tax varies from 1 goat to 8 sheep per tent according to the circumstances of the owner. The following is a common scale of barter in Mongolia:—

$$2 \text{ goats} = 1 \text{ sheep}$$
$$12 \text{ sheep} = 1 \text{ colt (over a year old)}$$
$$2 \text{ colts} = 1 \text{ pony}.$$

All disputes, civil or criminal, which arise within the Besi's jurisdiction are referred to him for decision. Khorlu-Núr lake is said to contain a great number of fish, but which are never disturbed by the Mongolians. The surface of the lake freezes in winter and after snow has fallen on it, it becomes the high road for travellers both on foot and horse-back. At Sukhai our Thingkali friends, who had come here for corn, settled their business and departed. As the sale of our merchandize, consisting of glass beads and such other valueless articles as the robbers had left, was very slow, we had no means of proceeding further and were obliged to wait at Sukhai for an opportunity. Happening one day to go to Gobi*, we fortunately met a Tibetan of Giángze, who finding us helpless treated us very kindly. He had some 20 years ago migrated to Saithang in Khorlu, where he married and settled and had now become a man of influence and position. He advised us to stay till the warm weather returned, when he promised to take us with him to his home and arrange for our journey onward: he engaged us to look after his camels in return for our food. He had come to Gobi to attend to a case which was pending in the Besi's Court. We remained in his service at Sukhai and Hoiduthára for 2 months and 29 days, during which time I took latitude and boiling point observations at both places: (Sukhai lat. 37° 17' 23'', height 8,770 feet); (Hoiduthára lat. 37° 20' 32'', height 9,200 feet). 5 peaks with patches of snow on them were observed from Sukhai bearing 30½°, 38½°, 47½°, 58° and 71½° and distant 18, 20, 23, 24 and 26 miles respectively. These peaks are on a long range of mountains having a direction east by south and west by north.

85. About 20 miles to the east-south-east of Gobi and at the eastern extremity of the Khorlu district, there is said to be a nomad camp named Golmo, containing about 40 tents and

---

* Through an oversight this part of the route has not been colored on the map.

EXPLORATIONS BY A——K IN GREAT TIBET AND MONGOLIA.

10 store-houses like those at Gobi. About 55 miles further to the east is Khukhu*, the seat of a Beli. Beli is a higher rank than that of Besi. Tuláng (Dulan-kit), the seat of the Whang (rája) is said to lie 40 miles to the east-south-east of Khukhu. The Whang is the chief officer in the Koko* Núr province, which embraces the Tuláng, Khukhu, Khorlu, Thaichinar, Jún, Bárong, Shiáng and Bánákhásum districts. Nomads of the last district are addicted to robbery. They are of Tibetan descent and are distinguished from the nomads of the other districts in that they live in black tents made of yáks' hair, while the Mongolians occupy tents made of a coarse woollen fabric. The latter are an honest, hospitable and peaceful people. From Dulan-kit, a road proceeding south-east for about 25 miles and thence north-easterly for about 40 miles, leads to the western side of the Koko-Núr lake or Cho Onbo (blue lake). The lake is about 280 miles in circumference and is said to contain a small island, called Cho Ning (heart of the lake), on which is a gomba inhabited by 20 Dábas: there is also a spring of fresh water. The Dábas of the island gather their supplies of food during the four months of winter; the water of the lake is then frozen and affords a convenient means of communication with the shore. A considerable number of fish are taken from the lake for sale at neighbouring settlements. Salt found incrusted on the banks of the lake is also an article of merchandize. The Ambáns of Sining, when on tour, halt at the lake for the sake of the fishing. At the south-eastern extremity of the lake is a large gomba, called Kumbum, containing 3,000 Dábas, which is a great seat of religious instruction for the Mongolians. This lake is considered sacred and Buddhists circumambulate it as a meritorious religious performance, a dangerous pilgrimage as the southern shore is infested by robbers. Tánkar or Tonkur a well known place of commerce is said to lie 100 miles to the east. 80 miles further to the east is Sining, where reside two Ambáns. Further to the east is Álásha, under the rule of a Whang. The present ruler is the son-in-law of the Emperor of China. Woollen carpets of every description are woven there.

86. Mongolians are Buddhists and hold Lhása to be a sacred city and the chief seat of learning: it is there only that the degree "Gisi" (learned) which is conferred by the learned members of the three Gombas—Sára, Daibung and Galdan—can be competed for. The examination is difficult and entails more than 12 years' continuous study, principally of religious books. The following preliminaries have afterwards to be gone through:—the candidate provides a feast for the Lámas and Dábas of the gomba to which he belongs, at which he expresses his intention of competing. Information is then sent to the other two gombas; and a committee of examiners from among the possessors of the Gisi degree in the three gombas is appointed. A Gisi ranks higher than a Dába, but lower than a Láma, and is held in high respect by men of all classes. He is not allowed to marry or to cohabit with woman. Mongolian Dábas are not under the same rules of celibacy as those of Tibet, but may marry; they must however wear the usual special garments when they worship or perform any religious ceremony. Their gomba is a large tent wherein they place images of gods. Mongolians of the Koko-Núr province pride themselves that amongst them was born a hero, named Tanjen Gombo, who having conquered Siling and Álásha finally became Emperor of China, and in whose family the empire still continues.

87. On the 28th February 1880, the settlers at Sukhai moved to Hoiduthára, 5 miles distant, to commence ploughing their fields. The sowing takes place in April and the harvest is reaped in September. ¾ of a mile from Sukhai a stream was passed coming from the north-west and falling into the Khorlu Gol river to the east; and 2½ miles further we crossed a small stream which joins the Khorlu-Núr lake. At Hoiduthára we spent 19 days herding camels; after which we were permitted to go to Saithang, and three camels were lent us for our baggage. From Thingkali to Hoiduthára the route has almost a northerly direction but thence it turns west.

88. Leaving Hoiduthára on the 19th March, we crossed, a mile from that place, the stream which as before mentioned flows into the Khorlu-Núr lake. As there is no water on the road for some distance, a supply had to be taken hence. Three quarters of a mile farther and a little to the left is Horga, which has five store-houses for grain; and 9¼ miles from Horga, we came to the dry bed of a stream coming from the west where we halted for the night. This water-course joins the stream crossed near Sukhai. Firewood was abundant, but there was no grass. Five peaks were observed bearing 180½°, 260°, 308°, 322½° and 356° and distant 10, 11, 11, 12, and 19 miles respectively.

---

* The names 'Khukhu' and 'Koko' are derived from Colonel Prejevalsky's map. The Explorer A——k says the names are identical and should be 'Khokho' which like 'Onbo', signifies 'blue'.

TRANSLATIONS FROM DIARY AND NOTES.

89. On the 20th March 1880, our route lay within a narrow valley and along the left bank of the dry water-course. After marching 8 miles we turned off the road to a spring about a mile to the left to obtain water. The road, 5¼ miles beyond the point where we had left it, quits the dry water-course and follows another which joins the former from the west. 3 miles to north-west from this place is a spring of fresh water. 2 miles further we stopped for the night.

90. On the 21st, having proceeded 5¾ miles, we observed a peak and a mound of red clay bearing 37° and 324½° and distant 11¼ and 3¼ miles respectively. The dry water-course ends here, and 3 miles beyond is a pass with an easy ascent. Thence, following a dry water-course for 4¼ miles, we came to a spring of salt water, and half a mile further to a path which branches off to the right to Igi Chaidam. This path though direct is seldom used by travellers owing to the scarcity of water. After another 4¾ miles the route diverged from the water-course and entered a somewhat open country. Here pasturage for camels is abundant and a deep hollow between large boulders full of snow supplies water to travellers during four months of winter. The route from Hoiduthára to this place is generally somewhat stony and is narrow in parts.

91. Next day, 6½ miles from our halting place, we observed four peaks bearing 305½°, 308°, 157°, and 188° and distant 32, 28, 21 and 14 miles respectively. Of these the first two are snowy peaks; the last two had been already observed from Thingkali. 16 miles further we arrived at Choñju situated in a grassy plain, and watered by a stream issuing from the mountains to the north-west and disappearing in the desert, after a south-eastern course, a few miles south of Choñju. We were told that some of the nomads of Bhága Chaidam come here to pasture their cattle during February, March and April. From Choñju a path branches off to the left to Thugthe, in the Thaichinar district, which is generally used by the inhabitants of that district when they require to purchase corn at Hoiduthára. We stopped at Choñju for two nights. To-day's route lay in a level plain. Firewood from bushes was abundant.

92. On the 24th, following up the stream for 2 miles, we crossed it at a place where it is 15 paces wide and 1¾ feet deep, and from the other side we observed two peaks bearing 194½° and 259½° and distant 13 and 8½ miles respectively. 5 miles further on we arrived at the base of a spur from the range of mountains to our left, and travelling thence 6 miles, observed the eastern corner of a lake called Bhága-Núr, bearing 267½° and distant 3 miles. This lake, of which the water is somewhat brackish, is an irregular oblong in shape, about 6 miles long and 4 miles broad. 11¼ miles beyond, the route brought us to Bhága Chaidam, where there are about 50 scattered tents. As there is no cultivation on this side of Horga supplies are dear: firewood is obtained from the distant mountains, and dry yâk and cow dung are also used for fuel: grass and water were abundant. Chaidam signifies a trading place or market, and such was Bhága formerly, as the Chinese resorted to it for borax, which is found incrustated on the margins of the Bhága-Núr and Igi-Núr lakes. We remained here two nights.

93. Leaving Bhága Chaidam on the 26th, and proceeding 7½ miles we arrived at a large spring of fresh water, from which place the route continues along the base of the mountains on the right; and 6¼ miles further, we crossed a pass with an easy ascent. This range of mountains terminates abruptly about 8 miles to the east. Descending gradually for three-quarters of a mile, we observed two high snowy peaks bearing 353½°, 350½° and distant 33 and 31 miles respectively, and proceeding 4¾ miles further over a level plain, we crossed the stream flowing south-east to Choñju. 3½ miles further, we struck the direct route to Igi Chaidam, which had branched off to our right, and there halted for the night.

94. On the 27th, we re-crossed the above mentioned stream, about 4 miles from our halting place, now flowing from the north, and saw some 15 tents of Mongolian nomads scattered along its banks. There is a hot spring about 2 miles to the north. 9 miles onward, we arrived at Igi Chaidam, where there are 100 scattered tents. This place formerly exported borax to China. Igi-Núr lake, close by, is 16 miles long and 8 miles broad and is supposed to be fed by springs only, several of which were visible from the road along its margin. Supplies are procurable although dear: grass and firewood are abundant. Observations of boiling point were taken here (height 10,480 feet), and two snowy peaks, bearing 33½° and 28°, distant 20 miles each, were also observed.

EXPLORATIONS BY A——K IN GREAT TIBET AND MONGOLIA.

95. On the 29th March 1880, proceeding 13 miles, the route crossed over a stream, 1¾ feet deep and 35 paces wide, flowing from the north and losing itself in the desert to the south. 3¼ miles further is Ijia, close to a range of hills, where there is a large spring of fresh water said by the inhabitants of the Khorlu district to be very wholesome. Ijia is covered with rich pasturage and is frequented by the nomads of Igi Chaidam during March. We stopped here for the night.

96. On the 30th, after proceeding 8½ miles, we crossed a low spur from the range of hills to our left, and 3½ miles further on we forded a brackish stream, 3 feet deep and 5 paces wide, running from a bearing of 32½°. 11 miles onward is a stream of fresh water, 1¼ feet deep and 25 paces wide, flowing to the south, from which a path leads to Mákha, a nomad camp about 30 miles to the west by south. This encampment of some 40 scattered tents, is in a dense jungle of trees of about the same height as those found in the Thaichinar district. It is from Mákha that the Mongolians of the neighbourhood obtain the material for the wooden framework of their tents. Proceeding up the bank of the stream for 2 miles, we arrived at Urel, 3 tents, where we passed the night. Grass and firewood were abundant.

97. On the 31st, having filled our leather bags with water, we left Urel at 8 A.M. and after a march of 11 miles crossed a low pass and camped for the night 2 miles beyond in an uninhabited place. Here we found no water or grass but firewood in small quantities was available. To-day's route was over sand and in parts over stony ground.

98. Leaving early the following morning, after 7½ miles we entered a large open plain; and journeying across it for 26¼ miles reached Chága also called Ulánggachar, an encamping ground, close to a spring of fresh water. From this place a road leads to Mákha to the south. There was no water or grass between Urel and Chága.

99. On the 2nd April, after proceeding 4 miles we came to an Obo, a place of worship, where there are a number of flags on an artificial mound; and some 15 tents are scattered about. 13½ miles further is Yembi, in Saithang.

100. Saithang is an extensive grassy plain surrounded on all sides by a sandy waste called Shialla. The plain is about 20 miles long with an average breadth of 17 miles, and is irrigated by several springs of fresh water. A few small pools of salt-water supply the inhabitants with salt. There are two lakes, of which the water is drinkable, one to the N.N.E. and the other to south-west of Yembi, about 9 miles apart, and which are joined by a small stream issuing from the former and flowing into the latter. They are nearly equal in size, about 4 miles long and 2½ miles broad, and are full of fish on which a kind of otter preys. There are some 300 tents scattered about Saithang; but this number is reduced to 50 in the winter when the cattle, especially the young ones, are, for protection against the extreme cold, driven into the small narrow valleys on either side of the northern range, which is about 30 miles distant: good pasturage abounds in these valleys.

101. Wild people exist in some of the valleys of the northern range. They have a thick and dark skin, are well built and apparently well fed. They wear no clothes except skins; nor do they dwell in either tents or huts, but live in caves and glens and under the shelter of overhanging rocks. They are ignorant even of the use of arms in the chase, and lie in wait for their prey near springs of water or where salt incrustates. They are said to feed even upon rats, lizards and other small animals. They are remarkable for their swiftness of foot, and when pursued even a horseman cannot easily catch them. Whenever they see a civilized man they run away in great terror. They are said to know how to kindle a fire with the aid of flint. They flay the animals they kill with sharp-edged stones. Sometimes, but very seldom, they steal goats and sheep grazing in the valleys.

102. The wild ass, chamois, yák, wolf, rabbit, brown bear, beaver, &c., are met with: the Bactrian camel and the horse are also found here in a wild state. It is believed that at a very remote period a Mongolian army from Thorkoth, invaded Tibet to assist the Lhása Government against its petty neighbours then ruling in Nari Khorsum and Ladak; and the specimens of these domestic animals, now existing in a wild state, are supposed to have sprung from stray animals of that army. The Mongolians of the vicinity believe themselves to be descendants of the followers of the same army, and say that the country before that invasion was uninhabited. All these animals excepting the wild horse are hunted, some for their flesh, some for their hides and others for both. Neither of these in the case of the wild horse are said to be useful.

TRANSLATIONS FROM DIARY AND NOTES.

103. It does not rain more than three times during the whole season; thunder and lightning are rare too; snow falls very seldom. From February to June dust storms, which occur almost daily, are very troublesome, one sometimes lasting for a week continuously: from the middle of June to the middle of September the springs remain unfrozen.

104. The Mongolians have built a kacha walled enclosure at Yembi for their Láma, who is looked up to by all as their spiritual guide. They are tolerably well off though there is no cultivation; for they obtain what is needed from Saitu, about five days' journey distant. There they exchange camels, goats, sheep, horses, wool and butter for corn: corn is also brought from Náichi and Náhuli. The articles of their diet are nearly the same as before described. Cooking and other utensils are obtained from China. The dress of both sexes is very similar; it consists of a long garment very like a large choga in shape. It is made of either cured skins, felt, coarse woollen cloth, or broadcloth of bright colors. The first is worn in winter, the second during the spring, the third in summer and the fourth on occasions of festivity.

105. Thorkoth, an extensive and rich tract of Mongolian territory, lies about a month's journey to the north-west of Saithang. It is governed by a Whang. For several generations past these Whangs are said to have died at an early age, leaving the management of the territory to their wives. The mother of the present young rája, fearing the same fate for her son, sent for several distinguished Lámas to perform some religious ceremony to insure a long life for him. A Tibetan Láma then in Saithang, a native of Cháng in Tibet, and believed to be an incarnation of the Láma of Thuden Gomba, in the Darge district, was also asked to join in the ceremony. He is a man well instructed in religious matters and had been previously summoned by the inhabitants around the Koko-Núr lake to pray for the prosperity of their country, and had now come to Saithang to perform a sacrifice with the object of warding off an incursion of the Bánákhásum robbers, about 1,000 in number, who had resolved to make a raid on that territory. This Láma refused to go to Thorkoth on the ground that he had other matters to attend to. He is revered by all the Mongolians at Saithang and many of them visit him daily and offer him presents. It is customary for visitors to kneel down three times before him and to offer him a khátág*, when he places his hand on their heads. He is very friendly towards Tibetans.

106. After spending some three months at Yembi in selling the merchandize left us by the robbers at Thingkali, and waiting for any traders proceeding to the Lob-Núr, we eventually resolved to go to Saitu. The merchandize we disposed of here consisted of small beads of red clay and of myrobalans. The latter found a ready sale at the rate of 2½ rupees a seer, but as the former were not articles in much request, being only worn by women in necklaces, we were a long while in disposing of them; we also sold our woollen chogas. All these articles fetched about Rs. 200 in silver, three horses and four colts. As one of our companions, M——g, had heard that the Hu Hu (Mahomedans of China) were at war with the Emperor of China, he was afraid to accompany me further and desired to remain in the Koko-Núr province for some years. He tried to instigate my companion L——c to desert me, and indirectly tried to persuade even myself to give up my design. Finding me determined to go to Saitu, he one day during my temporary absence despatched L——c to a distant place to fetch some goats due to us in exchange for some articles of merchandize, and availed himself of this opportunity to desert us, carrying away with him 150 rupees worth of silver, two horses and three colts, together with a small telescope. This happened in July 1880. Next day when I returned I found no one in my tent; but L——c's explanation on his return with the goats soon after, and the remembrance of the other's previous attempts to dissuade us from proceeding further left no doubt of his desertion. Our position now was very desperate as we had scarcely 50 rupees worth of things left. A friend who heard of the case sympathized with us and was ready to send men to seize him; but some travellers arriving at that time to visit the Láma informed us that they had met him at Urel and that he had told them to let us know that he would return after three months should he have sold the ponies. We had however no hope of seeing him again. Being reduced to such straits we were obliged to again take service; and we tended herds of ponies

---

* Khátág is a thin cloth made from the bark of a tree or of silk and is of various sizes, the smallest being a foot long and three inches broad and the largest a yard long and half a yard broad. The presentation of a khátág is a common mode of interchanging civilities. When a man writes to or visits a friend he encloses or presents the smallest one; but the size is increased in accordance with the rank and position of the person to whom it is presented. If one person goes to condole with another, or to attend a marriage ceremony, he presents a khátág. The non-observance of this custom is considered a mark of rudeness and want of etiquette.

and goats for about 5 months; but then getting tired of that work we determined to move on with the limited funds we possessed and when those should fail to beg our way.

107. On the 3rd January 1881, as some men were going to Saitu to exchange goats and sheep for corn, we obtained our employer's permission to go with them. He was a thorough gentleman, and on our departure, he gave us a horse worth Rs. 40 and warm clothes together with provisions. Observations for latitude and boiling point were taken at Yembi (lat. 38° 57′ 30″, height 9,690 feet).

108. Proceeding 3½ miles from the Láma's walled enclosure at Yembi, we crossed the stream, 2 feet deep and 15 paces wide, which joins the two lakes. From this place we observed a high snowy peak called Amandapára bearing 310° and distant about 30 miles, which the inhabitants of Saithang suppose to be the abode of Shibdag (the protecting god) of Saithang. At several places in Saithang, Obos (poles to which strips of cloth are attached) are erected where incense is burnt to propitiate that deity. 6½ miles further, we arrived at Harasirig, an encamping ground at the other extremity of the Saithang plain, where we halted for the night.

109. On the 4th, we left the encamping ground, and traversing the sandy tract, about 13¾ miles broad, forming the northern border of Saithang, we arrived at a dry water-course running from a narrow valley from the north-west. Proceeding up this ravine for 3 miles we crossed a pass with an easy ascent, and thence following another dry water-course for 3½ miles we passed over a spur, at the base of which this water-course meets a small stream of water. A mile further, we found a Mongolian tent on the right bank of the stream, which latter flows hence for 7¾ miles in such a narrow ravine that travellers have to walk over its frozen surface or wade through it, according to the season. The valley then opens into a sandy plain and near its northern extremity is an encamping ground where we stopped for two nights. Grass and firewood (from small bushes growing along this range) were abundant; we had to-day a fall of snow, about two feet in depth. We had heard at Saithang that about 3 miles to the west of this encamping ground was a tent occupied by an old woman, who with her husband had in their youth been carried away by Tánthus (men with white turbans) of the Lob-Núr district, formerly occupied by Mongolians, and we went to see her. She told us that the Lob-Núr lake, around which is a population of Tánthus, Mahomedans by religion, was distant about 250 miles to the west; that the route leading to it was uninhabited and water and grass could only be procured at certain places known to those who frequented it. She advised us to return to our tent before evening, because a *demo* (brown bear) had lately committed great ravages in the neighbourhood. We met no bear, but the old woman's son, who accompanied us for some distance, pointed out to us a wild man, on an opposite spur about 2 miles off, coming towards us, but who on perceiving us turned back. As he was at so great a distance I could not see him well enough to verify or add to the description already given. From this encamping ground we observed a high snowy peak close to Amandapára bearing 248½° and distant 34 miles.

110. On the 6th, after traversing for about a mile the bed of the stream, which disappears near the encamping ground, the road diverged from it, and 17½ miles further we arrived at a small spur from a sand ridge running east to west. From here a road branches off to Náiche city about 55 miles to the east. This city is said to contain a bazár surrounded by houses (built of unburnt bricks) about 1,000 in number, and is well known as a market for the sale of corn, the produce of the surrounding fields. Proceeding for 6¾ miles between two sand spurs we stopped for a night at the base of the sand ridge where we found neither grass, water nor firewood. Of the latter we had however brought a supply, and having found some snow in a sheltered place we melted it.

111. On the 7th, 1¾ miles from our halting place we crossed the sand ridge and traversing a sandy plain 11 miles broad, we arrived at Chángja, an encamping ground, on the left bank of a river. Here, we found grass and firewood and a few dwarfed trees. A cart-road runs up the left bank of the river to the south-east whence firewood and a sort of long grass are brought to the cities of Saitu and Náhuli. The carts are like those common in India but are drawn by horses.

112. On the 8th, following the left bank of the river for 3¾ miles, we crossed a low sand-hill, and 3½ miles further found a house, which had been built by some charitable person for the convenience of travellers, in one of the rooms of which was a shop for the sale of refreshments. From here a road branched off to Náhuli, about 20 miles north,

TRANSLATIONS FROM DIARY AND NOTES.

containing about 500 houses (of sun-dried bricks) and a small bazár for the sale of grain grown in the vicinity. 1½ miles further were two more houses for travellers, and 13¼ miles onward again, we reached the suburbs of Saitu, where we saw some cultivated fields and houses here and there. Passing through these for 1½ miles we crossed the river by a bridge 250 paces long and 5 paces broad with railings on both sides of it. This river, to which we heard no particular name assigned, and which therefore has been named Saitu, is here made to flow in two deep narrow channels by a large mass of masonry built in the middle, on which and on masonry on either side of the narrow streams the bridge is supported. The bridge consists of timber covered over with planks and a layer of "kankar" (a kind of limestone) so as to make it passable for carts. The river abounds with fish which are caught by angling. 300 paces from the eastern end of this bridge is the fort of Saitu.

113. Saitu (called Sachu by Mongolians) is a large fort within which are the palace of the Governor and many houses. It is situated on the right bank of the river, which after watering the patches of cultivation near Saitu ultimately disappears in the sandy waste to the north. It is irregular in form and construction and about 6 miles in circumference. The outer wall, which is throughout of sun-dried bricks plastered over with earth, is loop-holed, has bastion-towers and is protected by a ditch. Its western face is separated from the suburb which extends to Náhuli, by the river which is the only source of water supply. Saitu contains a long bazár with a kacha road passing through it. On either side of the bazár are single storied houses built of sun-dried bricks containing several rooms, one of which is set apart as a sleeping place for the servants; and round its wall a platform runs, about 3 feet high and 5 or 6 feet broad for the servants to sleep on, under which are small recesses for fires to warm the platform during winter. There are no apertures to carry off the smoke. The estimated number of houses in the fort and suburbs (excepting the western across the river) amounts to 2,000.

114. The religion of the inhabitants of Saitu is Buddhism; but it is not so strictly observed as in Tibet. They have no caste system.

115. The following is the scale of weights used in Mongolia and Saitu:—

$$10 \text{ Chen} = 1 \text{ Len}$$
$$16 \text{ Len} = 1 \text{ Jing} (= 50 \text{ tolas})$$
$$25 \text{ Jing} = 1 \text{ Dug}$$
$$10 \text{ Dug} = 1 \text{ Ten}$$

In exchange for a sheep, worth 4 chens of silver (= 1¼ rupees of Indian currency), 3½ dugs of wheat are given. *Ne* and millet are also sold at the same rate. Besides these, other grains, *viz.*, *kauli* (a kind of corn found in Saitu and used for distilling liquor), Indian corn, *masúr* (a kind of pulse), and *matar* (a pea) are cultivated. Rice is dear as it is imported from Yárkand. There are no water-mills for grinding corn, but mills worked by horse power are employed instead.

116. Saitu surpasses Tibet and Mongolia in the excellence and abundance of its fruits and vegetables; these are however inferior in flavour to those of Yárkand. Among the fruits and vegetables are the apple, pear, plum, cucumber, melon, water-melon, mulberry, walnut, guava, radish, carrot, turnip, mustard, &c. Sugarcane is unknown but a kind of honey-cake is brought from the north. Cotton is cultivated and manufactured into a kind of coarse cloth. Cho Gombo, the Governor of Laindu Choudu (one of the provinces of the Chinese Empire to which Saitu is subordinate) having come here on a tour of inspection, has lately established a manufactory for weaving silk cloth, and has also entertained ten good workmen for teaching the art of silk-weaving at Saitu. The chief articles of diet are bread, preserves, cooked esculent vegetables, meat and milk. Pigs and fowls are reared, because the flesh when boiled is much esteemed.

117. The climate of Saitu is generally healthy, and bears a great resemblance to that of Yárkand. The inhabitants of Saitu are not so stout or well built as the Mongolians: the color of their dress is generally black or blue, white being employed for mourning. They wear clothes padded with cotton in winter. They keep locks of hair on the top of their heads, which are plaited and hang down behind. The women wear a cap of the Chinese pattern and several coats of various colours put on in such an order that the sleeves of the innermost are the longest, extending to the wrist, whilst the sleeves of the others decrease in succession. Over these is worn a short coat which comes down a little below the hips and has sleeves reaching a little short of the elbows, and a loose pair of pyjamas (trousers) in

place of a petticoat completes the costume. Their feet are very small being not more than six inches in length. When a girl is three years of age, an iron chain of more than a seer in weight is hung round her neck, and when she attains her fifth year this chain is removed and her toes are bound with strips of cloth so as to cause them to turn inward: this unnatural twist of the toes sometimes produces sores. Women never expose their feet before men.

118. The "kurs" (an ingot of silver = about 156 rupees) is the current coin; there are two smaller silver coins of the same shape, one weighing five and the other ten 'len-', equal to Rs. 15-10 and Rs. 31-4 respectively. Ordinary lumps of silver are used for smaller change, which necessitates weighing and testing; and for smaller change than those even, brass coins are used, 500 of which equal one rupee.

119. On the 18th January 1881, we started in the company of some traders going to Thorkoth; but before we had proceeded a mile from the fort, we were overtaken by a horseman who ordered us to accompany him back to the Governor of Saitu. The Governor questioned us as to who we were and where we intended to go: he took us for thieves or spies from some foreign country and ordered us to remain at Saitu till we could procure security for good behaviour. He placed us under the control of a rich man in the fort and told him to watch our movements. As it was very expensive to keep ponies we sold ours at once; and not knowing what length of time we might be detained, we set up as fruit-sellers to obtain a livelihood. Here I suffered from a peculiar disease called by the natives "bam" in which red blotches appear on the legs, making it difficult to walk or even stand up. It is accompanied by fever and loss of appetite and in some cases by looseness of the teeth also. This complaint I was told is brought on by walking bare foot on a particular kind of soil, and if not properly attend to, disables a man for life from using his lower limbs. Various heating and intoxicating drugs were administered, and some plasters applied; but what I found most efficacious was radish juice rubbed over the afflicted limb, which was then wrapped round tightly with cloth and kept warm, this brought on perspiration and gradual relief. After seven months a friend from Saithang arrived here to visit Sange Kuthong (1,000 images), a sacred place of worship about 6 miles distant and bearing $122\frac{1}{2}°$; and being an old acquaintance of the person under whose charge we had been placed, he came to his house and recognising us obtained permission for us to return to Tibet. During the time we remained here we found no opportunity for taking latitude or boiling point observations. Seven days later we left Saitu with our former acquaintance and returned to Yembi which we reached on the 15th August 1881.

120. We remained at Yembi for 19 days, and as a direct return to Tibet with the limited means at our disposal, and from considerations of safety, was impossible, we took service with our friend who was going to Thuden Gomba in the Darge district, and started on the 3rd September with some Mongolian traders. Retracing our steps *viâ* Chága, Urel, Ijia, Igi Chaidam, Bhága Chaidam, Choñju and Sukhai, we arrived at Chákángnamaga on the 17th September.

121. Next day we marched 22 miles over a sandy plain to Mochiangsi encamping ground. Grass and firewood were obtained but there was no water.

122. On the 19th, after marching $1\frac{3}{4}$ miles we crossed a low sandy hill and traversing an undulating sandy plain 12 miles broad, we entered a level sandy plain. 6 miles further we crossed a salt-water stream coming from the south-east, and 9 miles further still forded a branch of the Bai Gol river, 2 feet deep and 20 paces wide, which, flowing to the west for some miles, intersects our previous route to the Chákángnamaga encamping ground, near Harahusun and where it is called by that name. 3 miles to the south from the left bank of the river is a house belonging to the Jhása of Jún. Near this house there are said to be some 50 tents, and the road from Lhása to Sining passes by it. This place is known as Jún Chaidam. We passed the night on the left bank and found grass and firewood in abundance.

123. On the 21st proceeding 3 miles we forded the Bai Gol river, 3 feet deep and 50 paces wide, which flowing to the west intersects our previous route near Thingkali. This river issues from the Aláng-Núr and Thosu-Núr lakes, and the two branches after flowing through the Shiáng district and uniting in the vicinity of Shiáng Chaidam, divide into two streams some miles east of the Jhása's residence. 9 miles from the Bai Gol river we entered the Bárong district. The Jún district, which extends from the salt-water stream to the Bárong boundary, contains some 500 tents, and is similar to the Thaichinar district in its

TRANSLATIONS FROM DIARY AND NOTES.

cultivation, forest, &c. 4½ miles from the Bárong boundary we arrived at Gakcharnamaga, a Mongolian nomad camp containing 30 tents. At the distance of 1½ miles from this encampment and bearing 132½° is Bárong Chaidam, containing 10 houses and some tents. It is the residence of the Jhása of Bárong, who has some cultivated land in its vicinity. We remained in this district for 14 days, while the chief of our party sent his servants to collect some property which he had deposited in some of the gombas in the neighbourhood. We here heard that M——g was at Bánákhásum where the black tent nomads reside; and we sent a man to persuade him to rejoin us. On this man's return we learnt that M——g had feigned illness and was afraid to return to us. He had purchased herds of goats, sheep and mares with the intention of settling in the district of Shiáng, and sent word to us to give up the journey for the present and to join him.

124. About 30 miles to the east is Shiáng Chaidam, in the Shiáng district, containing about 50 houses and the same number of tents. It has a small gomba inhabited by about 50 Dábas, and there is said to be cultivation in the neighbourhood. It is reported that this district was given to the Láma of Tashi Lumbo Gomba by the Emperor of China for performing a number of miracles before him. The Láma has full power over the district which is inhabited by Mongolians. The tract of country which includes the districts of Thaichinar, Khorlu, Jún, Bárong and Shiáng, is called Thábu Chaidam on account of the five chaidams, *viz.*, Igi Chaidam, Bhága Chaidam, Jún Chaidam, Bárong Chaidam and Shiáng Chaidam, being situated in it. To the east of Shiáng is Bánákhásum, a district full of robbers; and to the south-east of the latter is the Chiámogolok district, the inhabitants of which are also addicted to robbery. It is said that they once robbed an Ambán who was returning to China *viâ* Sining. To the north of Chiámogolok is a snowy range called Amnimañchenpoñra, lying east and west, some peaks of which are believed to be holy by the Buddhists who go round them as a religious performance. To the east of Chiámogolok is a large district called Amdo. The inhabitants of the last three districts—Bánákhásum, Chiámogolok and Amdo—bear a strong resemblance in language, manners and customs to Tibetans.

125. On the 7th October, after replenishing our stock of provisions and collecting such other articles as were needed, our party left Gakcharnamaga under the guidance of two Mongolians and proceeding 13¼ miles arrived at Hádho where there was cultivation and where we stopped for a night. Our employer had now 30 ponies with him, and as each of his servants had charge of some of them, we also were allotted a number to look after. The Láma here compelled us to travel on horse-back in order to get over this part of the journey quickly and thus avoid the robbers.

126. On the 8th, we entered a narrow valley and after proceeding ¾ of a mile, crossed a stream flowing to the north and following up its left bank for 14½ miles, we recrossed it and stopped for the night. A foot of snow fell here. There are no habitations, but during winter the nomads of the Bárong district bring their cattle here for pasture. We saw here a novel spectacle. A demo (brown bear) was found taking out *chipis* (marmots) from their den; as soon as he had got one out, he put it under his hind-quarters and thinking that he had thus secured his prey commenced his search for another. This necessitated his inclining forward which gave the poor captive opportunity to get up and escape. The bear continued his labour till they were all taken out, but at last found that all those he had captured before had escaped and the one he had last got hold of was his only prey.

127. The next day, after a difficult ascent of 3¼ miles, we reached the Namohoñ pass, across the Añgirtákshia range, and descending thence for 5½ miles along a stream we arrived at a place whence it flows to the south-east. An open valley about 8 miles wide and extending east and west now lay before us; and we learnt that at a distance of 50 miles to the east was a lake called Dongar Cho, about 20 miles in circumference, situated to the north of and at the base of the Amnimañchenpoñra range. Proceeding 3 miles across the valley, we forded the branch of the Bai Gol river, 1½ feet deep and 20 paces wide, which emanates from the Aláng-Núr lake. This lake is about 3 miles to the west, is about 5 miles long and 4 miles broad, and is fed by two streams from the south. The robbers of Bánákhásum and Chiámogolok districts adopt the route along this valley in their plundering excursions against the Mongolians to the west. 4 miles further we crossed one of the streams which fall into the lake, and on the banks of which the inhabitants of the Niamcho district sometimes wash for gold. Proceeding 5½ miles up this stream we stopped for the night. We found water and grass in abundance, but there was a scarcity of fuel.

128. On the 10th October 1881, after proceeding 4½ miles, we crossed a pass with an easy ascent, and 5 miles further reached another low pass. Descending 3¼ miles along the left bank of a stream, which then turns to a bearing of 237½°, we proceeded 2½ miles further and arrived at a place suitable for encamping: fuel, grass and water were abundant and the ground level and good. It was a good place for hunting and we succeeded in shooting some deer.

129. On the 11th, we marched 5½ miles along an elevated table-land and then descended for 1½ miles and crossed a stream flowing to the west. Ascending 3 miles we reached the top of a spur and thence descending along a tributary of the Ma Chu* for 3½ miles forded that river a little below its confluence. At a distance of 3 miles to the east this river falls into the lake called Cho Kiáring Kuring, 10 miles long and 3 miles broad, and issuing from the lake again it flows in an easterly direction and is said to pass by the town of Pechin (Pekin). This river was 4 feet deep and 300 paces wide. Proceeding 1¼ miles, we stopped for the night about half a mile to the east of a walled enclosure on a low isolated hill, where we found fuel, grass and water.

130. Next day our road had a gentle upward gradient for 3 miles, and then descending crossed the Ma Chu river twice in 1¾ miles and entered a plain called Karmathang, 15 miles long and 8 miles broad. Traversing this plain we arrived at a low pass, distant 9¼ miles from the left bank of the river, and descending gradually from it, we proceeded along the base of the hills to our left and ascending them arrived at a pass about 3 miles distant from the preceding one. Following down a stream for 1½ miles we turned to the south, and 1½ miles further crossed a small spur. This stream flows to the north-east and is one of the tributaries of the Ma Chu river. 4 miles more brought us to the left bank of another stream from the south-west, which rising in the Lámathologa range and watering the plain called Jingmathang joins the stream before mentioned. We halted for the night on the left bank where we found fuel and grass in abundance. In this plain and about 2 miles to the north-east of our halting place is a lake 1½ miles long and of about the same breadth.

131. On the 13th, a snowstorm caused us to miss the direct road and we followed up the left bank of the stream, and after 13 miles arrived at a pass over the Lámathologa range, (round like Lámas' heads) which contains several round peaks. Descending for a mile we arrived at a halting place bearing the same name as the range. We stopped here for the night: grass, fuel and water were abundant.

132. On the 14th, proceeding for 5½ miles along the right bank of a stream issuing from this range, we crossed the Dugbulág stream, 1½ feet deep and 15 paces wide, and flowing to the east, near the place where the stream joins it. We saw a large number of wild yáks grazing along the banks of this stream. These animals come so seldom in contact with any human beings that they did not even notice our presence, but I was informed that sometimes when excited they would attack passers by. The Dugbulág stream forms the northern boundary of the Niamcho district. 5½ miles further, we met two men of the Niamcho district, who informed us that some fifty mounted robbers from the Chiámogolok district had lately gone up the Dubulág valley to the west, to plunder travellers *en route* from Lhása to Sining. Continuing our march for 6½ miles, we crossed a small spur and proceeding thence 2¾ miles along the left bank of a stream, we stopped for the night near the northernmost winter encamping place of the Niamcho nomads. The Mongolian guides who accompanied us from Bárong were now no longer required, as the road could be easily traced; they were therefore dismissed. The road from Bárong Chaidam to this place is good and level excepting the hilly portions where it is rough and stony.

133. Crossing the stream on the 15th, and proceeding 6 miles along its right bank, we recrossed it a little below its junction with another stream from the south. The joint stream, about 1½ feet deep and 15 paces wide, flows hence to the south-west. Going up the stream flowing from south for 5 miles, we crossed a low pass where we saw several springs of fresh water which feed two streams, one flowing to the north and the other to the south along the route. 2¾ miles from the pass a stream from the west joined the one flowing along our route; and 5¼ miles onward another stream from the same direction fell into it. Here we found three tents of the Niamcho nomads, and halted for the night: grass and fuel were abundant.

---

* This river is distinct from those bearing the same name previously mentioned.

TRANSLATIONS FROM DIARY AND NOTES.

134. On the 16th October 1881, marching for $5\frac{3}{4}$ miles along the above mentioned stream, which is fed by three smaller streams, two from the east and the third from the west, distant 3, $4\frac{1}{4}$ and $5\frac{1}{2}$ miles respectively from the last halting place, we arrived at a hot spring. 9 miles further along the same stream, which receives in its course three more tributaries, one from the east, another from the north-east and the third from the south at the distances of 4, 7 and 9 miles respectively from the hot spring, we encamped for the night. The stream which we had followed now turned to a bearing of $242\frac{1}{2}°$: it was $2\frac{1}{2}$ feet deep and 25 paces wide. We passed *en route* some tents appertaining to the nomads of the Niamcho district and also found a number of them near the halting place. Grass and fuel were not easily procurable here, and to-day's road was rough and stony.

135. On the 17th, we went up the stream coming from the south and after $2\frac{3}{4}$ miles crossed a low pass. Descending thence for $\frac{3}{4}$ of a mile and proceeding $1\frac{1}{2}$ miles over level ground, we observed a snowy peak, believed to be sacred and named Gártojhio, bearing $304\frac{1}{2}°$, and distant 4 miles. At a distance of 2 miles to the west is the village of Niamcho, where there are about 100 tents and 50 houses, and which is the residence of the ruler of the district. This district has a population represented by about 1,000 tents; and the fields in the vicinity of Niamcho village are said to be cultivated to some extent. $2\frac{1}{4}$ miles further on, we crossed a stream, $1\frac{1}{2}$ feet deep and 15 paces wide, which flowing to the west joins the large stream mentioned before as going towards a bearing of $242\frac{1}{2}°$ and which finally empties itself into the Di Chu river. Niamcho lies a little to the west of this junction. Proceeding up the stream for $2\frac{1}{2}$ miles, we arrived at a halting place where grass and fuel were abundant. The road was stony and rough.

136. On the 18th, continuing our march up the stream, we crossed after a short distance a small stream from the south falling into it; and after $5\frac{3}{4}$ miles our route diverged from it and turned up another small stream from the south. $2\frac{3}{4}$ miles further, we stopped for the night at the foot of the pass where there was a scarcity of grass and fuel. The road to-day was uneven.

137. Next day a steep ascent of $1\frac{3}{4}$ miles brought us to the pass, which was covered with three feet of snow. After a difficult descent of $2\frac{3}{4}$ miles we followed the left bank of a stream which issues from this range, and after $4\frac{3}{4}$ miles arrived at Dhingo village, containing 10 houses and having some cultivation. This is the first village we met with on our route since we left Bárong Chaidam. Still following the stream for 2 miles, we passed a village of 8 houses nearly opposite to which a small tributary entered the stream from the north-west. Two miles further on the stream we were following joins another stream, 2 feet deep and 15 paces wide, coming from the east, and the united stream after flowing to the west turns abruptly to the south and falls into the Di Chu river. Marching three-quarters of a mile up the stream coming from the east we entered Tindhu village, containing 10 houses, where we halted for the night. The Niamcho district extends to the last mentioned pass: to the east of Niamcho are three more districts named Mogonzen, Garoche and Jachukha. Below the pass lie the Gába and Rablu parganas of the Darge district.

138. Leaving the village on the 20th, and proceeding up the stream for $1\frac{3}{4}$ miles, we arrived at a gomba named Kanzo, which contains a celebrated image of Jhio (a Buddhist god). This is believed to be a holy place and is inhabited by 150 Dábas. Crossing the stream to a village on the opposite bank and continuing up the valley for $1\frac{1}{4}$ miles, we passed another village on the same bank, and $2\frac{1}{4}$ miles further we turned up a stream from the south for $2\frac{3}{4}$ miles and then ascended a pass by a steep road of $\frac{1}{2}$ a mile. After a steep descent of $1\frac{1}{2}$ miles, we proceeded along a small stream for 2 miles to its junction with another from the east. About 3 miles up the latter and on its right bank is a large gomba, named Chioti, inhabited by 300 Dábas and having some 100 houses about it. The Láma of the gomba is one of the wealthiest persons in the Gába pargana: some time ago he visited China and brought back a cuckoo clock which is an object of much curiosity among his neighbours. Proceeding a mile down the stream, we arrived at Thiso village, containing 30 houses, where we stopped for the night. Supplies were procurable at all these villages and cultivation was seen in their vicinity. One crop of *ne* and wheat is raised annually.

139. On the 21st, continuing along the stream for $\frac{3}{4}$ of a mile, we came to Khutho village, containing 20 houses, and $\frac{3}{4}$ of a mile further to a gomba, called Thuden, having passed *en route* a village named Láso containing 8 houses. Thuden Gomba is a small monastery, and has only 50 Dábas. Observations for latitude and boiling point were taken

here (lat. 33° 16′ 29″, height 11,990 feet). This was the first opportunity I had of observing since leaving Yembi in September 1880. We remained here for about two months waiting for our employer, who was an inhabitant of this place, to pay us; he at last gave us some money and a letter for a friend of his at Kegu Gomba, asking him to help us on our way to Lhása.

140. Leaving the gomba on the 26th December 1881, we now had to travel on foot. Following the stream we first, after ½ a mile, passed Laindha village, containing 50 houses, and half a mile further came to Chiorten Kárpo, one of the sacred shrines in the Darge district. It is situated near the junction of the stream with the Di Chu river which latter here comes from a bearing of 332½°: observations for boiling point were taken here (height 11,440 feet). Opposite the chiorten, and on the right bank of the river, is a village named Thándha, containing 40 houses. A mile further we passed the village of Rángna situated on the left bank of the Di Chu, and little to our left, containing 15 houses. Having crossed the river, which was then frozen, and 175 paces wide, we came to Dwinda village, containing 50 houses, after 2¾ miles we passed the village of Dhokor on the opposite side of the river, containing 30 houses. 1¾ miles further we reached Jindha village, 30 houses, and 1¼ miles still further, arrived at the left bank of a stream which falls into the river. Opposite the junction is Bari village, containing 10 houses. Proceeding for half a mile up the left bank of the stream, which comes from the south-west, we passed opposite Deuda village, containing 30 houses. 1¾ miles further is a gomba named Bhonchi, and 1½ miles beyond that is Thombudha village, containing 20 houses, near the junction of and between a stream from the west and the one running along our route: here we stopped for the night. About a mile to the west of this village is a gomba named Rákna. To-day's road was stony and through valleys, and all the villages we passed had more or less cultivation about them.

141. On the 27th, after proceeding 2¼ miles up the stream we crossed another stream from the south-east, and 3¾ miles further, reached the top of a pass by a steep ascent. Descending for 1½ miles to a stream coming from the west, we ascended gently for a mile the opposite ridge, and after a stiff descent of 1½ miles and proceeding 1¾ miles along a stream, we passed Kegu Gomba, a little to our left, inhabited by 300 Dábas, and a quarter of a mile further reached Kegudo village, containing about 200 houses, where we halted. To-day's road was rough, and we passed *en route* several nomad tents. Kegudo is a large village, and in it are about 40 shops kept by Chinese and Tibetans; it is a place of trade. The chief articles exported to China are stags' horns, musk-pods and coarse woollen cloth, in exchange for which tea and silk cloth are imported. The stag is hunted during the spring as in that season its horns are young and soft. These horns are highly valued in China on account of their medicinal properties, and a pair of antlers sells there from Rs. 150 to Rs. 200. The letter which our late employer gave us for his friend at Kegu Gomba was delivered, and the latter recommended us to a trader going to Dárchendo. As we stopped here for 16 days we found an opportunity for taking observations for latitude and boiling point (lat. 33° 0′ 58″, height 11,860 feet).

142. Leaving on the 12th January 1882, in the service of the trader, we started for Dárchendo, along the route which branching off from the Chomora lake passes by this village. After 200 paces, we crossed a stream, 25 paces broad and 1½ feet deep, which flowing from the west empties itself into a stream coming from the south-east, which latter now turning to the east falls into the Di Chu river. Continuing for 3½ miles up the left bank of the stream from the south-east, we passed opposite a gomba, named Táng, situated little below the junction of a stream from the east, this gomba is inhabited by 30 Dábas. Proceeding 3¾ miles up the same bank we crossed a stream coming from the south-west. The general direction of our route from Bárong Chaidam to this place was south, but it now turned to the south-east. 3 miles further, we crossed the stream, 30 paces broad and 1½ feet deep, and thence observed at a distance of 6½ miles and bearing 169°, a snowy peak on a long range running east and west. Continuing up the right bank for 3½ miles we crossed a stream from the north, and three-fourths of a mile further on arrived at Bhenche Gomba, inhabited by 150 Dábas. Near the gomba were about 30 houses and some 40 tents appertaining to the nomads: here we stopped for the night.

143. On the 13th, proceeding up the stream for 1½ miles, we arrived opposite the junction of another stream with this stream, and three-quarters of a mile onward, we passed a gomba to the left of our route. 3¼ miles further, a stream from the north falls into the stream we were following and 4 miles onward a low pass was ascended. From Kegudo to

TRANSLATIONS FROM DIARY AND NOTES.

this place our route was good and led through a broad valley, but it now entered a narrow defile. Descending gently for a quarter of a mile, we reached a stream issuing from the pass and following it for 3½ miles, passed opposite a stream coming from the east. 1¼ miles onward, another stream from the south-west falls into the one running along our route; and 1¾ miles further is Khánsar village, containing 25 houses, where we stopped for the night. From Hádho in the Barong district to the pass just mentioned no trees or bushes were seen; but onward, the *padam* (a kind of fir), *chángma* (a kind of willow), *shán* (a tree not recognised) and wild rose-bushes were met with.

144. Next day proceeding 1¼ miles down the valley we crossed a stream from the south-west, near the junction of which were some fields and a hamlet of two houses. 1¼ miles further on, another stream from the west was crossed, opposite to which and on the left bank of the main stream is Shiongo Gomba, inhabited by 30 Dábas. Half a mile lower down and opposite a village containing 30 houses, this stream falls into the Di Chu river now flowing from the north-west. The river flows here in a narrow valley and was frozen here and there so that it could be crossed. Marching 5 miles along the right bank of the river we arrived at Siti village, containing 10 houses, having passed, 2¼ miles before reaching it, a small hamlet of 4 houses. 2 miles lower down is a small gomba on the left bank; and 2½ miles further, the route passes by Donthok Gomba built near the extremity of a spur to the right, and inhabited by 50 Dábas. Proceeding a quarter of a mile further, we crossed a stream falling into the Di Chu river, and 2¾ miles further still stopped at Dogung village, containing 10 houses, where supplies, firewood and grass were procurable.

145. On the 15th January 1882, we resumed our march and after 500 paces, crossed a stream which flowing from the south joins the Di Chu. The path which is at first rather steep and ill-defined, passed Sháo hamlet (2 houses), a stream from the right, and Donti hamlet (5 houses) and brought us to Dwinthang Gomba on the left bank of the river, distant 7½ miles from the last stage. A little above the gomba we crossed the river on the ice: it was about 180 paces wide. The gomba is said to contain 100 Dábas and is surrounded by 100 houses. Continuing for 3¼ miles along the left bank of the river and passing *en route* two hamlets, we arrived at a *dukha* (ferry), where the river is crossed by boats during the summer, opposite to a few huts on the right bank mostly inhabited by boat-men. Here a stream from the south-west joins the right bank of the river. 5¼ miles further on is Síla village, 30 houses, near the junction of a stream from the north-east, where we halted for the night. Supplies, firewood and grass were abundant. Observations for boiling point were taken here (height 10,390 feet).

146. On the 16th, proceeding three-quarters of a mile along the left bank of the river, we passed opposite a stream which falls into the Di Chu from the south, and half a mile further reached Rárang village of 20 houses. Opposite this village and on the right bank of the river is Dhingo Gomba having 30 Dábas; and 3¼ miles onward, is Chiti Gomba, containing 35 Dábas, situated on the left bank. Passing thence through scattered hamlets for 6½ miles, we came opposite to Chingo Gomba surrounded by 50 houses, and three-quarters of a mile further, arrived at the well-known temple, named Dolma Lhákháng surrounded by 30 houses, where we put up for the night and where observations for boiling point were taken (height 10,930 feet). About a quarter of a mile to the north of this temple is Losino village of 30 houses. Various kinds of corn and vegetables are cultivated along the banks of the Di Chu, *viz*., wheat, *ne* (a kind of barley), pease, *masúr*, (a kind of pulse), *sarsoñ* (a kind of mustard seed), turnip, radish, &c. About 50 miles to the south-east and on the right bank of the Di Chu river is the town Darge Gonchen, said to possess a large gomba, and palaces of the Darge Gialbu (rája). Some 15 years ago the inhabitants of the Niárong district, who are the most warlike of the Tibetans, invaded and conquered the town and pulled down several of the palaces. The rája is said to have a large printing establishment: the printing is executed by means of engraved wooden blocks; and this establishment contains such for almost all the books now existing in the Tibetan language. To economize space and material the blocks are engraved on both sides.

147. On the 17th, having proceeded ¾ mile along the left bank of the Di Chu, we passed the junction with it, on opposite sides, of two streams, one from the north-east and the other from the south; and 1½ miles further we crossed a stream from the north-east. Our road now diverged from the Di Chu which here takes a bearing of 127½°. After a steep ascent of 1½ miles up the slope of the range to our left, we came to Káphu Gomba, where there are 25 Dábas, we continued along the slope for 6¼ miles, and passing by

the hamlets of Bága (10 houses) and Rára (5 houses), crossed a stream flowing down from the north which joins the Di Chu about 3 miles to the south of the road. Continuing along the slope for 2½ miles, we passed Nágli Gomba (30 Dábas) and having crossed a spur, descended to a stream, 2 miles from the gomba, running to the east. Proceeding 3¾ miles along this stream we stopped at Chiri village for the night. This village contains 15 houses and has a hot spring near it. Firewood, grass and other supplies were procurable.

148. On the 18th January 1882, continuing along the stream for 4 miles, which thence flows southwards to the Di Chu, we crossed a spur running to the south, and then followed a stream issuing from it and falling into another stream from the south-east which joins the Di Chu. The river then turns south through a narrow valley, and is said to be very deep. 1¾ miles from the spur we passed Gainjo Gomba surrounded by 60 houses, and then proceeding up the stream from the south-east we passed Jongu Gomba surrounded by about 50 houses, and a stream coming from the north; we arrived at Dojam, a nomad camp, at the junction of two streams and distant 9½ miles from the spur. There were no fixed habitations here; but grass and firewood were abundant. We here learnt that we were likely to meet mounted robbers of the Chiámogolok district during our next day's march.

149. On the 19th, proceeding 7½ miles up the left branch of the stream, we reached a pass by an easy ascent, having crossed *en route* a small stream from the right. Leaving the pass, which is on the boundary of the Jokchen pargana of district Darge, we continued for 9 miles along a stream issuing from it which we crossed several times: this stream after receiving the water of three other streams, two from the south and one from the east, turns to the north-east and empties itself into the Ja Chu river. We passed several nomad encampments. 3¾ miles further, we crossed a pass by a slight ascent and descending half a mile we crossed a stream, which coming from the south and flowing for 2 miles along our route turns to the north. 3¼ miles further is a stream flowing from the south, and 1¼ miles onward is Jokchen Gomba on the bank of another stream from the same direction, which has about 200 houses and 100 tents in its vicinity: here we halted. We had a long march to-day as we wished to reach a safe encamping place to escape the robbers of whom we had heard yesterday. The three streams before mentioned as flowing to the north unite with the stream from the Miri Lá pass which latter empties itself into the Ja Chu river. They drain a generally level and open valley covered with rich pasturage, which affords sustenance to large herds of yáks, sheep and goats belonging to nomads who are numerous in the valley.

150. On the 20th we left the gomba and proceeding three-quarters of a mile crossed a small stream from the south. 2½ miles further, we reached the stream coming from the Miri Lá pass; marching up it within a somewhat narrow valley for 7 miles we gained that pass by a steep ascent of 1¼ miles. Near the foot of the pass 4 streams, from the right and left of our route, joined the one from it and formed the Miri Lá pass stream. This pass forms the boundary between the Jokchen and Yulung parganas of the Darge district. Descending abruptly for 1¾ miles and then marching 3 miles we came to a stream which issuing from a small lake (about a mile long and the same in breadth) to our right, flows to the north-east. 1¾ miles onward we forded a small stream which running to the north joins the one from the lake; and 4½ miles further, we crossed the united stream near its junction with another stream from the south-west. Proceeding down stream for 1½ miles, we arrived at Yulung, a nomad camp of 50 tents, among which was one house near the junction of a stream from the north. We stopped for the night and found fuel and grass in abundance. To-day we encountered 10 mounted robbers near the Miri Lá pass; but fortunately for us the sudden approach of a Tibetan Officer dispersed them. We would have halted near the lake but fearing a surprise we sought the protection of the nomad camp.

151. On the 21st, marching for 3 miles along the left bank of the stream, now bearing the name of the Yulung Chu, we passed opposite a stream which coming from the south-west joins it, and 5¼ miles lower down another stream from the same direction falls into it. 2¾ miles onward a stream comes from the north-east up which, about a mile from the route, is the residence of the Yulung Pon, or ruler of the Yulung pargana, where 5 or 6 houses and a number of tents were visible. Marching 3¼ miles along the left bank of the stream we observed a snowy peak, bearing 140¼° and distant 9½ miles, and 3½ miles onward crossed the stream, 35 paces wide and 2 feet deep. Following the right bank for 1¼ miles, we crossed a stream coming from the south, and there found some 10 nomad tents, situated in a small plain, at the southern extremity of which was a

TRANSLATIONS FROM DIARY AND NOTES.

thick forest containing a species of stunted oak, *deodár*, *bhoj* (a kind of birch), rhododendrons (bearing white flowers) and several kinds of plants and bushes. We halted near the encampment and found plenty of firewood and grass.

152. On the 22nd January 1882, proceeding 5 miles, we crossed two small streams from the south, distant half a mile from each other. Ascending gently for $2\frac{1}{2}$ miles to the top of a spur, opposite to which on the left bank of the river is a village distant $1\frac{1}{2}$ miles, we reached the boundary between the Darge and Rongbácha or Horko districts. This spur is well clad with forest, and sawyers from Dárchendo were engaged here in turning out timber for the use of the inhabitants of the surrounding places. From the village above mentioned the Yulung Chu stream turns to the north-east, and after a further course of some miles joins the Ja Chu river. Continuing for $1\frac{1}{2}$ miles along this spur we observed a snowy peak bearing 162°, distant $3\frac{3}{4}$ miles, and thence followed a stream which flowing 3 miles along our route turns to the east and ultimately falls into the Ja Chu river. 600 paces further, a stream from the west crosses the road and joins the above mentioned stream, and 2 miles onward a stream issues and flowing $3\frac{3}{4}$ miles along our route turns to the north and joins the same stream. $\frac{3}{4}$ of a mile from this turn, Riphug temple, which consists of a small cave adorned with flags, &c., to the left, was passed, and a quarter of a mile further we reached Lágarkhándo, where a well-known and very rich trader lives. Proceeding $1\frac{1}{2}$ miles, we passed Durkug village, containing large buildings, situated on the bank of a stream flowing to the north, and $1\frac{1}{2}$ miles onward crossed a stream, 30 paces wide and two feet deep, which flowing northerly joins the stream mentioned before which falls into the Ja Chu. Continuing our journey for $1\frac{1}{2}$ miles we reached Dáge Gomba, which has 1,000 Dábas and is surrounded by 300 private houses. This is one of the principal gombas in Tibet and is adorned with golden cupolas. Two miles onward is a village called Ringo, 40 houses, where we stopped for two days. Observations for latitude and the boiling point were taken here (lat. 31° 39′ 14″, height 10,550 feet). This village is surrounded by extensive cultivation, and to its south lies a long snowy range, which runs from Kegudo village eastward along the right of our route and extends to the Dáng Lá range on the west. Houses here are well built, as timber is easily procurable. Grass, firewood and supplies are abundant. The road from Kegudo village to this place was generally good excepting along the Di Chu where we found it rather stony and rugged.

153. On the 25th, we crossed the Ja Chu river over ice, 120 paces wide, near a small village about a mile from Ringo village. This river rises in the Jachukha district, to the north-west, to which it gives the name: it is crossed by boats in summer. From the left bank we observed a snowy peak at a distance of $4\frac{1}{2}$ miles, bearing $209\frac{1}{2}°$; and marching $3\frac{3}{4}$ miles along the river through fields and habitations, we saw a stream coming from the south, and joining the river. Half a mile further, we crossed a stream from the north-east, and proceeding thence 800 paces reached a hamlet to our left whence we observed a snowy peak, bearing 178° and distant 6 miles. A mile onward to our left was a gomba named Bhiar, and three-quarters of a mile further, we passed opposite another gomba named Nena, close to which a stream from the south joined the river. Still following the Ja Chu for $3\frac{3}{4}$ miles and passing a hamlet *en route*, we crossed a stream coming from the north, and $2\frac{1}{4}$ miles further saw a stream from the south falling into the river. Three-quarters of a mile thence we forded a stream from the north, on the left bank of which was a village where we stopped for the night. About half a mile to the north-west of the village and on the right bank of the stream is Kánzego, a large gomba inhabited by 2,000 Dábas and surrounded by 2,500 houses. It is so old and sacred that people of the neighbouring districts in order to confirm their declarations swear by its name. Rongbácha and the districts to the east of it are governed by two Chinese officers who have their head quarters at Kánzego. From here the Ja Chu takes a south-easterly course; some miles further on it cuts through the southern snowy range, and waters the Niároug district, the inhabitants of which are very brave and are said to have conquered the neighbouring districts, and to have even baffled the Chinese troops sent against them some 15 years ago: at last the Lhása Government won over their chiefs by bribery and thus subdued them.

154. On the 26th, having marched $2\frac{1}{2}$ miles, passing *en route* a hamlet of 20 houses, we observed two snowy peaks close to each other, bearing $135\frac{1}{2}°$, $137\frac{1}{2}°$ and distant 14 miles. $3\frac{1}{4}$ miles further, we crossed a stream (near a hamlet) coming from the north and falling into the Ja Chu. Ascending thence 2 miles and then descending three-quarters of a mile, we crossed another stream coming from the north, which flowing to the south for half a mile joins a stream coming down from a pass ahead. The joint stream flowing to the south

for some miles receives a third stream issuing from the southern snowy range and then falls into the Ja Chu. Proceeding half a mile further we reached a small village on the right bank of the stream from the pass where we stopped for the night. We had a short march to-day as we wanted some of our companions who had been detained by their friends at Kánzego to join us.

155. On the 27th January 1882, proceeding up the stream for 3 miles we reached a pass, the boundary between the Rongbácha and Dau districts, by an easy ascent, and descending thence 3¼ miles we crossed a stream coming from the south. 1½ miles lower down we passed a gomba, named Jior, and three-quarters of a mile further the hamlet of Khánsar of 10 houses. Still continuing to descend for 3¼ miles and passing two hamlets *en route*, we arrived at the junction of a stream from the north with a stream from the west, close to a village having the residence of an official of the Dau patti. Proceeding three-quarters of a mile along the stream, we passed the residence of the Gialbu (rája), surrounded by 30 houses, and 1¼ miles further on a stream from the south-west joined the one along the route. Continuing down stream for 6¾ miles and passing *en route* 3 hamlets, we crossed a stream from the south, on the right bank of which is the village named Dwinda containing 25 houses, where we stopped for the night. To-day's path was stony and rugged.

156. On the 28th, still following down stream, after 1½ miles we crossed a stream coming from the south; thence marching 7¾ miles, and crossing *en route* a low spur and passing by two hamlets, we forded a stream from the south-west. Marching on for 5½ miles, through fields and habitations, we crossed another stream from the south-west. From this place the stream takes a circuitous course round spurs of hills from the south. Proceeding half a mile further, we reached Gori village, where we halted, and where grass, firewood and supplies were procurable. To-day's road was for the most part good.

157. On the 29th, after proceeding 2¼ miles, we crossed a stream from the south. 1¼ miles further we reached a hamlet close to the low pass which forms the boundary between the Dau and Dángo districts, and about 2 miles onward arrived at the gomba of Dángo, inhabited by 2,000 Dábas and surrounded by about 1,000 houses. This gomba is also far famed and is adorned with golden cupolas. Three-quarters of a mile further we crossed a stream flowing to the north, and a little beyond arrived opposite the junction of a large stream from the north with the main stream. Ascending about a mile to a spur we proceeded along it for 1¾ miles, and thence descending gently for 3 miles arrived at the village of Báthog, containing 15 houses, on the left bank of a small stream from the south which joins the main stream. Proceeding 5 miles along the main stream through fields and cultivation, we crossed a stream from the south-west, and 2½ miles further forded the stream itself, here 70 paces wide and 3 feet deep, to a village on the left bank. Continuing our journey we passed, after 1¼ miles, opposite a stream from the south-west, and 2½ miles further arrived at a village of 10 houses where we stopped for the night, and where grass, firewood and supplies were procurable. To-day's road was stony and rugged.

158. The next day, after proceeding a mile down the stream and then up a stiff ascent for three-quarters of a mile, we came to a village on the top of the spur forming the boundary between the Dángo and Tau districts, and descending thence to a hamlet half a mile distant we crossed 3 miles further, a large stream coming from the north and joining the main stream. Continuing our journey for 10 miles and passing *en route* 6 hamlets, we reached the village of Yáthok, containing 25 houses, situated near a stream from the north, where we halted for the night. All the villages along to-day's route were situated on the left bank of the stream, and the opposite bank was covered with forest trees.

159. On the 31st, we left Yáthok village and having crossed a stream arrived at the village of Dathok, 10 houses, distant 1¾ miles. 2¼ miles from Dathok we crossed a stream from the north having passed a hamlet *en route*, and 2¾ miles further forded another stream from the north-east, having passed 2 hamlets on the road between these two streams. Marching 1½ miles along the left bank of the main stream we passed opposite a stream coming from the south-west, and a quarter of a mile further reached a stream from the north, on the right bank of which about a quarter of a mile to our left was a gomba, named Nichong, occupied by about 800 Dábas. The stream which we had followed from the Dau patti and which was locally called by various names from places watered by it, is here known as Tau Chu: a quarter of a mile below the gomba it turns to the south-west, and passing through the district of Niárong falls into the Ja Chu, and the united river lower down is

TRANSLATIONS FROM DIARY AND NOTES.

named the Nag Chu. 4¾ miles from the gomba, having passed 2 hamlets *en route*, we crossed a stream coming from the south-east which flowing to the west joins the Tau Chu. Going up its left bank for 2¼ miles we observed that a stream from the north-east joined it, and 6 miles further, we arrived opposite Giáro village situated on the right bank of the stream. The hill sides from this village onward are covered with thick forest of the same kinds of trees met with near Yulung. To-day we passed a number of hamlets situated on the banks of the stream.

160. On the 1st February 1882, marching up the stream for a mile, we passed a village containing 15 houses, and two miles higher up crossed a stream coming from the south-west. 2½ miles further we crossed another stream from the same direction, and 1½ miles beyond reached the foot of a pass, named Minia Lá, which has a steep ascent of three-quarters of a mile. This pass forms the boundary between the Tau and Minia districts and crosses the southern range which had lain along the right of our route and which hence turns to the south. Descending half a mile from the pass, we found a stream which issues from it, and following it through an uninhabited part of the Minia district for 5¾ miles, we arrived near the junction with it of a stream from the north-west. Proceeding 6 miles along the right bank we passed opposite a hamlet, and two miles further reached the village of Khánsar (15 houses) where we stopped for the night. The route from Giáro to Khánsar passes through heavy forest, and the robbers from the Niárong district generally plunder travellers in the neighbourhood of the pass. About a year ago, it is said, they robbed and murdered a Chinese trader in its vicinity. Some cultivation was seen near Khánsar village.

161. The next day after going a quarter of a mile down stream, we crossed to the left bank at a place where it was 15 paces wide and 1¾ feet deep. Continuing along it for 4¼ miles, we passed a small gomba, occupied by 10 Dábas, and 2½ miles further on, crossed a stream coming from the north, near a hamlet. 3 miles further having passed a hamlet *en route*, we arrived at the junction of the stream along our route with another from the south-east. The joint stream flowing hence to the south-east joins the Nag Chu river. Having crossed the stream from the south-east, 15 paces wide and 1½ feet deep, we marched up its left bank, and passing *en route* 2 small hamlets, forded, 2¾ miles from the junction mentioned before, a stream coming from the south. A mile further on, a stream from the north joined the one along our route; thence passing by 2 hamlets we arrived, 3¾ miles further on, at the junction with it of two streams, one from the south and the other from the north. 3 miles further up the left bank, we crossed to the village of Sháo, 15 houses, situated on the right bank, where we stopped for the night. Supplies, firewood and grass are procurable. Cultivation was scanty in the vicinity of the villages on this side of the Minia Lá pass. Each hamlet had near it one or more old, stone built, square towers which were necessary in former times as safeguards against bands of plunderers who then infested the country.

162. On the 3rd, having gone 3 miles we crossed a stream from the east near a hamlet (5 houses). Half a mile further on, a stream from the south-east joined the one we had followed and thence by a stiff ascent of ¾ of a mile we gained a pass whence we observed two snowy peaks, bearing 79° and 116°, distant 7¾ and 8½ miles respectively. Descending gently to a stream, distant ½ a mile, we proceeded along it for 1½ miles to its junction with another small stream from the north, and the joint stream thence turned to the south. 1¼ miles further on, we crossed a stream, 20 paces wide and 1¾ feet deep, from the east; and 704 paces onward we forded a stream from the south-east. 2¾ miles further we crossed a stream which coming from the south-east joins the above mentioned stream, and 1½ miles onward reached a pass by an easy ascent. Descending for a mile we arrived at the confluence of three small streams issuing from the pass and proceeding along the united stream for 2¾ miles, we crossed a stream coming from the east. Proceeding 1¾ miles further, along the stream from the pass, we saw a hamlet on the right bank, and thence leaving the stream and turning to our left proceeded for 1¼ miles, and near a small village crossed a stream which flowing to the west joins the stream mentioned before. Crossing a low pass we arrived after 2¼ miles at Tombadu, 10 houses, near the junction of two streams which come from the north-east and east, where we stopped for the night. Our path was undulating, and we passed several nomad tents and a breeding establishment for horses belonging to a Tibetan official. Supplies, firewood and grass were abundant.

163. On the 4th, we crossed a spur about a mile distant, and descending thence for half a mile, we forded a stream coming from the north. 1¼ miles further, we crossed

a stream, formed by the junction of two small ones coming from the north and south-east respectively. Proceeding up the south-eastern branch for 1½ miles a stream coming from the north-east joined it, and 1½ miles further, we reached a low pass. Descending about half a mile, we forded a stream flowing to the south and one mile further crossed a stream from the east which flowing to the south-west joins the one mentioned before. 1¼ miles further we reached a low pass, named Sáma Lá, and proceeding along an elevated tract for 4 miles, crossed a stream and thence ascended for 700 paces to the Gi Lá pass. This pass also crosses over the snowy range which here divides into two ranges running to our right and left, and from it a path branches off to Lhása by way of Lithang and Báthang. Descending along a stream for 3 miles we crossed another, which coming from the west joins the one flowing along our route, and 2¼ miles further, we forded a stream from the east joining the main stream. Continuing our progress 3½ miles we arrived at Chithog Giachug (a posting stage where a relay of horses is kept) opposite to a stream coming from the west. Here are some 25 houses where travellers can lodge and obtain food on payment, and a stage-house for Chinese Officers. These rest-houses are very comfortable and well furnished and their managers are ready to supply anything on demand; but as all articles have to be brought from Dárchendo they are dear. To-day snow fell, and the path from the Gi Lá pass was rugged and stony and lay through a narrow valley. We found no village or hamlet between Tombadu and Sáma Lá, but saw some nomad tents here and there; from the latter place even these were not met with.

164. Leaving Chithog on the 5th February 1882, we crossed after three-quarters of a mile a stream from the north-east and proceeding 3 miles further arrived opposite the junction of a large stream from the south with the one along our route, whence we observed 5 snowy peaks, bearing 68°, 79°, 86½°, 107½°, and 116½°, distant 5¼, 5¾, 6¼, 7 and 7½ miles respectively. 4¼ miles further we crossed the main stream by a bridge 15 paces wide, and proceeding ¼ of a mile further, we arrived at the gate of Dárchendo city.

165. Dárchendo (named Táchiálo by the Chinese) is a small city situated in a very narrow valley resembling the English letter T in form, enclosed on all sides by snowy mountains which rise in precipices of stupendous height. It contains two bazárs, extending north and south for about ¾ of a mile along the banks of the stream, each of which consists of a row of shops on either side of a paved roadway about 15 feet wide. At the end of these two streets a large stream from the west joins the one flowing through the city and the joint stream then flows to the east. The two streets near their termination, extend some way up and down the right bank of the stream from the west. There are four gates, one at each end of the two bazárs, with doors made of thick boards; and the stream is bridged over in a number of places with timber to facilitate communication between the bazárs. The houses are built of stone and timber and are generally high and double-storied. There are four gombas at the four corners of the city. The city is governed by a Chinese officer entitled Thain (literally "sky" and therefore may be taken to mean highest officer), assisted by several inferior officers. A Tibetan officer called Chiákla also resides here and has a subordinate jurisdiction over the original inhabitants of Dárchendo. It is a market chiefly for tea which is brought by coolies from a distance of some 20 days' journey, and is hence carried by beasts of burden to various places in Tibet and even to Kashmir itself. When moist it is shaped into bricks*, each weighing about 5 lbs., and costing from 6 annas to 3 rupees per brick according to the quality of the tea. In our journey from Kegudo to Dárchendo we met several traders returning to their homes with tea estimated to aggregate not less than 300,000 lbs.

166. The climate of the city in winter is very severe owing to a continuous fall of snow for weeks, while in the hot weather it is comparatively warm from the circumstance of the city being situated in a very narrow valley and surrounded by high mountains. Chinese and Tibetan traders are very numerous, being about equal in number. The language and religion of the native inhabitants of the city resemble those of the Tibetans, but their social and other customs are like those of the Chinese.

167. With the exception of small gardens for raising ordinary vegetables no cultivation is carried on in the Dárchendo valley. Corn and different kinds of vegetables and fruits are brought from some distance eastwards where the soil is better suited for

---

* These bricks are known in western Tibet and Kashmir by the name of 'dámu'; the price of a 'dámu' of tea in Leh varied some 20 years ago from 5 to 8 Rs.

TRANSLATIONS FROM DIARY AND NOTES.

culture. Some small bushes alone grow on the hill sides and a few stunted trees have been planted here and there in the vicinity of the houses. Timber and firewood are brought down the large stream from the south, which joins the main stream about 4½ miles before reaching the city. The streams abound with fish which are caught by angling. The same currency and weights as used at Saitu obtain here, but besides them the Indian rupee is also current.

168. Having heard that two Jesuit Fathers lived outside the city, close to the northern and southern gates, I determined to visit them in order to enquire about the safest and surest route to India, and also to try to obtain through them means to prosecute my journey. One day I met one of them who received me very kindly, but as in the course of conversation he did not raise the question of my means I did not think it advisable to trouble him. He however presented me with six rupees, and gave me an introductory letter to his brethren at Báthang and Darjeeling, and advised me to return by way of Tibet in preference to that by China, as the former, he said, would take only 40 days to reach India and furthermore required no passport which would be necessary for the latter. Returning to my quarters I glanced at the Father's letter and found that he and I disagreed in our dates, for what he had put down as the 11th I made out to be the 12th February: unfortunately I had no opportunity of seeing him again. We remained at Dárchendo 11 days during which we were unable to take observations for latitude owing to the cloudy weather and continuous fall of snow; but we took boiling point observations (height 8,310 feet).

169. On the 16th February 1882, we left Dárchendo and retracing our steps for 2½ miles took boiling point and latitude observations, the latter of which were however doubtful, as clouds were passing over the meridian at the time: (height 8,930 feet). At nightfall we arrived at Chithog Giachug where we halted.

170. The next day we reached the Gi Lá pass, where observations of the boiling point were taken (height 14,690 feet), and thence we took the Báthang route along a stream which runs to the west, and after 2½ miles arrived at Cháchukha Giachug, where there were two houses and a rest-house where we stopped for the night.

171. On the 18th, having proceeded 2 miles we saw a stream, which coming from the south-east joins the one along our route, and three-quarters of a mile further reached Thicho village of 15 houses. Marching 2¼ miles onward, we crossed to the left bank of the stream near a hamlet, and three-quarters of a mile further passed opposite its junction with the one from the Sáma Lá pass. Continuing along the left bank for 4½ miles, we arrived at Ánya Giachug, which has 30 houses and a stage-house. Following down the same stream and passing the junctions with it of four others, of which the first comes from the east and the others from the north, at distances of 2½, 3, 5 and 5½ miles respectively, we reached Thondo Chiorten, also called Háche, surrounded by eight houses, situated opposite the last junction. To-day we passed several hamlets with cultivation about them along both sides of the stream (now become a small river) and halted near the chiorten. The following morning was new year's day of the Tibetan year, and in keeping with the custom of the country we gave ourselves a holiday.

172. On the 20th, we resumed our march and after proceeding along the left bank for 2 miles were informed that the route which we had adopted was wrong. We therefore crossed the stream, 35 paces wide and 2 feet deep, and marching back half a mile up its right bank reached its junction with another stream from the north-west. Going a quarter of a mile up the right bank of the second stream, we crossed to the left bank and continuing along it for 4¼ miles we re-crossed it by a wooden bridge, 25 paces long; the stream was estimated to be 1½ feet deep. A quarter of a mile further a stream from the west joined it, and 2¼ miles onward we reached Golokthok Giachug, having a stage-house and 20 houses, opposite to the junction of a stream from the north-east with the main stream. After a quarter of a mile we passed the village of Golokthok, and proceeding 5¾ miles up the stream, we arrived at an encamping ground, where we halted. To-day we passed many hamlets with cultivation around them and found the inhabitants continuing the festivities of the new year's day. The encamping ground was surrounded by forest. The path was good; grass and firewood were abundant.

173. On the 21st, by a stiff ascent of 2¼ miles up the stream, we reached a pass; and descending gently for three-quarters of a mile we crossed a stream which flows to the

south past the gomba of Kashi, 30 houses, situated on its left bank about a mile away. After a steep ascent of a mile from the stream, we gained the Kashi Lá pass, where observations for boiling point were taken (height 14,710 feet). Descending about 2½ miles to a stream coming from a bearing of 102½°, we followed it for 1½ miles to its junction with a stream from the south. Proceeding down the latter for ½ a mile another from the north joined it and 1¾ miles further, we passed Urong Dongu Giachug, having 15 houses and a stage-house. Half a mile onward, two streams coming from the north and south respectively joined that along the route and 3 miles lower down a stream from the south emptied itself into the same. Three-quarters of a mile further we crossed to the left bank and stopped at the hamlet of Zíra (3 houses). To-day's road passed through a forest; and there were no hamlets or cultivation along it.

174. On the 22nd February 1882, after proceeding three-quarters of a mile we passed opposite the junction of a stream from the east, and half a mile further saw on the right bank a hamlet named Urongshi (10 houses), the residence of the chief of the Urongshi district, which latter extends from the Kashi Lá pass on the east to the Nagchukha village on the west. Continuing for 4¾ miles along the left bank, we arrived at Kharingbo Giachug, 15 houses and a stage-house, situated near a stream from the south, and 3¾ miles further, crossed to the right of the stream along our route. About a mile thence we crossed a stream from the north, by a wooden bridge, and along the next 5¼ miles having crossed the main stream three times by wooden bridges, we reached Nagchukha village. About half a mile before reaching the village the depth of the stream was found to be 2½ feet and the width about 25 paces.

175. Nagchukha village (properly bazár) is situated on the banks of the Nag Chu river, and consists of some 40 shops scattered here and there and surrounded by high mountains covered with grass and thick forest trees. The forest is full of wild animals among which a species of stag with a thick, flat, long tail is remarkable. The inhabitants are very fond of breeding hogs and hunting-dogs: the former are of two kinds, the Chinese or broad-eared breed and the common kind found in India. Two crops are annually raised here; one consists of barley and wheat, and the other comprises millet, *dau*, turnips and other edible roots.

176. To cross the river previous sanction of the headman of the village is required. We, therefore, went to him to obtain his permission, but as soon as he heard our request he suspected us to be thieves, as he said that every one in the country was celebrating the new year festival, and that no one but thieves cared to travel. He ordered us to stay there four days, during which time he would get information from the ruler of the city of Dárchendo, whether any theft had lately been committed in the city. After four days we were set at liberty, and having paid two annas to the keeper of the bridge, we crossed the river, which is about 100 paces wide. This river as mentioned before is formed by the junction of the Ja Chu and Tau Chu rivers and flowing to the south it is said it falls into the Di Chu which flows through the Chinese Empire. Observations for latitude and the boiling point were taken at Nagchukha village (lat. 30° 2′ 13″, height 8,410 feet).

177. Leaving the village on the 28th, and crossing the river as stated above, we marched northwards along its right bank for half a mile, and thence turned up a stream from the west. Crossing this stream, 15 paces wide and 1½ feet deep, after a quarter of a mile, and continuing our progress for 1½ miles, we crossed a stream which falls into it from the left. Proceeding 6 miles up the latter we reached Margen Dongu Giachug, 5 houses and a stage-house, where we stopped for the night. With the exception of a hamlet on the right bank of the river, no habitation was seen along to-day's route. Supplies, grass and firewood were procurable here.

178. On the 1st March 1882 continuing up the stream and proceeding 4¼ miles, we reached the junction with it of a stream from the west, 1¾ miles further we crossed a pass by a steep ascent and descending three-fourths of a mile arrived at a small giachug, consisting of 3 houses. Ascending 1¾ miles we reached another pass by a steep ascent and continuing our journey down it for 3¾ miles, arrived at a giachug, 5 houses and a stage-house. Marching 1¾ miles further we passed the gomba of Golok, containing 25 houses, about a mile to the south of our route, and three-quarters of a mile onward reached the junction of a small stream from the north with a larger one from the north-west which flows to the south-east. Proceeding 2 miles up the latter stream and having crossed, where

TRANSLATIONS FROM DIARY AND NOTES.

it was 25 paces wide and 1¾ feet deep, to the right bank, we arrived at Golokthok Giachug, which has a stage-house and 15 houses, where we passed the night. To-day's road was rugged, stony and undulating, and from the pass last mentioned, lay in the Lithang district. Cultivation was found here; and grass, firewood and supplies were abundant. Small-pox was prevalent in this vicinity and to prevent its spreading a kind of snuff was administered by Chinese physicians. This snuff has the same effect as vaccination, as its use brings out a few pimples here and there over the body, accompanied by a slight fever: these pimples dry up in time and the dried up matter which falls from them is used in preparing the antidote mentioned above.

179. On the 2nd March 1882, proceeding 4 miles we reached the top of a spur by a slight ascent. Marching 1½ miles along a stream which issues from the spur, we arrived at a small giachug where a stream from the east falls into the one along our route. 1½ miles further we crossed, where it was 15 paces wide and 1½ feet deep, to the right bank and proceeding a quarter of a mile thence passed over another stream from the west. These streams unite a little to the left of the route and thence flow to the south. Marching 1¼ miles up the latter stream we arrived at Támáráthong Giachug, which has a stage-house, seven houses and 10 tents belonging to nomads, and is situated at the junction of three streams coming from the north-east, west and south-west respectively. We stopped here for the night. Our route to-day was good: it passed through a forest and we met with no cultivation. Supplies, grass and firewood were procurable here.

180. On the 3rd, we proceeded 3½ miles up the stream from the south-west and reached a pass by a slight ascent, where there is a small giachug consisting of a single house. Descending 3½ miles we crossed a stream, which issuing from the northern range flows to the south, and one mile further arrived at another small giachug, where there was a house and 10 nomad tents. Ascending 1½ miles at a steep gradient we gained the top of a pass; and descending thence for a mile we proceeded 4 miles along a stream which issues from the pass, and reached Hapchukha Giachug, where there are 10 houses and a stage-house; here we halted. No hamlets or cultivation but scattered tents of nomads were seen along the route. Supplies, grass and firewood were procurable.

181. The next day proceeding a quarter of a mile along the stream, we forded it to the right bank. This stream flowing a little to the south-west falls into a stream, which coming from the north-west flows to the south. Going up the latter for ½ a mile, we crossed a stream falling into it from the north, and 5½ miles further we passed over to the right bank; it was here 30 paces wide and 2½ feet deep. Here a stream from the west joined it and near the junction is a small giachug of one house. From Hapchukha to this place we passed about 100 tents of nomads, and we were told that a little to the north of this junction washing for gold was carried on, and that the gold found there was very fine in color and quality. Proceeding 3½ miles further up the stream from the west, we crossed a pass by a slight ascent and marching for 5¾ miles over undulating ground, along the base of spurs from the range to the right, arrived at Lithang, a small city containing about 2,500 houses.

182. Lithang, one of the richest towns in Tibet, is situated to the north of a plain and at the end of a spur from the northern range. This plain is watered by a stream, named Li Chu, which flows to the south-east. The plain is covered with grass and contains several springs of fresh water. Its greatest length is about 15 miles, and the greatest breadth about 8 miles, and is peopled by a large number of nomads. There is no cultivation, and corn is brought from a distance of about three days' journey to the south; while rice and *gur* (a coarse kind of sugar) are brought from Yúna (Yunnan), a large tract of country belonging to China and distant some 300 miles to the S.E.

183. Here as in Lhása the popular festival of Chionga Chiopa is celebrated during the first month of the year. This month is called Molam Chemo, or the month of asking blessings, owing to a belief that favors asked for in it are sooner granted by the gods than those sought at any other time. A large earthen figure, triangular in shape, called Chiopa, is made and painted with various colours. The figure, together with a number of smaller ones similar in construction and arranged around it, is placed in the verandah of the gomba: this gomba is said to be inhabited by 2,500 Dábas. A fair commences on the 16th day of the new year, *i.e.*, the day of the full moon (in March), and lasts two days, during which a large gathering of the inhabitants of the neighbourhood takes place. The town has a

long bazár said to contain about 100 shops kept by Chinese and Tibetans. Observations for boiling point were taken at this place (height 13,400 feet). A road branches off from here to Darge Gonchen.

184. On the 7th March 1882, 3¼ miles from Lithang, we crossed a stream which flows to the south. On its right bank lies a spring of hot water and about this spring is a kind of saline incrustation. Half a mile to the north of the spring is a *Rito** (a place of retirement for religious contemplation), with some out-houses for attendants, where the Láma of Lithang resides. 2¾ miles further we crossed the Li Chu stream, about 3 feet deep, by a wooden bridge 75 paces long, to a small giachug on its right bank. Proceeding 7¼ miles up a stream from the south-west, we arrived at Jiambothok Giachug, where there is a stage-house and four houses: here we halted. Supplies, firewood and grass were procurable. No hamlets or cultivation were met with along the route.

185. Next day, a mile from the giachug, we crossed the stream and 3½ miles further up reached the Gára Lá pass, where observations for boiling point were taken (height 15,400 feet). Descending 1¾ miles to a small lake we followed a stream issuing from it for 3 miles and passed another small lake from which also a small stream emanates and joins the one along our route, close to a small giachug. Proceeding 2½ miles we observed three snowy peaks bearing 292½°, 306½°, 275½°, distant 11, 11½, and 15 miles respectively, and a mile further on crossed a stream which coming from the south joins the one along our route; the latter then flows to the north. Half a mile further, we reached a spur by an easy ascent, and descending thence along a stream for 3½ miles arrived at Gáralárcha Giachug, where there was a stage-house, three houses and some nomad tents; the giachug is situated on the left bank of the stream, a little below the junction with it of a stream from the south. We remained here for the night and found firewood and grass in abundance: supplies were procurable. The road to-day was stony and with no hamlets or cultivation along it.

186. On the 9th, following the stream for 2 miles we crossed another stream coming from the north, and 1¾ miles further forded another from the south-west. Continuing our progress for a mile we reached the point where the stream along our route joins the large one, which issuing from the Gára Lá pass had turned northwards to wind round the bases of spurs. Marching 1½ miles down stream we crossed it, 35 paces wide and 2½ feet deep, and arrived at Ráno village of 10 houses, where a chief resides. From this place the stream flows to the south and the route ascends for 2 miles up a stream to a pass to the north-west, and descending 1¾ miles crosses a stream, 30 paces wide and 2 feet deep, flowing to the south. Proceeding a mile further we reached Máne Ringbo, a long wall extending a mile and faced with thin, rectangular, smooth, stone slabs, on which sacred formulæ and religious precepts are engraved. Continuing our journey for 3¾ miles along an undulating path, we crossed a small stream which coming from the north and flowing for half a mile to the south joins a stream, 40 paces broad and 3 feet deep, from the west. A little to the east of this junction is a hamlet which contains 10 houses. Proceeding 3¾ miles up the left bank of the stream, we arrived at Naida Giachug having a stage-house and 10 houses. 3 miles distant and bearing 317½° is Gombone, a place of pilgrimage at the foot of the mountains. We stopped at Naida Giachug for the night. We passed a few hamlets with some cultivation near them and found a number of nomad tents near Naida.

187. On the 10th, having crossed a stream flowing down from Gombone, we followed up the left bank of the main stream for 10½ miles, within which distance two streams from the south and three from the north at 4¼, 5½, 6¼, 7¾, and 10½ miles respectively, joined it. We here observed a high snowy peak, bearing 29¾° and distant 6¼ miles, and continuing our journey for 1¼ miles, crossed a stream from the north, and 1¼ miles further passed over to the right bank of the stream; about ½ a mile further we forded a stream from the south-west, and arrived at Ráthi Giachug, where there was a stage-house and 5 houses. Grass and firewood were abundant. The path was good, and we passed through a forest of *padam* trees. There were many nomad tents scattered along the route.

188. On the 11th, the route diverged from the stream and after a gentle ascent of 3½ miles crossed a stream which, coming from the west, joins the stream we had forded near Ráthi. Continuing the ascent for 2¼ miles further we reached the Ráthi Lá pass, the boundary between the Lithang and Báthang districts, where observations for boiling point

---

* Erroneously entered on map as 'Láma's Temple'.

TRANSLATIONS FROM DIARY AND NOTES.

were taken (height 15,340 feet). A stream issues from the pass which flowing down to the west for 2 miles joins a larger stream. Descending 3 miles from the pass to a stream we proceeded along it for 1½ miles and arrived at the left bank of the larger stream which coming from the north flows to the south. Going up the left bank of this for 2½ miles, we forded a stream from the east and 2¾ miles onward crossed the stream, which is 25 paces wide and 2 feet deep, to the right bank. A mile further we reached Táshu Giachug, where there is a stage-house and 15 houses, on the bank of a stream which coming from the north-west joins the main stream. The path was rugged and stony: no cultivation was met with, but nomad tents were pitched along the stream. Grass and firewood were abundant.

189. The next day proceeding 6¼ miles up the stream which comes from the north-west we reached a pass by a steep ascent. We passed *en route* two tributaries of this stream, one coming from the south-west and the other from the north. Descending 1½ miles from the pass we found a small lake to the left of our path, whence a stream emanated and flowed along our route. Continuing our journey for 1½ miles, we crossed a stream from the north-east and 3 miles further passed another from the south. Three-quarters of a mile onward we reached Pángthámo Giachug, having a stage-house and five houses, situated in the midst of a thick forest. The path was rugged, stony and undulating.

190. On the 13th March 1882, after proceeding half a mile we crossed a stream which coming from the north joined the one along our route. 6 miles further brought us to a small hamlet with some cultivation near it, and 5¼ miles beyond to a hot spring, where five tanks with high curtain and partition walls are built, and around which were a number of tents belonging to persons who had come to bathe: the bathing is continued for at least a week. Proceeding 1¾ miles further we reached Chioti Gomba, in Báthang, where we rested for three nights.

191. This gomba lies near the junction of the stream along our route with another from the north. This stream a little above the junction is crossed by a wooden bridge and is about 35 paces wide and 3½ feet deep. The gomba, which is protected by strong, high curtain walls, is about half a mile in circumference and is inhabited by about 1,000 Dábas. The inhabitants of the Saingan patti, in the Báthang district, who live along the banks of the Di Chu, about a day's journey above the village of Báthang, are said to be very turbulent, having on several occasions robbed travellers.

192. Báthang is a considerable village or rather a small town in a valley enclosed by hills, and is situated for the most part on a level strip of ground on the right bank of the stream near its junction with the main stream. There are about 2,000 houses including 50 shops. On the left bank of the stream is a house belonging to a Jesuit Father. Two crops are generally raised here as in Nagchukha. Observations for latitude and boiling point were taken here (lat. 30° 0′ 30″, height 8,150 feet). The general direction of our route from Dárchendo to Báthang was westerly.

193. On the 16th, proceeding 4½ miles along the left bank of the stream and passing a gomba and three villages *en route* we crossed a stream coming from the south-east. Ascending for a mile to the top of a spur by an easy gradient we observed that about 2 miles to the north the stream we had followed and a stream from the north-west joined the Di Chu, which latter here flowed down from the north. Proceeding 4 miles along the left bank of the river we crossed a stream coming from a bearing of 147½°, and 1¾ miles further another from 142¼°. Continuing our journey for 7¾ miles we reached the ferry and village of Dubána, where there are about 30 houses and a stage-house; here we stopped for the night. The path was rugged, stony and undulating; for the first 11 miles there were a number of hamlets. Observations for boiling point were taken here (height 7,700 feet). There was a scarcity of grass, but firewood was abundant.

194. The next day we were detained for some hours as the ferry-boats were not available. At 10 A.M. we crossed the Di Chu, here about 300 paces wide and having a rapid current, to a hamlet of 10 houses on the right bank, and proceeding 1½ miles down the river we crossed a stream coming from the west. Still keeping to the right bank of the Di Chu for 7¾ miles, we reached a hamlet near the junction of a stream from the south. The river now turned south by east and the route leaving it followed up the stream for 1½ miles to a hamlet, containing 10 houses where we halted; firewood and grass were abundant. The path was rugged, stony and undulating.

EXPLORATIONS BY A——K IN GREAT TIBET AND MONGOLIA.

195. On the 18th March 1882, proceeding 5½ miles up the stream through a populated country, we reached a pass by a slight ascent. Descending half a mile we arrived at Konzukha Giachug, 15 houses and a stage-house, situated near the boundary between the Báthang and Mákham districts. Continuing to descend for 2¼ miles through a thick forest we reached a stream, 25 paces wide and 2 feet deep, flowing from the south; and marching up its left bank for 4 miles arrived at a village where we stopped for the night. Supplies, grass and firewood were procurable.

196. On the 19th, we proceeded 5¾ miles up the stream along a level path and reached a small giachug. Continuing our journey for 2¼ miles we crossed a spur by a slight ascent and descending thence a mile forded a stream which comes from the south. Thence we reached another spur by a steep ascent of a quarter of a mile; and descending 1¾ miles arrived at a Lhákháng on the left bank of a stream from the north. 1¾ miles further, this stream joined another flowing to the south, near a hamlet of 10 houses, and half a mile up this second stream Lhamdun Giachug, containing a stage-house and 20 houses, was reached: near this place is a temple dedicated to Namba Nácho; and a route branches off hence to Chiákta Cháka, where salt is found. To the south-west of Chiákta Cháka is a snowy range named Khákárpo culminating in some peaks held sacred which pilgrims circumambulate by way of adoration. We stopped at this village for two nights on account of a fall of snow.

197. On the 21st, we resumed our journey and proceeding 1¼ miles up the stream we crossed it to its right bank; it is here 20 paces wide and 1½ feet deep. Continuing our journey for 3¾ miles up the stream, through an inhabited part of the country, we crossed a pass by a slight ascent. Descending 1½ miles, we observed two snowy peaks on the Khákárpo range, bearing 211° and 221½°, distant 20¾ and 19½ miles respectively, and continuing the descent for 1½ miles, we crossed a stream, 20 paces wide and 1½ feet deep, coming from the north-east, near its junction with another from the north-west and a mile to the south of a giachug. Marching 5¼ miles up the north-western stream, we crossed a pass by an easy ascent and descending 3¾ miles along a stream issuing from it arrived at Phula village, having a stage-house and 20 other houses, near the junction of the stream with a stream from the north-west. We stopped here for the night.

198. Proceeding the next day for a mile up the stream we crossed it, 35 paces wide and 2 feet deep, to the right bank; and marching 12¼ miles up that bank arrived at Gárthok or Mákham. This is a large village, containing about 700 houses with a large gomba and a building for the residence of the two Jong Pons, and has some cultivation near it. We remained here for two nights and took latitude and boiling point observations (lat. 29° 41′ 7″, height 11,920 feet). Gárthok is under the Government of Lhása. The general direction of our route from Lhamdun to this village was north-west.

199. On the 24th, proceeding a mile up the stream, we reached the junction with it of a stream from the north-west. 2¼ miles up the latter stream, we found that another stream from the south-west joined it. As we intended to enter India through Assam we here left the Lhása route* which goes up the stream from the north-west, and followed a footpath up the stream from the south-west towards Zayul, a district about 100 miles N.E. of Sadiya. Proceeding 2½ miles, we reached a pass by a slight ascent and travelling along the ridge for 1½ miles descended gently for 5¼ miles along a stream, which flows in a narrow valley, to the village of Láo, containing 20 houses, situated opposite to the junction of a small stream from the east with the one along our route. We stopped here for the night.

200. On the 25th, marching down the narrow valley for 8 miles, we arrived at the junction of the stream with the river called Chiámdo Chu, which comes from the north-west. The stream in this distance received three small tributaries—two from north-west and one from east. The valley is well cultivated and has a number of houses scattered about it. A quarter of a mile down the river a stream from the east joined it, and 1¼ miles further on we arrived at Samba Dukha (ferry), where are five houses belonging to the men in charge of the bridge. Observations of the boiling point were taken here (height 9,450 feet). The arrange-

---

* This route proceeds north-westerly for about 180 miles, viâ Dáyág, till it reaches Chiámdo on the left bank of the Chiámdo Chu: thence it turns south-westerly for about 110 miles (crossing en route the Giáma Nu Chu river) and joins the route we eventually adopted near Lho Jong.

TRANSLATIONS FROM DIARY AND NOTES.

ment for crossing consists of a thick leather rope stretched very tight from an elevated point on one bank to a lower level on the opposite bank. The rope is secured round stout poles half buried in the ground, and is strong enough to bear the weight of men and animals. The method of crossing is very simple. A rope is carefully fastened to a niche at one end of a semi-circular (bent) piece of wood; the latter is brought on to the thick leather rope, and the former rope after being securely attached round the body is fastened to the other end of the bent wood which is then made to slide down bearing the passenger to the opposite bank in a minute. For re-crossing the river another rope is similarly stretched in a suitable locality close by. The length of the rope bridge was estimated to be about 130 paces. Crossing the bridge and proceeding $3\frac{1}{2}$ miles along the right bank of the river, we arrived at the junction of a stream from the west. The river turns hence to the south-east, and is said to pass by Rin Chiako, a place of pilgrimage in Burmah. Going 2 miles up the stream we reached Jio village, containing about 15 houses, where we stopped for the night. The path was narrow, rugged and stony.

201. On the 26th March 1882, ascending 2 miles we gained the spur by a steep ascent, on top of which to the left of the route lies a gomba, called Jio; and continuing the ascent for three-quarters of a mile we reached the pass of Jio Lá. Descending thence $2\frac{1}{4}$ miles to a stream flowing from north-west, close to a hamlet containing 3 houses, we followed it for $2\frac{3}{4}$ miles, and crossed it, here 15 paces wide and 2 feet deep, to the right bank. Continuing along it for $1\frac{1}{2}$ miles, we forded a small stream from the west, and $3\frac{1}{4}$ miles further reached a spur by a slight ascent. Here we observed that a stream coming from a lake near the Ghotu Lá pass joined the one along our route and their joint stream flowed east towards the Chiámdo Chu river. Continuing our progress for $2\frac{1}{2}$ miles up the latter stream, we arrived at Cha Chiorten, on the right bank, close to where a stream from the north joins it. This chiorten which is one of the sacred places in Tibet is surrounded by 30 houses. We found here two species of the chough; one species, common in Tibet, has beak and legs red and feathers black, and the other has feathers spotted or pie-bald but beak and claws black. Both of these were numerous here and the cultivators had to keep a watch over their fields to preserve the seed which had lately been sown from being eaten up by them. We stopped here for 3 days on account of snow, and observations for boiling point were taken (height 10,640 feet). Two miles to the south of the chiorten and on the top of a hill is a gomba occupied by 30 Dábas.

202. On the 30th, proceeding $10\frac{1}{4}$ miles through a thick forest along the stream, which receives 6 small tributaries—2 from the right and 4 from the left—we arrived at an encamping ground where we stopped for the night.

203. On the 31st, proceeding over snow for $1\frac{1}{4}$ miles, we found a frozen stream coming from the south, and 2 miles further on reached a lake from which that stream issued. A stiff ascent of $1\frac{1}{4}$ miles brought us to the Ghotu Lá pass, then covered with snow, and a difficult descent of 2 miles also over snow, took us to a small frozen lake, a stream emanating from which flowed along our route. Continuing to descend for half a mile along it, we found that it received a tributary from the south-east and $5\frac{1}{4}$ miles further on another from the north. We stopped near this junction in a forest of *deodar* trees for two nights as we were suffering badly from ophthalmia brought on by glare and fatigue.

204. On the 2nd April, proceeding $1\frac{3}{4}$ miles, we crossed a stream from the south-east, and continuing our progress for $3\frac{1}{4}$ miles further arrived at the village of Dáyul, 15 houses, on the right bank of the stream along our route. Half a mile thence we crossed by a wooden bridge a stream, 60 paces wide and 3 feet deep, coming from north. Ascending 500 paces we reached the gomba of Dáyul which is surrounded by 100 houses, including a large house, the residence of a Jong Pon: Dáyul is situated in a narrow valley in the midst of a thick jungle abounding with wild sheep and musk deer. The price of musk as sold in the pod is at 2 Rs. per tola: large quantities of this article are carried from these parts to China. Patches of cultivation were found here. We were informed that no person was allowed to go beyond the district of Dáyul, which latter extends from the Jio Lá pass to the Koli Lá pass, on account of the small-pox which was then raging in the district; but as the Jong Pon of Dáyul was going to Sanga Chu Jong, distant in a direct line only about 65 miles due west yet not capable of being reached except by a detour of over 100 miles, we were allowed to accompany him. Observations for latitude and boiling point were taken here (lat. 29° 12′ 13″, height 11,450 feet).

EXPLORATIONS BY A——K IN GREAT TIBET AND MONGOLIA.

205. Leaving the gomba on the 4th April 1882, we crossed after half a mile a stream which coming from the south-west flows to the east and joins the stream which runs to south-east. Marching 5¼ miles up another stream, which receives three small tributaries, we crossed a spur from the Koli Lá pass and ascending 2¼ miles further reached the pass itself. Descending 1½ miles to a stream we proceeded along it 1¾ miles and arrived at Koli village, 8 houses, where we halted for the night.

206. On the 5th, proceeding 2½ miles along the right bank, we crossed a small stream coming from the north. The joint stream leaves the route and flows to the south-west towards the Giáma Nu Chu river. Marching three-quarters of a mile thence we reached the gomba of Jior and about the same distance further arrived at the village of Jior containing 25 houses, where we stopped for the night. To-day we had a heavy fall of snow.

207. The next day we left the village and after a stiff descent of 5¼ miles reached Thángshu Dukha (ferry), height by boiling point 7,160 feet, and crossed the river Giáma Nu Chu also called Nu Chu, which is deep and rapid and about 200 paces wide. We crossed here on planks which were propelled by oars, and kept from being carried down the current by some of the boatmen holding on to a rope stretched across the river. This river is formed by the junction of several streams which issue from the range between the Áta Gang Lá* and Nub Gang Lá† passes, and is said to flow in a narrow valley running from north-west to south-east, and finally to pass by Riu Chiako, a noted place of pilgrimage in Burma. About 12 miles to the north-west of Thángshu Dukha, a large stream coming from the north, through the Chárong district, joins the Nu Chu. A quarter of a mile from the right bank, we arrived at a small gomba where we remained for two nights. There was a scarcity of firewood and grass.

208. On the 8th, ascending 3¼ miles we passed by a village containing 15 houses. 2¾ miles further we reached a spur and descending thence for 2½ miles arrived at Yu village where we halted. Grass was scarce, but firewood was abundant.

209. The next day having marched 4½ miles, we arrived at the village of Hákha containing 15 houses, and descending thence for a mile reached the village of Ji, where we stopped for eight nights. This village is situated near the junction of two streams, from north and south, with a stream emanating from a small lake below the Tila Lá pass. This stream receives in its course numerous tributaries from right and left, and 10 miles to the east joins the Nu Chu. About 2 miles to the north of the village, and on the left bank of the stream, is a gomba inhabited by 30 Dábas; and towards the south is the snowy range of Rirapphási which is regarded by Tibetans from all parts of the country as an object of deep veneration; and they circumambulate it in great numbers as a religious exercise. Near this village patches of cultivation were found. The Jong Pon's official business detained him here.

210. Having heard that the Tila Lá pass would soon be practicable, as the snow was melting, we left the village on the 17th April and proceeding half a mile crossed the stream, 25 paces wide and 2½ feet deep. Marching for 1¾ miles up its left bank we arrived opposite the junction of a stream from the south, and thence observed two snowy peaks of the Rirapphási range, bearing 207¾° and 212½°, and distant 4 miles. Continuing our journey for 6¼ miles and passing *en route* two small hamlets, we crossed a stream from the west, and from its right bank observed a snowy peak bearing 287¼° and distant 4 miles. We stopped here for the night and found grass and firewood in abundance.

211. The next day proceeding 11 miles up the stream, which receives in this distance four tributaries—two from the left and two from the right—we arrived at the village of No-yu, containing 20 houses, and surrounded by a thick jungle.

212. On the 19th, proceeding 7¾ miles up the stream, and passing *en route* three small streams from the right and left, we reached the village of Niakho, containing 15 houses. 1¾ miles further we crossed a stream from the south-east and halted near it for the night.

213. On the 20th, marching 2½ miles up the stream, we observed a frozen lake to the left of our route and ascended thence 1¼ miles over snow to the Tila Lá pass (height by

---

* In the north of the Zayul district.

† On the boundary between the Lhárugo and Arig districts (see para. 271).

TRANSLATIONS FROM DIARY AND NOTES.

boiling point 16,110 feet). The district of Nuchu Giu lies between the two passes Koli Lá to the north-east and Tila Lá to south-west. Descending for 1½ miles over snow to a stream proceeding from the pass, and following it for 6 miles, through a thick forest, we crossed a stream from the north-east and stopped near its junction for the night.

214. On the 21st April 1882, marching 3¼ miles along the stream, we arrived at the hamlet of Rika, containing six houses; and 1¼ miles further, in which distance the main stream received two tributaries from the north and one from the south-east, we reached a small hamlet, a little beyond which is another tributary from the north. 6¾ miles beyond we arrived at another small hamlet of three houses, situated near the junction of a stream from the south, where we halted for the night. Grass and firewood were abundant.

215. On the 22nd, marching 2½ miles along the stream we arrived at the gomba of Dowa (height by boiling point 8,300 feet) surrounded by 25 houses, situated near the junction of the stream with the river called Zayul Chu coming from the north. Hence a route branches off to the fort of Sanga Chu Jong, distant about 50 miles to the north, where two Jong Pons reside and which is said to have some 250 houses near it. Continuing for 10 miles along the left bank of the river and passing *en route* two small streams from right and left, some small hamlets and a rope bridge, we crossed a stream, 30 paces wide, coming from the east. A mile further we crossed another stream, 25 paces wide and two feet deep, and a quarter of a mile further still reached the hamlet of Chikung, four houses. Opposite the hamlet and on the right bank of the river, is Gáwa village containing 15 houses, with patches of cultivation watered by a small stream, which joins the river half a mile to the north. We stopped at the hamlet for the night and found grass and firewood abundant.

216. On the 23rd, proceeding 8½ miles along the left bank of the river, which in this distance receives four tributaries from right and left, we crossed by a wooden bridge to the right bank. The river is about 80 paces wide, is deep and has a rapid current. A mile further along the right bank we reached the hamlet of Dabla, containing 10 houses, and a quarter of a mile further crossed a stream coming from the north. Marching thence for a mile we arrived at a small hamlet, where we stopped for the night. Paddy fields were observed for the first time; grass and firewood were abundant.

217. On the 24th, marching 17¾ miles along the river and having crossed it twice, we arrived at a small hamlet, where we halted. In this distance the river is fed by six small streams, coming from the right: we also passed a small hamlet on the left bank opposite which on the right bank was a Lhákháng or temple. Grass and firewood were abundant.

218. On the 25th, proceeding 2¼ miles we crossed a large stream, 65 paces wide, which comes from the north-west. Half a mile further, we crossed the Zayul Chu river by a wooden bridge about 100 paces long, and continuing our journey for 3 miles forded a stream from the east. 1½ miles further on, a small stream from the south joined the river; and 5¼ miles onward we reached the junction of Rong Thod Chu and Zayul Chu rivers. Half a mile thence we crossed a stream from the east a little below which a rope bridge spans the river, and arrived half a mile further at Shíkha in the district of Zayul.

219. Shíkha is the winter residence of the officers of the Zayul district. The buildings, about 25 in number, constructed after one pattern by the zamindárs for these officials, lie in the lands of the village of Ríma. They are made of timber and some of them are two stories high. The officers who reside here are:—a Jong Pon, a Shián-u (the civil and magisterial officer of a district), a Jám Pon (custodian of the bridges in the district), with a number of subordinates and attendants. This place is also the resort in winter of traders from all parts of Tibet. The district of Zayul, which is said to extend from the Tila Lá to the Áta Gang Lá pass, is bounded on all sides by lofty ranges[*] of snowy mountains. The spurs which shoot off from them are thickly covered with large trees and long grass; the latter of which affords good nourishment to wild and domestic animals. I was surprised to hear that though the forest was full of game no venomous serpents or carnivorous beasts were to be found. The following are the domestic animals bred by the inhabitants: oxen, *jobos* and *jomos* (male and female animals obtained by cross breeding between a bull and a female yâk, or *vice versâ*), horses, hogs and fowls. Cows are never milked because it is supposed to render the calves weakly; but the milk of the *jomo* is in general use. The climate of the district is mild. Goitre is a common disease from which very few escape.

---

[*] The range to the north is known as the Neching Gángra range (see map).

220. The inhabitants of the district are very simple in their habits. The dress of both sexes is made from a kind of striped cloth woven from a mixture of hemp and wool. The men shave their heads like Dábas and Lámas, but the women dress their hair in two long plaits, which are wound round the head and tied together in front. The hair thus arranged looks like a cap from a distance. They use no umbrellas, but make hats of straw or reed to protect their heads against sun or rain. Their language differs very much from that of the Tibetans, which however they understand very well, and their mode of expressing themselves is amusing, as they speak in a very loud tone of voice and with many gesticulations. They profess Buddhism, but rarely visit gombas or other sacred places and have full belief in the sacrifice of pigs and fowls, which they offer to propitiate gods during times of distress. They burn their dead like the Hindus of India. The chief articles of diet are rice, unleavened bread, meat, a kind of paste made by boiling flour of various grains, and some vegetables mostly found growing wild. They mix a large quantity of chillies with their food. They raise two crops; one of these, reaped in October and November, comprises paddy, *kodo* (a small grain called mandwa in India), Indian corn, millet, dau, and varieties of pulse grains, such as kulath, masúr, matar and urd: the other crop which is harvested in April and May, consists of barley, *ne*, wheat, and sarsoń (a kind of mustard). Of fruits, the lemon, plantain, walnut and peach only are found in the district.

221. This district is much frequented by traders from the Mishmí or Náhong tribe, living in the forests bordering this district. The articles of merchandise which they bring for exchange are *shugshing* (the bark of a plant used for making paper), *ram* (a kind of grass which yields blue colours), *choi* (a kind of grass which yields yellow colour), *shingcha* (the root of a plant exported to China for colouring silk, and which according to some is also used there as medicine) and deer skins. Besides these productions of their own country, they bring various kinds of cloth and money from Assam, and exchange them for salt and horned animals. They also kidnap children from Assam, and sell them as slaves here. We saw here an old man 70 years of age, a native of India, who said that he had been taken captive with eight others by the Mishmis some 50 years ago and all were sold for one horned animal each. This district is considered by Tibetans as the warmest place in their country and therefore any person who is guilty of a crime requiring transportation for life is sent here by the government of Lhása to undergo that sentence. These culprits are branded over their foreheads.

222. No sooner had we entered Shíkha, than we were made to pay a rupee to the Jám Pon (the custodian of the bridges) as a ferry toll, and were soon afterwards seized by the Shián-u, who ordered us to remain in quarantine for 22 days, owing to our coming from the district where small-pox was raging. The road from Gárthok to this place was narrow, undulating, stony and rugged and its general direction was south-west. Observations for boiling point were taken here (height 4,650 feet), but we had no means of taking observations for latitude as the mercury had leaked away near the pass of Koli Lá.

223. On the 23rd May 1882, we resumed our journey and having retraced our steps to the rope bridge, we crossed over to the right bank of the river which is here about 250 paces wide, deep and rapid. Proceeding 1 mile we found that a stream from the east joined its left bank near a small village containing 15 houses. Continuing our journey for 4½ miles we arrived at the hamlet of Singu, containing seven houses, and three-quarters of a mile onward crossed a small stream from the west by a wooden bridge about 15 paces long. Three-quarters of a mile further we reached the village of Sáma, containing seven houses, situated on the border of the Mishmi country and about 16 miles to the north of the hamlet of Zayulmed on the Tibetan boundary on that side. We here endeavoured to make arrangements to cross the Mishmi country and to reach Assam but were told that if we trusted ourselves to the Mishmis we were sure to be murdered, as they were little better than savages.

224. Finding it unadvisable to return by this direct route to India, we were obliged to adopt the circuitous one by Lhása; but hearing that the Áta Gang Lá pass on the latter route, was at that season impracticable on account of snow, and as the small amount of money then in our possession was not sufficient to cover the expenses of that long journey, we employed ourselves in going about from house to house in the villages of Singu, Sáma, Ríma and Duning, reciting from Tibetan sacred books and thus succeeded in collecting some twenty rupees.

TRANSLATIONS FROM DIARY AND NOTES.

225. On the 9th July 1882, we resumed our journey, and proceeding 1¾ miles from the rope bridge up the right bank of the Rong Thod Chu river, we crossed a stream coming from the west, and 1½ miles further arrived at the hamlet of Dungtang, 3 houses, where we halted. The headman of this hamlet had a slave, about 30 years of age, purchased from a Mishmi, who had brought him from Assam some 16 years ago.

226. On the 10th, continuing up the right bank of the river for 2½ miles, we crossed a stream by a wooden bridge 25 paces long, and a quarter of a mile further reached the village of Bonathang. 1½ miles further, we passed opposite Thaling hamlet situated near the junction of a stream coming from the east, and 2 miles onward arrived at the hamlet of Tími, where we halted.

227. On the 11th, 2¾ miles from the hamlet, we crossed a stream coming from the south-west, and 1¼ miles further reached the hamlet of Di, 7 houses, where we passed three nights.

228. On the 14th, after proceeding ½ a mile, we crossed a small stream coming from the west, and marching three-quarters of a mile further arrived opposite a gomba, named Chiángsi, situated on the left bank of the river. Continuing our journey for 2¼ miles we crossed a stream by a wooden bridge 20 paces long, and 4 miles further arrived at the hamlet of Thoyu, 3 houses. Here we remained two nights. We here saw a lad, 7 years of age, from Assam, who had been sold as a slave by a Mishmi last year.

229. On the 16th, having crossed two streams from the west within 3¼ miles, we arrived at the hamlet of Tithong, 3 houses. Opposite to this hamlet a stream from the north-east joins the river, and up the former a path goes to the nomad camp of Luba about 25 miles distant and to the north of the Neching Gángra range. The hamlet of Tithong contains a large house built for the Shián-u of the Zayul district, who occupies it for three months in the rainy season. I was detained here for two nights on account of the illness of my companion L——c.

230. On the 18th, after three-quarters of a mile, we reached the gomba of Jungu surrounded by eight houses, and 6 miles further, having passed *en route* two small streams from the south-west, we crossed a stream by a wooden bridge 25 paces long. This stream comes from the west and nearly opposite to it another from the east joins the river. Continuing 2¼ miles up the right bank of the river, we arrived at the gomba of Murgu surrounded by 10 houses.

231. On the 19th, proceeding 2½ miles, we forded a stream coming from the west, and thence leaving the regular route, which crosses the river, we proceeded 2 miles to the north-west to the village of Sonling, 15 houses. The inhabitants of this village are esteemed the wealthiest in the Zayul district. About 45 miles to the north-west is a sacred peak called Pemakaun, which is rarely visited by pilgrims as they have to pass through the country of the Lhobas who are much addicted to robbery. These Lhobas inhabit the Lhoyul district to the north-west of the Mishmi country. Their manners and customs are similar to those of the Mishmi though their language is somewhat different. They bring the same articles of merchandise as the Mishmies and exchange them for salt at Sonling. We stopped here for three nights: height by boiling point 6,200 feet.

232. On the 22nd we retraced our steps to the point where we had left the route, and having crossed the river by a rope-bridge 70 paces long, we resumed our journey in company with some other travellers who were going northwards to the district of Nagong. 3¾ miles up the left bank of the river we passed opposite the junction of a stream from the west, and half a mile further reached the hamlet of Isámedh close to which a stream from north-east falls into the river. Proceeding 4½ miles thence we crossed a stream coming from north-east, opposite to the junction of which is the hamlet of Rangyul containing 5 houses. A mile further we arrived at Isátodh, where we stopped for the night. Rice-fields were numerous between Dabla and this place.

233. On the 23rd, proceeding 4¼ miles up the Rong Thod Chu, we passed opposite the confluence of a stream coming from the west, and a quarter of a mile further came to an abrupt and difficult descent of 300 paces with steps leading down: we were informed that there was a circuitous route for laden animals. Three-quarters of a mile onward

we forded a stream coming from north-east, and 2¼ miles thence arrived at an empty house, opposite to the junction of a stream, where we halted.

234. On the 24th July 1882, marching for a mile up the left bank, we forded a stream coming from the north-east, and ascending thence at an easy gradient for 3 miles along the hill side by a very bad path, we came to the junction of two streams, one from the north-west and the other from the north-east, forming the Rong Thod Chu river. A difficult descent of half a mile brought us to the left bank of the stream from the north-east, which we crossed by a rope bridge* about 40 paces long and halted on its right bank for the night.

235. On the 25th, proceeding 5¼ miles along a bad path which lies a little above the narrow bed of the stream that comes down from the north-east, and passing *en route* 2 streams, one from the north and the other from the south, we reached the village of Modung, containing 5 houses, where a very rich man resides. We halted here 3 nights.

236. On the 28th we resumed our journey along the bank of the stream, and within three-quarters of a mile crossed 2 streams coming from the north. Continuing for 2½ miles up the stream, we found that a large stream coming from the east joined it and heard that at the distance of 8 miles and on the right bank of this stream was the village of Sugu, 8 houses. 2 miles further up the right bank of the stream, we arrived at the hamlet of Lasi, 3 houses, and three-quarters of a mile further, crossed a stream coming from the north-west. Proceeding thence for about a mile we reached the village of Áta where we remained for 6 nights. Elegant wooden cups are made here. This is the most northern village in the Zayul district where cultivation is carried on. Grain is cheap and the inhabitants of the Nagong district come here to purchase. It is said that from the spurs of the mountains on the west the snowy peaks of the Neching Gángra range on the east are visible. These peaks are objects of religious veneration to Tibetans. Observations of the boiling point were taken here (height 7,950 feet).

237. On the 3rd August, we crossed the stream, which, when we had gone 1¾ miles further, we observed issued from a glacier. The path winds for 5½ miles along the south-eastern side of the glacier, which stretches from the north-west, and by a stiff ascent of 1¼ miles comes to a small stream and by a further rise for three-quarters of a mile to the encamping ground of Chutong, where we halted. From Shíkha to this place, with the exception of cleared and cultivated spots in the vicinity of villages, the hill sides are covered with forest trees.

238. On the 4th, proceeding three-quarters of a mile, we reached a pass by a steep ascent and there observed a snowy peak bearing 325½° and distant 3¾ miles. Descending 1½ miles we came to the southern edge of the continuation of the glacier mentioned before and crossed it, here three-quarters of a mile wide, and following up the western edge for 1 mile we came to the pass of Áta Gang Lá over the Neching Gángra snowy range. Proceeding 2½ miles over the glacier and 1¾ miles along a stream emanating from it, we arrived at a small unoccupied house, probably built for the accommodation of travellers, near the junction of a stream from the north-west with the one along the route. We stopped here for 5 nights owing to a continuous fall of rain. Observations for boiling point were taken here (height 14,690 feet). Some 5 tents belonging to nomads were seen in the vicinity.

239. On the 9th, proceeding 3 miles along the right bank, we forded a stream 50 paces wide and 2 feet deep which issuing from a small glacier to the east falls into the stream along our route. A little further on another stream from a lake to the west, about 2 miles long and three-quarters of a mile broad, joined the stream which lower down is named the Nagong Chu river. Continuing our journey for 3 miles, we arrived at the village of Lhágu, containing 20 houses, where we halted for the night. A little cultivation was visible here. The road was smooth. Grass and firewood were abundant. The river here forms a large pool on account of a small glacier from the west impeding its course, but finds an outlet under its eastern extremity: the route continues along it.

240. On the 10th, proceeding three-quarters of a mile, we reached the edge of the glacier mentioned above and skirted it for a mile. Continuing for 2 miles along the right bank of the river we crossed a stream 25 paces wide, coming from the east, and half a

---

* This rope bridge consists of two stout ropes stretched parallel to each other with cross ropes tied to them and hanging at convenient distances, on which planks are laid.

TRANSLATIONS FROM DIARY AND NOTES.

mile further reached a village of 10 houses opposite to the junction of a stream from the west. Marching 3¾ miles along a spur up a slight ascent we arrived at the small hamlet of Kháñsar, and 2¼ miles further reached the temple of Nagougjhio. Descending thence half a mile we crossed a stream by a wooden bridge 30 paces long. This stream comes from the north-east and flowing to the west for 1¼ miles joins the river a little above a bridge made of masonry and timber over the latter. This bridge is about three-quarters of a mile long, and the river for some miles above and below it flows in a low level valley and presents the appearance of a broad sheet of water. Ascending for half a mile from the stream we arrived at the gomba of Shiuden situated in a lovely spot on high level ground overlooking the river. This gomba has 100 Dábas and is surrounded by about 150 houses. Having arrived from Zayul we were suspected by the official here of being escaped convicts; but some days after our arrival a rich man from Ríma happening to visit the gomba obtained permission for us to proceed. A route branches off from this place to the fort of Sanga Chu Jong to the east. Observations for boiling point were taken here (height 13,650 feet).

241. On the 20th August 1882, we resumed our journey and, proceeding 6¼ miles along the river, arrived at the village of Ránya, 10 houses. Within this distance the river received 3 small tributaries from east and west. Marching 1¾ miles further we reached a stream which flowing to the west for 2 miles joins the river close to the village of Rahu, 8 houses, and the joint river thence turns to the west and flows through the Pomedh country. A shorter route to Lhása, practicable for foot passengers only, passes through Pomedh and Kongbo; but on account of the sickness in the Zayul and Lhása districts the inhabitants of Pomedh and Kongbo had applied for and obtained permission from the Government at Lhása to close the route that year. Having crossed the stream mentioned above, which is 20 paces wide, we rested for the night at the temple of Naukhazod. Grass and firewood were abundant.

242. On the 21st, re-crossing the stream to the left bank and proceeding for 11½ miles, we arrived at a small lake from which the stream issued. This stream received besides 4 small tributaries within that distance from the east and the west. Proceeding 1 mile, we crossed a low pass by a slight ascent. The district of Nagong is said to extend from the Áta Gang Lá to this pass. Three-quarters of a mile beyond the pass, we forded a stream, which coming from the west flows along the right of our route. Here we found some tents appertaining to the nomads and halted for the night. Grass and firewood were abundant.

243. On the 22nd, marching for 5½ miles along the left bank of the stream, we crossed a small stream coming from the west and reached the hamlet of Goñkha containing 5 houses. Continuing on for 2 miles, we crossed a wooden bridge about 30 paces long over a stream which coming from the north-west flows to the east for a mile and then falls into that along our route. On the left bank of this stream and close to the route is the village of Dongsar, containing about 40 houses and a gomba; and about 2 miles higher up and half a mile from the same bank is a gomba, named Au-takpa, surrounded by 40 houses. The village of Dongsar is situated in an extensive and well cultivated valley. We remained here for 4 nights and took service with a rice merchant who had brought that article from Zayul and was taking it to Shiobádo (distant about 100 miles further on the same route that we were following) for sale; the rice was carried on mules. Boiling point observations were taken here (height 13,850 feet).

244. On the 26th, we resumed our journey along the left bank of the stream, and after proceeding 2 miles passed the junction of a small stream from the east. 1½ miles further on, another stream from the east joined it, and 3 miles thence we arrived opposite the gomba of Dángo situated on the right bank of the stream. A bridge 45 paces long communicates with the gomba, from which a road leads to the fort of Pashu Jong distant about 50 miles due north. Continuing along the left bank for 4½ miles, we arrived at the village of Diu, containing 8 houses, where we rested for the night. Grass and firewood were abundant. From Áta Gang Lá to this village the road was generally speaking good.

245. The next day, after going half a mile we crossed a small stream which flows into the stream along our route. 1½ miles further on we reached the village of Buñ-yu, 8 houses, and half a mile onward we crossed another stream coming from the west. The main stream here turns to the east and flows into the Giáma Nu Chu river. Marching for 4 miles up a tributary of the main stream, coming from the Buñ-yu Lá pass, we halted for the night. Grass and firewood were abundant.

246. On the 28th August 1882, ascending for a mile over snow we reached the pass of Buñg-yu Lá, and descending thence for 1½ miles to a stream we followed it for 5¾ miles to its junction with another from the west. At this junction were some nomad tents where we remained for two nights on account of rain. Grass and firewood were abundant. The Buñg-yu Lá pass is on the boundary between the districts of Dainsi and Pashu.

247. On the 30th, marching for 2½ miles along the left bank of the stream, we found that a stream from the south-east joined it, and a quarter of a mile further we crossed to the right bank by a wooden bridge about 25 paces long. Having proceeded for 4¼ miles along the stream, which in this distance received two tributaries from right and left, we reached the junction of a stream from the north. The joint stream hence turned to the west and the path going up the stream from the north for 4 miles brought us to an encamping ground near the junction of a stream from the west. Here we rested for the night. Grass and firewood were abundant. From Diu to this place the road was rugged and stony.

248. On the 31st, having forded a stream from the west, 1¼ miles from our last halting place, we came 1½ miles further to a pass by a steep ascent; and 4½ miles down a stream emanating from the pass, which in this distance receives two small streams from the left and right, we arrived at the hamlet of Tapsing, 5 houses, where we stopped for the night. Grass and firewood were procurable. There were no villages or cultivation between Buñg-yu and Tapsing.

249. On the 1st September, continuing 1½ miles along the stream we found that it flowed into a larger one coming from the west and going off towards the Giáma Nu Chu river. A route goes down this stream to the fort of Pashu Jong, which is about 16 miles to the north-east. Crossing this stream, 20 paces wide and 1½ feet deep, and proceeding up another from the north for 4 miles we reached some nomad tents at the foot of a pass and there halted for the night. Grass and firewood were procurable.

250. On the 2nd, ascending gradually for 1½ miles, we arrived at the pass and descending thence for 7 miles along a small stream issuing from it, we crossed a large stream by a bridge named Giok Jam 45 paces long. This is the same stream which took its rise from the Buñg-yu Lá pass and flowing in a northern direction for some miles along our route turned to west: winding round the range connecting the two last mentioned passes it changes its course to the east, and flows into the Giáma Nu Chu river. Near this bridge and on either bank of the stream are several hamlets at one of which we remained for two nights. Grass and firewood were procurable. Cultivation is carried on here, and peaches and apricots were found in abundance. Observations for boiling point were taken here (height 11,040 feet). A toll of 4 annas is levied from each passenger across the bridge.

251. On the 4th, ascending for 1½ miles we reached a gomba, named Baimbu, and continuing for 6½ miles to ascend a stream from the north-west, we arrived at the village of Rángo, 10 houses; a mile thence, we crossed a stream which coming from the south-west joins the one along our route. 2 miles further we reached the gomba of Niopha, surrounded by 10 houses. This day we travelled through an inhabited part of the country. Grass and firewood were procurable.

252. On the 5th, proceeding for 1¾ miles, we reached a pass by a slight ascent. Here the district of Pashu ends and that of Lho Jong begins. The road through the former district was undulating, rugged and stony. Travelling for 7¾ miles through a narrow valley, we crossed a pass by a slight ascent. Within this valley we passed four small streams which issuing from the eastern mountains form a large stream which flows below the large gomba of Jiáphug to the west and after some distance turns abruptly to the south and joins the large stream which emanates from the Buñg-yu Lá pass. Descending for 3½ miles along a stream which takes its rise from the pass, we arrived at the gomba of Ong situated near the junction of a stream from the north-east, where we halted for the night.

253. On the 6th, continuing along the stream for 2 miles we crossed a small stream which comes from the east, and proceeding for 4 miles through an inhabited country, we arrived at the village of Chukpodesa situated at the junction of the stream along our route with another from the west. The joint stream flowing to the east for some miles joins the Giáma Nu Chu river. Two miles to the north of this village and on the left bank of the stream is the fort of Lho Jong, where two Jong Pons reside. Near the fort is a large gomba, a giachug and 150 houses. The general direction of our route from Shíkha in the

TRANSLATIONS FROM DIARY AND NOTES.

district of Zayul to this village was northwards. We stopped at the fort for the night and took boiling point observations (height 13,140 feet). We here struck the high road from Dárchendo to Lhása*, from which we had diverged at Gárthok with the intention of returning to India through Assam. The following is a list of the giachugs, with their estimated distances from each other in Lis†, *en route* from Gárthok to Lho Jong fort:—

Risi	60
Nimágo	70
Dáyági Sácham	60
Rasi	60
Asi	60
Dáyág	60
Jiamdo	60
Gham	50
Wángkha	50
Bágáng	60
Pángdha	60
Mongpho	70
Chiámdo (on left bank of the Chiámdo Chu)	80
Lungdha	90
Lágang	90
Nulda	80
Mari	90
Shang-ye Jam (on left bank of the Giáma Nu Chu)	80
Lho Jong	120

254. On the 7th September 1882, we left the fort and retracing our steps to Chukpodesa village crossed the stream coming from the west by a wooden bridge 15 paces long. Proceeding 8¼ miles by a smooth and level path up the stream, which waters the fields of the villages on both sides of it, we arrived at its source, and 2 miles thence reached a pass by a slight ascent. Our route now entered the district of Jithog. Descending for 7¼ miles along a stream which rises from the pass we reached the gomba of Jithog, having 200 houses and a stage-house situated near it, close by the junction of a large stream from the south-west with the one along our route. We rested here for the night.

255. On the 8th, following down the above stream for 12 miles and passing *en route* several small villages and two gombas, we crossed it a little above its confluence with another from the west, by a wooden bridge 25 paces long. The joint stream flows hence to the east and falls into the Giáma Nu Chu river. Crossing the stream from the west by a wooden bridge 20 paces long and proceeding up it for 3¾ miles, we arrived at Shiobádo, near the junction of a stream from the south-east, which possesses about 200 houses, a small bazár, a gomba and a stage-house, and is the place of residence of some Chinese officials. As the rice merchant's journey ended here we now took service with a trader from Chárong who was going to Lhása. Boiling point observations were taken here (height 12,470 feet).

256. On the 9th, marching for 5½ miles up the stream from the west we reached its junction with another from the south; and continuing for 4 miles further we gained a pass by a steep ascent and entered the district of Pemba. Descending a mile to a gomba to the right of the route and thence following a stream for 3½ miles, we arrived at its confluence with another from the south. Here we found some 20 tents of nomads who remain during the rainy season to pasture their cattle. The stream hence turned to the north and the route continuing westward up an ascent for 5 miles brought us to an encamping ground where we passed the night. Grass and firewood were abundant.

257. On the 10th, after a steep ascent of three-quarters of a mile, we gained a pass and descending thence 3¼ miles we crossed a stream 12 paces wide flowing to the north, on the left bank of which is the giachug of Bari and a stage-house. Continuing for 4 miles up this stream, which thence turned to the north, we proceeded up an ascent for 2 miles and arrived at an encamping ground, where we remained the night. Grass and firewood were abundant.

---

* See para. 199.
† 4½ *Lis* are approximately equal to 1 English mile.

EXPLORATIONS BY A——K IN GREAT TIBET AND MONGOLIA.

258. On the 11th September 1882, ascending for half a mile we arrived at a pass and descending from it for 3½ miles found a stream coming from the south-east : some nomad tents were near the route. Continuing 4½ miles along this stream, we crossed a small stream from the north-east, and proceeding 6 miles further, we crossed the stream by a wooden bridge 25 paces long. 2 miles thence, we arrived at Lháche, where there are a gomba, 10 houses, a giachug and a stage-house. We stopped here for the night. From Shiobádo to Lháche the route is good but passes through a sparsely inhabited country. The nomads of Potodh, the tract across the snowy range to the south of our route, sometimes rob travellers. The stream here receives a tributary from the south-west and turns to the north.

259. On the 12th, proceeding 1¾ miles up the stream from the southwest, we crossed it by a wooden bridge 15 paces long. 1¾ miles further we reached a pass by a steep ascent and descended thence for a mile to a stream which comes from the south-west. Proceeding 7¾ miles along this stream, and passing *en route* 3 small streams from the left, we arrived at the large gomba of Pemba. There are about 100 houses, a giachug and a stage-house, and some cultivation. We stopped here for the night.

260. On the 13th, proceeding 3¼ miles along the stream we crossed it by a wooden bridge 40 paces long. Marching three-quarters of a mile we crossed a small stream coming from the south, and 2½ miles further passed another from the same direction. 4½ miles lower down the stream we reached the gomba of Chiákro, 1½ miles beyond which the stream turned to north-east. Marching for a mile, we crossed a stream which rises from the Shiár Gang Lá pass and then turning to the north-east flows into the stream before mentioned. About one mile to the west of the junction is the gomba of Bárgo. Continuing up the Shiár Gang Lá stream for 2 miles, and passing *en route* 2 small streams joining it from the south, we arrived at the giachug of Urgentámdha, where we stopped for the night. There are about 15 houses, a stage-house and a small lhákháng. Grass and firewood were procurable. The path from the Lháche Gomba to this place is level, and lies through an inhabited part of the country.

261. On the 14th, proceeding 6¼ miles, we crossed the Shiár Gang Lá pass by a steep ascent. Our route now entered the district of Arig. Descending for 4½ miles along a stream which rises from the pass, we crossed it a little above its junction with another stream from the north-west. We halted here for the night. Grass and firewood were procurable.

262. On the 15th, proceeding 5¾ miles along the stream from the pass, we crossed a small stream coming from the north-west by a wooden bridge 15 paces long. Following the stream for 1¼ miles, and crossing it twice in that distance by bridges each about 25 paces long, we arrived at the Namgialgon Giachug, where there were 4 houses, a stage-house and a small gomba. Continuing on for 2¾ miles, we observed a snowy peak bearing 203½° and distant 4¾ miles, and 2¾ miles further reached the place where the stream along our route empties itself into a large stream coming from a bearing of 117½° as also does a smaller one from the south-east : there is a gomba near this junction. Proceeding three-quarters of a mile, we came to a small lake to the right of the route, opposite to which a stream unites with the one along our route ; and 2¾ miles thence reached the giachug of Nuldokár. Grass and firewood were abundant and land was cultivated. Here we halted for the night.

263. On the 16th, proceeding 1¼ miles, we reached Arig Gomba surrounded by 20 houses where boiling point observations were taken (height 12,480 feet), and 400 paces further we crossed a stream coming from the north. Three-quarters of a mile further a small stream from the north was forded and opposite to its junction a stream from the south-east joined the one along the route. ¾ of a mile thence we reached Ji village where we replenished our stock of provisions. 1¼ miles further on, a stream from the south falls into the main stream. Continuing for 1¼ miles along the right bank we crossed a small stream from the north, and 1 mile further another from the west. Proceeding thence 3½ miles and crossing the stream twice in that distance by wooden bridges each 65 paces long, we reached Áládo Giachug with 7 houses and a stage-house. Here we halted for the night.

264. On the 17th, proceeding 500 paces, we crossed a large stream which rising from the Nub Gang Lá pass falls into the one along our route : the united stream then turns to the south, where it is known as the Daksong Chu, and after being joined by the Kongbo Giámda Chu falls into the Sángpo about 20 miles above Gya-la-Sindong. Marching 7¾

TRANSLATIONS FROM DIARY AND NOTES.

miles up the Nub Gang Lá stream and passing *en route* 3 tributaries from the right and left, we arrived at Álágák Giachug, two houses and a stage-house, where we halted for the night. Grass and firewood were abundant.

265. On the 18th September 1882, marching 7½ miles up the left bank of the stream, which in that distance receives 4 small tributaries from right and left, we arrived at the Áláchiago Giachug, where there are 5 houses and a stage-house. Here we passed the night.

266. On the 19th, we resumed our journey and proceeding 10 miles up the left bank of the stream, we crossed a stream from the north by a wooden bridge. Within this distance we passed some nomad tents; and the stream received 4 small streams from the south. Continuing on for 7 miles, we arrived at Áládochug Giachug, 6 houses and a stage-house. There was a scarcity of firewood but grass was abundant. We halted here for the night.

267. On the 20th, after proceeding half a mile we observed a snowy peak bearing 215½° and distant about 1½ miles. Marching for 4 miles up stream and up a steep ascent we gained the pass of Nub Gang Lá where boiling point observations were taken (height 17,940 feet). Here our route entered the district of Lhárugo. Descending from the pass for 1¼ miles we reached a small lake whence a stream issued, which 2 miles further flowed through another small lake. Continuing for 8¼ miles along this stream, which in this distance receives three tributaries from right and left, we arrived at the giachug of Cháchukha, 5 houses, a stage-house and some scattered tents. We stopped here for the night; grass and firewood were procurable.

268. On the 21st, proceeding 8½ miles down stream, which receives two tributaries within that distance, we crossed a pass over a spur by a slight ascent, and descending thence along a stream we reached after 6¾ miles the left bank of the stream before mentioned. Crossing the stream by a bridge 25 paces long and proceeding 800 paces further, we arrived at Lhárugo Giachug, where there are 60 houses, a stage-house and a gomba. It lies between two streams, the one we had followed from the east and another and a larger one from north-west: the united stream hence flows to the south-east. From this giachug a road branches off to Lhása by the gomba of Dugong or Digung. We stopped here for two nights. There was a scarcity of grass and firewood. Observations for boiling point were taken here (height 13,690 feet). The general direction of our route from Lho Jong to this place was westwards.

269. On the 23rd, proceeding 800 paces, we forded the stream from the north-west, 50 paces wide and 2½ feet deep, and marching for 7½ miles up a tributary which joins its right bank, we reached a pass, named Árcha Lá, by a steep ascent. Descending 1¼ miles, we observed a snowy peak bearing 167½° and distant 7½ miles, and continuing the descent 1½ miles further, we arrived at Árcha Giachug where there are about 12 houses, a gomba and a stage-house. Three-quarters of a mile further on we crossed a stream by a bridge 24 paces long, which rising from the Árcha Cho lake flows to the south-east. Following up the right bank for 2¼ miles, we arrived opposite the junction of a stream from the north-west and 1½ miles further came to the eastern extremity of the lake where we stopped for the night. Observations for boiling point were taken here (height 14,680 feet). Grass and firewood were abundant. The lake is about 4 miles long and 1½ miles broad, and is fed by three streams from the south and one from the west. The tract of country around affords rich pasturage to herds of cattle belonging to nomads of the neighbourhood.

270. Next day we proceeded 3¾ miles along the southern margin of the lake and thence ascending its third tributary from the south for 5¼ miles, we forded the stream, 20 paces wide and 2 feet deep. Continuing up a stream joining it from the south for 5¼ miles, which within that distance receives a tributary from the west, we reached Gole Giachug, where there are 3 houses and a stage-house; grass was abundant, but firewood scarce. We stopped here for the night.

271. On the 25th, proceeding up stream 3¼ miles, we reached the pass of Tola Lá by a steep ascent. Observations for boiling point were taken here (height 17,350 feet). Descending a stream issuing from the pass for 7½ miles we reached Donthog Giachug, where we halted for the night. At Donthog there are 7 houses and a stage-house situated near the junction of a small stream from the west with the one along the route. The country between Álágák and Donthog Giachugs is uncultivated.

272. On the 26th September 1882, proceeding down the stream for 6¾ miles, we passed by a gomba, which had 20 houses and some patches of cultivation near it. Continuing on for 7 miles, within which distance the stream received 3 tributaries from right and left, we arrived at Laru Giachug where we stopped for the night. There were some 25 houses, a stage-house and a gomba at this giachug.

273. The next day, following the stream for 16 miles, in which distance 4 tributaries from right and left fall into it, we crossed it by a bridge 70 paces long, where a toll of 6 annas is levied from each passenger, we reached the small town of Giámda situated above the confluence of 2 streams, the one we had followed from the north and another from the west: the joint stream flows to the east and is known as the Kongbo Giámda Chu. The town consists of about 100 small houses with a main street lined by about 200 shops running through it, the shops are kept by Tibetans, Chinese and Nepalese. At Giámda is the mint where Tibetan money is coined. Cultivation is carried on in the vicinity, and wheat, barley and other coarser grains are raised. We stopped here for 2 nights. Observations for boiling point were taken (height 10,900 feet).

274. On the 29th, proceeding 8¼ miles up the stream from the west, and passing *en route* a hamlet, we reached the gomba of Sángsar near the junction of a stream from the north-east. Marching thence half a mile, we crossed the stream by a wooden bridge 50 paces long, and continuing our progress for 5½ miles up the right bank we arrived at Gam Giachug. Within the last distance the stream is fed by 3 small tributaries which join its left bank. At the giachug are 10 houses and a stage-house. We halted here for the night.

275. On the 30th, proceeding 12 miles up the right bank of the stream, which receives 3 tributaries from right and left within that distance, we reached the junction of a stream coming from the north-west. Continuing along the same bank for 6¼ miles, and passing *en route* 2 streams, we crossed the stream which here comes from the south, near the junction with it of another from the west. We stopped here for the night.

276. Leaving the next day, and proceeding 4¾ miles up the right bank of the stream from the west, we passed opposite Nimáring Giachug on the left bank of the stream, and 3 miles further we arrived at the confluence of a stream from south-west with that along the route and which here flows from the north-west. Continuing our progress for 8 miles up the stream from south-west, and passing *en route* a small stream from south, we reached the Gia Lá pass by a steep ascent. This pass is on the south-western boundary of the Kongbo district, which latter commences from the Tola Lá pass. Tibet is divided into three parts; the first called Nari Khorsum stretches from Ladakh to Mariam Lá; the second, called Ú Cháng, from Mariam Lá to Gia Lá, containing Lhása, Shigáche &c.; the third called Dokham or Kham, from Gia Lá to Dárchendo. Descending 2½ miles from the pass along a stream rising from it we stopped for the night. Grass was abundant, but there was a scarcity of firewood.

277. On the 2nd October 1882, following the stream for 7¼ miles, which within that distance receives 3 small tributaries from right and left, we arrived at Chomoráwa Giachug, 10 houses and a stage-house. We here left the road* to Lhása and took a path, named Uri Bár-Khor, which is only trodden by pilgrims from Lhása when going round the range of mountains to the south of the city. This pilgrimage is considered so obligatory that even the Great Láma himself has to perform it. Parting company with the trader and proceeding up the right bank of a tributary from south for 7¼ miles and passing *en route* 2 small streams from the east, we gained a pass by a slight ascent. Descending thence for 2¾ miles along the stream which issues from the pass, we found some nomads and remained with them for 2 nights.

278. The nomads here were engaged in burying animals which had died from a certain disease named *Sándo* supposed to be caused by an insect about half an inch long. The head of this insect is black and its body is of a dull yellowish colour. The insects are common all over Tibet; they swarm under grass which for a distance around becomes so dangerous that any animal that grazes on it is at once attacked by fever which almost always proves fatal. The fever afterwards becomes contagious and attacks other animals and even the men who herd

---

* There are four giachugs, *viz.*, Whezarsang (Euzer), Rinchenling, Meduggonkhar (Medu Kongkar), Dechen (Dhejen Jong) on this road between Chomoráwa and Lhása.

TRANSLATIONS FROM DIARY AND NOTES.

them or eat their flesh. We were told that all animals which die of this disease are found with their heads towards the north and their tails crooked. Persons who suffer from it are first attacked by fever followed by boils which appear under the armpits and in the elbow and knee-joints. Very few animals or persons recover from it. The only measure adopted by the inhabitants is one of a precautionary nature; they eat scorched insects, which fortifies their system against the poisonous effects of the living ones. These insects are not easily discovered, as they remain always hidden under the grass, and the only time for unearthing them is winter, at which season the place where they exist is found free from snow. People put on the spot a large copper vessel turned downwards and kindle a fire over and around it: after a time the vessel is removed when a number of these insects are found scorched underneath. One such insect is given to a man. They are also given to animals, mixed with salt.

279. On the 4th October 1882, proceeding 10 miles along the stream we arrived at the gomba of Jingcho, where cultivation was seen. From the pass to this gomba the stream receives 5 small tributaries from right and left. Continuing for 3½ miles along the stream, we crossed it by a wooden bridge 25 paces long, and half a mile further on passed Kánadeba, where there were two large three-storied houses, the residence of some rich persons. Marching thence for 1¼ miles along the stream, we reached the fort of Hoka (Horga) Jong surrounded by about 250 houses, and there halted for the night.

280. On the 5th, a quarter of a mile from the fort, we crossed the stream which a little lower down joins a stream named Mik Chu coming from the north-east and flowing to the south-west towards the Cháng Chu or Sángpo river. Marching thence for 4½ miles we ascended a spur whence we observed two snowy peaks, bearing 134½° and 156½°, distant 4½ and 8 miles respectively. Descending for 4 miles along a stream we arrived at the village of Yáchu near the junction of a stream named Yáchu coming from the north. Having crossed this stream, which also joins the Mik Chu, by a wooden bridge 30 paces long, and ascended for 3¼ miles we arrived at another pass over a spur, and thence descending 2¼ miles we reached the hamlet of Khátha containing 5 houses, situated on the left bank of the Cháng Chu, also named Sángpo, where we stopped for the night. The general direction of our route from the Lhárugo Giachug to this hamlet is south-west: it was wide throughout but generally rugged and stony. Observations for boiling point were taken here (height 11,260 feet). The Cháng Chu which rises near the Mánsarowar lake is called by different names in various places: in Nari Khorsum it is named Támchiok Khamba; in the Cháng district Nari Chu, and in some part of the district of Lhokha which extends from the Gia Lá to the Gong Kha Jong fort, it is named Cháng Chu or Sángpo. The general direction of the river is eastwards: the force of its current a little below Khátha is very strong. In its further course it receives contributions from innumerable streams and water-courses which take their rise from the southern and western slopes of that portion of the range which lies between the Äta Gang Lá pass on the east and the Gia Lá pass on the west. It is said that the river finally inclines to the south and receiving a tributary of nearly half its dimension from the east named the Zayul Chu, flows into India.

281. On the 6th, proceeding 5½ miles up the left bank of the river, we crossed a small stream coming from north-east and 3 miles further we arrived at the gomba of Zángri Khammedh surrounded by 20 houses. Proceeding thence 1 mile we reached the fort of Zángri Jong surrounded by 30 houses and situated near a tributary of the river. About 3 miles to the south and on the right bank of the river is Shíkhár Jong fort surrounded by 35 houses. From Zángri Jong the road leaves the river and ascending the hills on the right for 4¾ miles reaches Daisithi Gomba, a place of pilgrimage. There are about 40 houses near this gomba. We halted here for the night.

282. The next day, descending 2¼ miles and thence following the left bank of the river for 7½ miles, we reached the gomba of Hon-Ngarí Thanjang (Naridácháng). It is a large high building on an isolated mound, the latter has about 200 houses around it. Grass and fuel are procurable. We halted here for the night.

283. On the 8th, marching 1¼ miles we came to a stream that falls into the Sángpo from the north: here we crossed the river, which is 200 paces wide and very deep. On the right bank of the river is Niáko Dukha (ferry), where there is a large house belonging to the owners of the boats. There was formerly an iron bridge at this place which I was told was destroyed by lightning. Proceeding 3 miles from the ferry we arrived at Chetáng, a large town containing 1,000 houses, a bazár, a gomba and a fort. From here a

EXPLORATIONS BY A——K IN GREAT TIBET AND MONGOLIA.

route branches off to Lhása, by way of Samaye and Dhejen Jong (Detsin), which latter is about 45 miles from this town. Boiling point observations were taken at Chetáng (height 11,480 feet). We halted here for 3 nights.

284. On the 11th October 1882, proceeding up the right bank for a mile, we crossed a tributary of the river. Marching thence 1¼ miles, we passed the temple of Chyasá (Chense) Lhákháng and about 1½ miles further on, arrived opposite Gerpa Duga ferry (Gába Dukha). 2 miles higher up is the village of Dhomda (Tánda), on the left bank of the river. Continuing on for 14¾ miles we arrived opposite the gomba of Samaye, bearing 13° and distant 4½ miles. Samaye is a large gomba surrounded by 1,000 houses and shops.

285. The next day we reached the hamlet of Dushio, 2 miles from our halting place, and about the same distance further a stream from the north joined the river. Proceeding 1¼ miles we visited Chinduchoka Gomba, in the vicinity of which were 10 houses, and 3½ miles thence we passed the gomba of Jera and the chiorten of Jiambáling, the former of which was about 1 mile to the south and the latter 3 miles south-east of the route. Continuing on for 15 miles along the right bank of the river we arrived at Chitishio Jong where there are about 1,000 houses, a fort and a small bazár. This place is well known on account of the woollen cloth manufactured. We halted here for the night.

286. On the 13th, proceeding along a spur for 2¾ miles, we observed the gomba of Dorje-dág, bearing 42½° and distant 2¾ miles. This gomba is situated on the left bank of the river and is surrounded by about 100 houses. Marching 4 miles further we reached Taishion village and 1½ miles thence the village of Chishio. Half a mile onward we passed the large gomba, called Rá-medh, surrounded by 100 houses, and 2½ miles thence we arrived at the temple of Nianga Lhákháng. Continuing our journey up the right bank of the river for 9 miles, we reached the chiorten of Gong-kha, near which were some 200 houses, and 1½ miles further we passed the Gong-kha Jong fort, surrounded by 600 houses. 2 miles further on is the hamlet of Lhásang and 1¾ miles still further that of Kína where we stopped for the night. About a mile to north-east of the last hamlet is the Ki Chu river which flowing from north-east joins the Cháng Chu. Boiling point observations were taken at Kína (height 10,510 feet).

287. On the 15th, ascending 1½ miles to a spur we observed 2 snowy peaks, bearing 263½° and 259½°, distant 21 miles each, and descending thence for 1¾ miles, we arrived at the village of Jiang-thang, containing 10 houses. Proceeding 4¼ miles further the route diverged from the Cháng Chu river which comes from the west. The general direction of the route from the hamlet of Khátha to this place was to the west and along the bank of the river which in this portion of its course has a very slow current. Turning hence to the south and proceeding for half a mile, we arrived at Khambabarji stage-house, which we had visited when going to Lhása some 4 years ago. We ended our route survey here as this place was fixed by Pandit Nain Singh. Leaving Khambabarji we arrived at Darjeeling on 12th November. In this portion of the route we suffered severely on account of heavy snow.

J. B. N. HENNESSEY,

DEHRA DUN,
1st March, 1884.

Dy. Surveyor General,

In charge Trigonometrical Surveys.

TABLE I. Abstract of Latitudes from Observations with a Sextant and Mercurial Horizon.

LATITUDES.

Year and Date of Observation		Station and District	Direct distance between consecutive stations	Name of Star	No. of Observation	Latitude by each Star		N − S	Mean resulting Latitude	Remarks
						North of Zenith or N	South of Zenith or S			
			Miles			° ′ ″	° ′ ″	′ ″	° ′ ″	
1879 June	27	Lhása, Bhánágshio Street	...	α Scorpii (Antares) ...	1		29 38 13		29 39 0	
,, September	20	Chamchánang vil. on right bank of Migi Changpo, District Phondu	45	α Pis. Aus. (Fomalhaut)	1		30 15 42			
,, ,,	,,	Ditto	...	α Ursæ Minoris (Polaris) Upper ...	1	30 17 18	30 15 42	+ 1 36	30 16 30	
,, ,,	23	Yár Khorohon, District Dam	17	β Ceti ...	1		30 30 8			
,, ,,	29, 30	Shiabden Gomba, District Nagchakha	74	α Ursæ Minoris (Polaris) Upper ...	2	31 29 15	31 27 16			
,, ,,	30	Ditto ditto	...	α Aquilæ (Altair) ...	1					
,, October	1	Ditto ditto	...	α Pis. Aus. (Fomalhaut)	1		28 1			
,, ,,	,,	Ditto ditto	...	α Ursæ Minoris (Polaris) Upper ...	1	31 29 15	31 27 39	+ 1 36	30 30 55	
,, ,,	4	Khamlung E. G., District Jána	34	α Ursæ Minoris (Polaris) Upper ...	1	31 58 31			31 28 27	
,, ,,	11	Maurusen Khua E. G.	128	α Pis. Aus. (Fomalhaut)	1		33 47 44		31 57 44	
,, ,,	,,	Ditto	107	α Ursæ Minoris (Polaris) Upper ...	1	33 49 6	33 47 44	+ 1 22	33 48 25	

Note.—E. G. stand for Encamping Ground.

EXPLORATIONS BY A——K IN GREAT TIBET AND MONGOLIA.

TABLE I—(Continued). *Abstract of Latitudes.*

Year and Date of Observation		Station and District	Direct distance between consecutive stations	Name of Star	No. of Observation	Latitude by each Star		N – S	Mean resulting Latitude	Remarks
						North of Zenith or N	South of Zenith or S			
			Miles			° ′ ″	° ′ ″	° ′ ″	° ′ ″	
1879 October	19	Khokhosili E. G.	...	β Ceti	1		35 9 38			
,, ,,	,,	Ditto	...	α Ursæ Minoris (Polaris) Upper	1	35 11 36	35 9 38	+ 1 58	35 10 37	
,, ,,	25	Añgirfákshis E. G.	34	α Pis. Aus. (Fomalhaut)	1		35 32 39			
,, ,,	,,	Ditto	...	β Ceti	1		33 6			
,, ,,	,,	Ditto	...	α Ursæ Minoris (Polaris) Upper	1	35 34 16	35 32 53	+ 1 23	35 33 35	
,, November	29, 30 / 1, 2	Naichi N. C., District Naichi	23	α Ursæ Minoris (Polaris) Upper	4	35 53 8				
,, October	30	Ditto ditto		α Canis Majoris (Sirius)	1		35 51 14			
,, ,,	,,	Ditto ditto		α Canis Minoris (Procyon)	1		51 6			
,, November	31 / 1, 2	Ditto ditto		Sun (Both Limbs)	3		51 42			
,, October	31	Ditto ditto		α Pis. Aus. (Fomalhaut)	1		51 41			
,, November	1	Ditto ditto		β Ceti	1		52 1			
,, ,,	2	Ditto ditto	55	β Orionis (Rigel)	1	35 53 8	51 29 / 35 51 32	+ 1 36	35 52 20	

NOTE.—N. C. stand for Nomad Camp.

LATITUDES.

TABLE I—(Continued). *Abstract of Latitudes.*

Year and Date of Observation	Station and District	Direct distance between consecutive stations (Miles)	Name of Star	No. of Observation	Latitude by each Star — North of Zenith or N	Latitude by each Star — South of Zenith or S	N – S	Mean resulting Latitude	Remarks
1879 Nov. 11, 12, 13, 15, 18, 19, 20	Golmo N.C., District Thaichinar		α Pis. Aus. (Fomalhaut)	7		° ′ ″ 36 24 38		° ′ ″	
,, 11, 12, 13, 14, 15, 16, 17, 19, 20	Ditto		α Ursæ Minoris (Polaris) Upper	9	36 26 7				
,, 12, 13, 14, 15, 16, 17, 19, 20	Ditto		β Ceti	8		24 47			
,, 12, 19, 20	Ditto		α Orionis	3		24 9			
,, 19, 19, 20	Ditto		α Canis Majoris (Sirius)	3		24 8			
,, 12, 19, 20	Ditto		α Canis Minoris (Procyon)	3		24 17			
,, 19, 20	Ditto		β Orionis (Rigel)	2		24 54			
		59			36 26 7	36 24 29	+ 1 38	36 25 18	
1879 December 2, 3, 7, 8, 9	Thingkali, District Thaichinar		α Pis. Aus. (Fomalhaut)	5		36 23 38			
,, 2, 3, 7, 9, 11	Ditto		β Ceti	5		23 20			
,, 2, 3, 7, 9, 10, 11	Ditto		α Ursæ Minoris (Polaris) Upper	6	36 25 24				
,, 3, 8, 11	Ditto		β Orionis (Rigel)	3		23 37			
,, 3, 8, 11	Ditto		α Canis Majoris (Sirius)	3		23 30			
,, 3	Ditto		α Canis Minoris (Procyon)	1		23 5			
,, 11	Ditto		α Orionis	1		23 23			
		67			36 25 24	36 23 26	+ 1 58	36 24 25	

EXPLORATIONS BY A——K IN GREAT TIBET AND MONGOLIA.

TABLE I—(Continued). Abstract of Latitudes.

Year and Date of Observation	Station and District	Direct distance between consecutive stations	Name of Star	No. of Observation	Latitude by each Star — North of Zenith or N	Latitude by each Star — South of Zenith or S	N − S	Mean resulting Latitude	Remarks
		Miles			° ′ ″	° ′ ″	° ′ ″	° ′ ″	
1879 December 22, 30, 31 } 1880 January 5, 7, 8, 9 }	Sukhai N. C., District Khorlu	...	α Ursæ Minoris (Polaris) Upper	7	37 18 21				
1879 December 23, 31 } 1880 Jan. 4, 5, 7, 8, 9, 11, 25 } ,, February 7, 14 }	Ditto	...	β Orionis (Rigel)	11		37 16 31			
1879 December 28, 31 } 1880 January 6, 7 } ,, February 7, 8 }	Ditto	...	α Canis Majoris (Sirius)	6		16 33			
1879 December 30, 31	Ditto	...	β Ceti	2		16 35			
1880 January 6, 7 } ,, February 7 }	Ditto	...	α Orionis	3		17 12			
,, January 7	Ditto	...	α Canis Minoris (Procyon)	1		16 15			
,, ,, 28, February 7	Ditto	...	α Ursæ Minoris (Polaris) Lower	2	17 49				
,, February 14	Ditto	...	α Orionis	1		17 28			
,, ,, ,,	Ditto	...	β Ursæ Minoris Upper	1	17 48				
					37 17 59	37 16 46	+ 1 13	37 17 23	
1880 March 1, 12	Hoiduthám vil., District Khorlu	...	α Canis Majoris (Sirius)	2		37 19 43			
,, ,, 9	Ditto	...	β Ursæ Minoris Upper	1	37 20 35				
,, ,, 12	Ditto	...	α Canis Minoris (Procyon)	1		20 9			
,, ,, 13	Ditto	216	α Ursæ Minoris (Polaris) Lower	1	21 41				
					37 21 8	37 19 56	+ 1 12	37 20 32	

LATITUDES.

TABLE I—(Continued). *Abstract of Latitudes.*

Year and Date of Observation	Station and District	Direct distance between consecutive stations	Name of Star	No. of Observation	Latitude by each Star		N−S	Mean resulting Latitude	REMARKS
					North of Zenith or N	South of Zenith or S			
		Miles			° ′ ″	° ′ ″	° ′ ″	° ′ ″	
1880 May 22, June 3	Yembi, District Khorlu	...	α Ursæ Minoris (Polaris) Lower	2	38 58 6				
,, July 31, June 15, 26 10	Ditto ditto	...	α Scorpii (Antares)	4		38 57 32			
,, June 2, 9	Ditto ditto	...	α Virginis (Spica)	2		57 30			
,, ,, 3, 13	Ditto ditto	...	β Ursæ Minoris Upper	2	57 45				
,, Aug. 13, 28	Ditto ditto	...	α Ursæ Minoris (Polaris) Upper	2	57 34				
,, Sep. 2, 13	Ditto ditto	...	α Aquilæ (Altair)	2		56 20			
,, ,, 4	Ditto ditto	...	β Ceti	1		57 35			
					38 57 48	38 57 14	+ 0 34	38 57 31	
1881 Nov. 17	Thuden Gomba, District Darge	...	α Canis Majoris (Sirius)	1		33 15 49			
,, ,, 23, Dec. 16	Ditto ditto	...	α Ursæ Minoris (Polaris) Upper	2	33 17 21				
,, Dec. 12, 14	Ditto ditto	...	β Ceti	2		15 23			
		18			33 17 21	33 15 36	+ 1 45	33 16 29	
1882 Jan. 10	Kagudo, District Darge	230	α Canis Majoris (Sirius)	1		33 0 11		33 0 58	
,, ,, 22	Ringo vil, District Rongbácha	179	α Ursæ Minoris (Polaris) Lower	1	31 40 1			31 39 14	
,, Feb. 16	Station on hills about 3 miles S. of Dárchendo, District Minia	49	Sun (Upper Limb)	1	30 21 19	30 21 19		30 22 6	

NOTE.—The direct distance between Sukini N. C. and Thuden Gomba is 281 miles.

EXPLORATIONS BY A——K IN GREAT TIBET AND MONGOLIA.

TABLE I.—(Continued). *Abstract of Latitudes.*

Year and Date of Observation		Station and District	Direct distance between consecutive stations	Name of Star	No. of Observation	Latitude by each Star — North of Zenith or N	Latitude by each Star — South of Zenith or S	N − S	Mean resulting Latitude	Remarks
			Miles			° ′ ″	° ′ ″	° ′ ″	° ′ ″	
1882 Feb.	22	Nagchukha on left bank of Nag Chu River, District Nagchukha	...	α Canis Minoris (Procyon)	1		30 1 35			
,, ,,	,,	Ditto ditto	...	α Virginis (Spica)	1		0 28			
,, ,,	,,	Ditto ditto	112	β Ursæ Minoris Upper	1	30 3 33				
						30 3 33	30 1 2	+ 2 31	30 2 18	
,, Mar.	14	Chioti Gomba, District Báthang	...	α Canis Majoris (Sirius)	1		30 0 5			
,, ,,	,,	Ditto ditto	34	α Canis Minoris (Procyon)	1		29 59 20			
							29 59 43		30 0 30	
,, ,,	21	Gárthok or Mákham, District Mikham	...	α Virginis (Spica)	1		29 39 58			
,, ,,	22	Ditto ditto	40	Sun (Upper Limb)	1		40 41			
							29 40 20		29 41 7	
,, Apr.	1	Dáyul Gomba, District Dáyul	...	Sun (Upper Limb)	1		29 11 26		29 12 13	
					Index Correction		Mean ± ¼ Mean	+ 1 34 ± 0 47		for South / North.

NOTE.—The latitude by each star was obtained *after* applying the Index Error of the Sextant as determined at each station; a residual Index Error appears however to remain, and twice this error is shown in the column N − S; this has been assumed to be eliminated in the mean result at all stations where both North and South objects were observed; where the objects had only one of these aspects, the correction of ± 47″ to South / North latitude has been applied in determining the mean results.

March, 1884.

HEIGHTS.

TABLE II. *Heights above sea level deduced from Boiling Point Observations.*

Place and District	Height in feet	Place and District	Height in feet
Lhása,* Bhánágshio Street	12,600	Station on hills about 3 miles S. of Dárchendo, District Minia	8,930
Phembu Gong Pass, District Phembu	16,320	Gi Lá Pass, District Minia	14,690
Chak Pass	15,840	Kashi Lá Pass	14,710
Phondu on right bank of Rong Chu River	13,340	Nagchukha on left bank of Nag Chu River, District Nagchukha	8,410₅
Chamchúnang vil. on right bank of Migi Cháng-po River, District Phondu	13,230	Lithang, District Lithang	13,400₂
Márnio Lá Pass, District Reting	14,960	Gára Lá Pass, Do.	15,400
Láni Lá Pass	15,750	Ráthi Lá Pass	15,340
Yár Khorchen, District Dam	14,460₂	Chioti Gomba, District Báthang	8,160₂
Shiábden Gomba, District Nagchukha	14,930₄	Dubána Ferry, left bank of Dí Chu River, District Báthang	7,700
Khamlung E. G., District Jáma	15,050	Gárthok or Mákham, District Mákham	11,920
Giáro E. G. on left bank of Saung Chu River, District Yágra	14,540	Samba Dukha Ferry, left bank of Chiámdo Chu River, District Mákham	9,450
Yágratodh E. G., District Yágra	14,950	Cha Chiorten, District Dáyul	10,640₂
Dáng Lá Pass, Do.	16,380	Dáyul Gomba, Do.	11,450
Átag-hapchiga E. G.	15,080	Thángshu Dukha Ferry, left bank of Giáma Nu Chu River, District Nuchu Giu	7,160₂
Maurusen Khua E. G.	14,230	Tila Lá Pass	16,110
Maurus River, Left bank	14,660	Station on left bank of Zayul Chu River, near Dowa Gomba, District Zayul	8,300
Uláng Miris River, Left bank	14,640	Shíkha in Rima vil., District Zayul	4,650₂
Khokhosili E. G.	13,430	Sonling vil., District Zayul	6,200
Chu Már River, Right bank	14,040	Áta vil., Do.	7,950
Do. Left bank	14,050	Áta Gang Lá Glacier; station near Pass	14,690
Añgirtákshia E. G.	13,690	Shiuden Gomba, District Nagong	13,650
Naichi N. C., District Naichi	12,010₁₁	Dongsar, District Dainsi	13,850
Shiárthoge N. C., Do.	10,370₂	Giok Jam Bridge, left bank of stream, Dist. Pashu	11,040
Golmo N. C., District Thaichinar	8,790₂₄	Lhojong, District Lhojong	13,140
Thingkali, Do.	7,720₁₁	Shiobádo, District Jithog	12,470
Sukhai N. C., District Khorlu	8,770₇₆	Arig Gomba, District Arig	12,480
Hoiduthára vil., Do.	9,200₃	Nub Gang Lá Pass	17,940
Igi Chaidam on N. bank of lake, District Khorlu	10,480₃	Lhárugo Giachug, District Lhárugo	13,690
Yembi, District Khorlu	9,690₁₅	Ár Cha Cho Lake, S.E. bank, District Lhárugo	14,680
Thuden Gomba, District Darge	11,990	Tola Lá Pass	17,350
Chiorten Kárpo on left bank of Di Chu River, District Darge	11,440	Giámda, District Kongbo	10,900
Kegudo, District Darge	11,860₂	Khátha vil. on left bank of Cháng Chu or Sángpo River, District Lhokha	11,260
Síla vil. on left bank of Di Chu River, Dist. Darge	10,390	Chetáng* Bazár, District Lhokha	11,450
Dolma Lhákháng on left bank of Di Chu River, District Darge	10,930	Kína vil. on right bank of Cháng Chu or Sángpo River, District Lhokha	10,510
Ringo vil., District Rongbácha	10,550		
Dárchendo, Bazár on left bank of stream, District Minia	8,310₃		

NOTE.—The heights here given are to the nearest 10 feet, where a subscript is added it signifies the number of boiling point readings from which the height has been obtained. E. G. stand for Encamping Ground and N. C. for Nomad Camp.

* The heights of these two places, as given on the Map, are Pandit Nain Sing's values, determined in 1874-75, *i.e.* Lhása 11,910 feet and Chetáng 11,480 feet.

March 1884.

TABLE III. *Observations of Temperature of the Air.*

AT LHASA, BHANAGSHIO STREET.

Date	6 A.M.		9 A.M.		Noon		3 P.M.		6 P.M.	
	Temperature Fah.	Remarks	Temperature Fah.	Remarks	Temperature Fah.	Remarks	Temperature Fah.	Remarks	Temperature Fah.	Remarks
1879 June 5	Degrees ...	.....	Degrees ...	.....	Degrees 68·4	Clear; S.W. wind	Degrees 72·4	Clear; S.W. wind	Degrees ...	.....
" 6	...	.....	60·4	Clear; W. wind	70·4	Clear; W. wind	76·4	Cloudy; W. wind	73·9	Cloudy; W. wind
" 7	53·9	Clear; S.W. wind	59·7	Clear; S.W. wind	...	.....	...	.....	...	.....
" 8	55·4	Clear; S.E. wind	61·4	Clear; S.E. wind	70·9	Clear; S.E. wind	...	.....	...	.....
" 11	...	.....	...	.....	75·9	Clear; W. wind	...	.....	...	.....
" 12	...	.....	...	.....	...	.....	77·4	Cloudy; W. wind	...	.....
" 13	49·7	Clear; S.E. wind	65·9	Clear; S.E. wind	74·4	Cloudy; S. wind	73·9	Cloudy; slight drizzle; strong S. wind	71·4	Clear; S.W. wind
" 14	54·9	Clear; W. wind	69·4	Clear; W. wind	76·6	Cloudy; W. wind	77·4	Cloudy; W. wind	74·4	Cloudy; W. wind
" 15	50·7	Cloudy; S.E. wind; rain last night	69·4	Cloudy; S. wind	74·4	Clear; S. wind	76·4	Clear; S. wind	69·4	Clear; S. wind
" 16	48·4	Clear; S.E. wind	56·4	Clear; S.E. wind	65·9	A few clouds; S.E. wind	68·4	A few clouds; S.E. wind	62·4	Clear; S.E. wind
" 17	49·9	Clear; E. wind	59·4	Clear; E. wind	66·9	Clear; E. Wind	69·2	Clear; E. wind	62·9	Clear; E. wind
" 18	50·4	A few clouds; S.E. wind	59·4	A few clouds; S.E. wind	69·4	A few clouds; S.E. wind	74·4	A few clouds; S.E. wind	68·4	A few clouds; S.E. wind
" 19	54·4	Cloudy; E. wind	59·4	Cloudy; E. wind	68·4	Cloudy; S.E. wind	70·4	Cloudy; S.E. wind	68·4	Cloudy; S.E. wind
" 20	52·4	Cloudy; E. wind	56·9	Cloudy; E. wind	68·4	Cloudy; E. wind	71·4	Cloudy; E. wind	68·4	Cloudy; E. wind
" 21	50·9	Cloudy; S. wind; rain last night	56·4	Cloudy; S. wind	65·4	Cloudy; S. wind	71·4	Cloudy; S. wind	67·4	Clear; S. wind
" 22	54·4	A few clouds; calm; rain last night	57·9	Very cloudy; calm	64·4	A few clouds; E. wind	72·4	A few clouds; E. wind	67·4	A few clouds; E. wind

TABLE III—(Continued). Observations of Temperature of the Air.
At Lhasa, Bhanagshio Street—(Continued).

Date		6 A.M.		9 A.M.		Noon		3 P.M.		6 P.M.	
		Temperature Fah.	Remarks	Temperature Fah.	Remarks	Temperature Fah.	Remarks	Temperature Fah.	Remarks	Temperature Fah.	Remarks
1879 June	23	Degrees 56·4	Clear; S.E. wind	Degrees 66·4	Clear; S.E. wind	Degrees 74·4	Clear; S.E. wind	Degrees 77·4	Cloudy; raining; S.E. wind	Degrees 70·4	Very cloudy; raining; S.E. wind
,,	24	55·4	A few clouds; E. wind	57·4	A few clouds; E. wind	67·4	A few clouds; E. wind	74·4	Cloudy; drizzling; E. wind	68·4	A few clouds; E. wind
,,	25	51·4	Cloudy; E. wind	58·4	Cloudy; calm	65·4	Cloudy; calm	68·4	Cloudy; N.E. wind	62·4	Cloudy; raining; N.E. wind
,,	26	49·4	Cloudy; raining; N.W. wind	52·9	Cloudy; N.W. wind	64·4	A few clouds; W. wind	66·4	A few clouds; W. wind	58·4	Cloudy; raining; W. wind
,,	27	53·4	Cloudy; calm	61·4	Cloudy; W. wind	66·4	Cloudy; W. wind	69·4	Cloudy; W. wind	62·4	Raining; W. wind
,,	28	49·4	A few clouds; N. wind	51·4	A few clouds; N. wind	62·4	Clear; N. wind	64·4	Clear; N. wind	62·4	Cloudy; calm
,,	29	51·4	A few clouds; N. wind	60·4	A few clouds; N. wind	65·4	A few clouds; N. wind	68·4	Clear; N. wind	64·4	Clear; N. wind
,,	30	51·9	Clear; E. wind	59·4	Clear; E. wind	66·4	Cloudy; calm	70·4	Cloudy; E. wind	65·4	Cloudy; E. wind
July	1	53·9	Cloudy; mild E. wind	61·4	Cloudy; N. wind	69·4	Cloudy; N.W. wind	71·4	Cloudy; N.W. wind	69·4	Cloudy; N.W. wind
,,	2	50·9	Raining; W. wind	68·9	Raining; W. wind	71·4	Cloudy; W. wind	74·4	Cloudy; W. wind	69·4	Cloudy; W. wind
,,	3	52·4	A few clouds; W. wind; rain last night	63·4	A few clouds; W. wind	73·4	A few clouds; W. wind	77·4	Cloudy; W. wind	67·4	Raining; W. wind
,,	4	49·4	Cloudy; E. wind	54·4	Cloudy; E. wind	65·9	Cloudy; E. wind	74·9	Cloudy; E. wind	65·4	Raining; E. wind
,,	5	51·4	Cloudy; S.E. wind	54·9	Cloudy; S.E. wind	64·9	Cloudy; S.E. wind	70·9	Cloudy; S.E. wind	64·4	Cloudy; S. wind
,,	6	53·4	Cloudy; calm	55·9	Cloudy; S.E. wind	64·4	Cloudy; S.E. wind	66·4	Cloudy; S.E. wind	60·4	Cloudy; S.E. wind
,,	7	51·4	A few clouds; S. wind	56·4	A few clouds; S. wind	77·9	A few clouds; S. wind	70·9	A few clouds; S. wind	64·4	A few clouds; S. wind
,,	8	51·4	Clear; E. wind	63·4	Clear; E. wind	68·4	A few clouds; E. wind	70·4	A few clouds; E. wind	65·4	Clear; E. wind

TABLE III—(Continued). *Observations of Temperature of the Air.*

AT LHASA, BHANAGSHIO STREET—(Continued).

Date		6 A.M.		9 A.M.		Noon		3 P.M.		6 P.M.	
		Temperature Fah.	Remarks	Temperature Fah.	Remarks	Temperature Fah.	Remarks	Temperature Fah.	Remarks	Temperature Fah.	Remarks
1879 July	9	Degrees 53·4	Clear; N.W. wind	Degrees 64·4	Clear; N.W. wind	Degrees 69·4	A few clouds; N. wind	Degrees 72·4	A few clouds; N. wind	Degrees 64·4	Hailstorm; N. wind
„	10	57·4	Cloudy; mild N. wind	60·4	Cloudy; N. wind	68·4	Cloudy; N. wind	74·4	Cloudy; N. wind	65·4	Cloudy; N. wind
„	11	52·9	Cloudy; E. wind; rain last night	63·4	Cloudy; E. wind	64·4	Cloudy; E. wind	71·9	Cloudy; E. wind	67·4	Cloudy; E. wind
„	12	51·4	Cloudy; calm; rain last night	56·4	Cloudy; E. wind	69·4	Cloudy; E. wind	74·4	Cloudy; E. wind	66·4	Cloudy; E. wind
„	13	49·4	Cloudy; S. wind; rain last night	52·4	Cloudy; S. wind	64·4	Cloudy; S. wind	69·4	Cloudy; S. wind	63·4	Cloudy; S. wind
„	14	52·4	Cloudy; calm	56·4	Cloudy; N.E. wind	67·4	Cloudy; N.E. wind	71·4	Cloudy; N.E. wind	63·9	Cloudy; N.E. wind
„	15	49·4	Cloudy; calm; rain last night	52·4	Cloudy; S.E. wind	66·9	Cloudy; S.E. wind	69·9	Cloudy; S.E. wind	63·9	Cloudy; S.E. wind
„	16	54·4	Cloudy; E. wind	57·4	Cloudy; E. wind	64·9	Cloudy; E. wind	72·4	Cloudy; E. wind	64·4	Cloudy; calm
„	17	57·4	Cloudy; calm	59·4	Cloudy; W. wind	67·9	Cloudy; W. wind	73·4	Cloudy; W. wind	66·4	Cloudy; W. wind
„	18	54·4	Cloudy; calm	57·4	Cloudy; N. wind	67·4	Cloudy; N. wind	69·4	Cloudy; N. wind	67·4	Cloudy; N. wind
„	19	53·4	Cloudy; W. wind	57·4	Cloudy; W. wind	64·4	Cloudy; W. wind	69·4	Cloudy; W. wind	67·4	Raining; W. wind
„	20	51·4	Cloudy; S.W. wind	57·4	Cloudy; S.W. wind	64·4	Cloudy; S.W. wind	67·4	Cloudy; S.W. wind	66·4	Cloudy; S.W. wind
„	21	50·9	Cloudy; N. wind; rain last night	56·4	Cloudy; N. wind	64·9	Cloudy; N. wind	66·4	Cloudy; N. wind	64·4	Cloudy; N. wind
„	22	48·9	Cloudy; E. wind; rain last night	53·4	Cloudy; E. wind	64·4	Cloudy; E. wind	66·4	Cloudy; W. wind	64·4	Cloudy; W. wind
„	23	49·4	Cloudy; W. wind	56·4	Cloudy; W. wind	64·4	A few clouds; W. wind	66·4	A few clouds; W. wind	64·4	A few clouds; W. wind

TEMPERATURE.

TABLE III—(Continued). *Observations of Temperature of the Air.*

AT LHASA, BHANAGSHIO STREET—(Continued).

Date	6 A.M. Temperature Fah.	6 A.M. Remarks	9 A.M. Temperature Fah.	9 A.M. Remarks	Noon Temperature Fah.	Noon Remarks	3 P.M. Temperature Fah.	3 P.M. Remarks	6 P.M. Temperature Fah.	6 P.M. Remarks
1879	Degrees		Degrees		Degrees		Degrees		Degrees	
July 24	51·4	A few clouds; W. wind	56·4	A few clouds; W. wind	66·4	A few clouds; W. wind	68·4	A few clouds; W. wind	65·4	A few clouds; W. wind
,, 25	50·9	A few clouds; E. wind	64·4	A few clouds; E. wind	66·4	A few clouds; E. wind	69·4	A few clouds; E. wind	65·4	A few clouds; E. wind
,, 26	51·4	A few clouds; E. wind	65·9	A few clouds; W. wind	67·4	A few clouds; W. wind	70·9	A few clouds; W. wind	66·4	A few clouds; W. wind
August 27	55·4	A few clouds; S. wind	61·4	A few clouds; S. wind	64·4	A few clouds; S. wind	...	......	...	......
,, 28	51·4	Very cloudy; S.W. wind	57·4	Cloudy; W. wind	60·9	Cloudy; W. wind	63·9	Cloudy; W. wind	58·4	Cloudy; W. wind
September 4	49·4	Cloudy; calm	53·4	Cloudy; N. wind	65·4	Cloudy; N. wind	66·4	A few clouds; N.E. wind	61·9	A few clouds; N.E. wind

AT GOLMO, DISTRICT THAICHINAR.

November 11	...	......	30·4	A few clouds; S.W. wind	42·9	Very cloudy; S.W. wind	...	Cloudy; S.W. wind	41·9	Clear; N.E. wind
,, 12	...	......	34·9	A few clouds; W. wind	42·9	Very cloudy; W. wind	45·4	Cloudy; W. wind	...	......
,, 13	...	......	37·4	Clear; W. wind	47·4	Clear; W. wind	46·4	Clear; W. wind	...	......
,, 14	...	......	32·4	Clear; N.W. wind	46·2	Clear; W. wind	50·9	Clear; W. wind	...	......
,, 15	...	......	31·4	A few clouds; S.W. wind	47·9	A few clouds; S.W. wind	50·4	A few clouds; S.W. wind	...	......
,, 16	...	......	26·9	Cloudy; W. wind	43·4	A few clouds; W. wind	45·4	Clear; W. wind	...	......
,, 17	...	......	34·4	Clear; E. wind	41·4	Clear; N.E. wind	44·9	Clear; E. wind	...	......
,, 18	...	......	32·9	Clear; W. wind	41·4	Clear; W. wind	44·4	Clear; W. wind	...	......
,, 19	...	......	27·9	Clear; mild W. wind	38·9	Clear; mild W. wind	42·4	Clear; mild W. wind	...	......
,, 20	...	......								

TABLE III—(Continued). *Observations of Temperature of the Air.*

AT THINGKALI, DISTRICT THAICHINAR.

Date	6 A.M. Temperature Fah.	6 A.M. Remarks	9 A.M. Temperature Fah.	9 A.M. Remarks	Noon Temperature Fah.	Noon Remarks	3 P.M. Temperature Fah.	3 P.M. Remarks	6 P.M. Temperature Fah.	6 P.M. Remarks
1879 November 28	Degrees ...	......	Degrees 27·4	Clear; S.E. wind	Degrees 36·2	Clear; N.E. wind	Degrees 36·4	Clear; N. wind	Degrees ...	......
„ 29	...	......	24·9	Clear; high S.E. wind	33·4	Clear; high S.W. wind	32·9	Cloudy; high S.W. wind	...	......
„ 30	...	......	26·9	Clear; S.E. wind	36·4	Clear; E. wind	38·9	Clear; E. wind	...	......
December 1	...	......	21·9	Clear; high W. wind	29·4	A few clouds; high W. wind	31·9	A few clouds; high W. wind	...	......
„ 2	...	......	28·4	Clear; W. wind	37·9	Clear; W. wind	39·9	Clear; W. wind	...	......
„ 3	...	......	26·4	Clear; high E. wind	38·4	Clear; high E. wind	41·4	Clear; E. wind	...	......
„ 4	...	......	25·9	Very cloudy; high W. wind	37·4	A few clouds; high W. wind	39·4	Clear; high W. wind	...	......
„ 6	...	......	29·4	A few clouds; high E. wind	34·9	Cloudy; S.E. wind	34·9	Cloudy; W. wind	...	......
„ 7	...	......	31·4	A few clouds; N.E. wind	36·9	A few clouds; N. wind	39·4	Clear; N. wind	...	......
„ 8	...	......	26·9	Clear; high E. wind	34·9	Clear; strong N.E. wind	33·9	Clear; strong N.E. wind	...	......
„ 9	...	......	25·4	Clear; W wind	31·4	Clear; W. wind	35·4	Clear; W. wind	...	......
„ 10	...	......	23·9	Clear; mild N.E. wind	35·4	Clear; mild N.E. wind	40·4	Clear; mild N.E. wind	...	......
„ 11	...	......	26·4	Clear; E. wind	33·9	Clear; high E. wind	36·9	Clear; high E. wind	...	......

AT SUKHAI N. C., DISTRICT KHORLU.

December 21	24·9	Clear; E. wind	...	......	34·4	Clear; E. wind	37·4	Clear; E. wind	...	......
„ 22	24·9	Clear; mild N. wind	...	......	31·9	Clear; mild N.W. wind	34·9	Clear; mild W. wind	...	......
„ 23	...	......	12·4	Cloudy; mild E. wind	34·9	Clear; S.E. wind	35·4	Clear; S.E. wind	...	......

TEMPERATURE.

TABLE III—(Continued). Observations of Temperature of the Air.

At Sukhai N. C., District Khorlu—(Continued).

Date	6 A.M. Temperature Fah.	6 A.M. Remarks	9 A.M. Temperature Fah.	9 A.M. Remarks	Noon Temperature Fah.	Noon Remarks	3 P.M. Temperature Fah.	3 P.M. Remarks	6 P.M. Temperature Fah.	6 P.M. Remarks
	Degrees		Degrees		Degrees		Degrees		Degrees	
1879 December 24	...	......	22·9	Clear; N.W. wind	39·9	Cloudy; N. wind	37·9	Cloudy; N. wind	...	......
,, 25	...	......	29·9	Cloudy; mild S.E. wind	43·4	Cloudy; mild S.E. wind	45·9	Cloudy; mild S.E. wind	...	......
,, 26	...	......	21·4	Cloudy; high N.E. wind	28·9	Cloudy; high N.E. wind	32·4	Cloudy; E. wind	...	......
,, 27	...	......	24·9	Cloudy; snowing; mild S. wind	30·4	Cloudy; snowing; S.E. wind	31·9	Cloudy; snowing; S.E. wind	...	......
,, 28	...	......	13·9	Clear; E. wind	20·4	Clear; E. wind	21·4	Clear; E. wind	...	......
,, 29	...	......	20†	Cloudy; S.W. wind	26·9	Cloudy; S.E. wind	27·4	Cloudy; S.E. wind	...	......
,, 30	...	......	*	Cloudy; snowy; S.W. wind	23·4	Cloudy; snowing; S. wind	23·9	Cloudy; S. wind	...	......
,, 31	...	......	*	A few clouds; W. wind; fall of snow on surrounding hills last night	19·4	A few clouds; S.E. wind	21·4	A few clouds; S. wind	...	......
1880 January 1	...	......	...	A few clouds; S.W. wind	...	A few clouds; N.E. wind	20†	A few clouds; S.E. wind	...	......
,, 2	...	......	*	A few clouds; W. wind	23·4	A few clouds; S.W. wind	25·9	A few clouds; S.E. wind	...	......
,, 3	...	......	20†	A few clouds; S.E. wind	30·4	Cloudy; S.E wind	34·9	Cloudy; S. wind	...	......
,, 4	...	......	*	Clear; E. wind	26·9	A few clouds; S.E. wind	29·9	A few clouds; S.E. wind	...	......
,, 5	...	......	*	A few clouds; N.E. wind	27·9	A few clouds; S.E. wind	31·4	A few clouds; S. wind	...	......
,, 6	...	......	...	A few clouds; E. wind	24·4	A few clouds; E. wind	28·9	A few clouds; E. wind	...	......
,, 7	...	......	*	A few clouds; mild W. wind	29·4	Cloudy; S.E. wind	32·9	Cloudy; S.E. wind	...	......
,, 8	...	......	*	A few clouds; mild E. wind	26·9	A few clouds; N.E. wind	33·4	A few clouds; strong W. wind	...	......

* In these cases the mercury receded into the bulb where it of course could not be read; but by estimate it is concluded that the prevailing cold was more than 18° below 0° of Fahrenheit's scale.
† These are approximate.

TABLE III—(Continued). *Observations of Temperature of the Air.*

AT SUKHAI N. C., DISTRICT KHORLU—(Continued).

Date	6 A.M.		9 A.M.		Noon		3 P.M.		6 P.M.	
	Temperature Fah.	Remarks	Temperature Fah.	Remarks	Temperature Fah.	Remarks	Temperature Fah.	Remarks	Temperature Fah.	Remarks
	Degrees		Degrees		Degrees		Degrees		Degrees	
1880 January 9	...	......	*	Cloudy; S.E. wind	27·4	A few clouds; E. wind	31·4	A few clouds; W. wind	...	......
,, 10	...	......	*	Cloudy; W. wind	22·4	Cloudy; S. wind	28·4	Cloudy; S. wind	...	......
,, 11	...	......	20†	Cloudy; W. wind	33·4	Cloudy; S.W. wind	34·9	A few clouds; S. wind	...	......
,, 12	...	......	*	A few clouds; E. wind	27·4	A few clouds; S.E. wind	31·9	A few clouds; S.E. wind	...	......
,, 13	...	......	*	A few clouds; E. wind	26·9	A few clouds; E. wind	29·4	A few clouds; E. wind	...	......
,, 14	...	......	*	Cloudy; E. wind	29·9	Cloudy; W. wind	29·9	Cloudy; E. wind	...	......
,, 15	...	......	*	A few clouds; N. wind	24·9	A few clouds; N. wind	28·9	Cloudy; N. wind	...	......
,, 16	...	......	*	Clear; S. wind	27·9	A few clouds; S. wind	31·9	A few clouds; S. wind	...	......
,, 17	...	......	*	Cloudy; N.E. wind	27·9	Cloudy; S.E. wind	29·9	Cloudy; strong E. wind	...	......
,, 18	...	......	*	A few clouds; N.E. wind	24·9	A few clouds; E. wind	28·9	Cloudy; E. wind	...	......
,, 19	...	......	20†	Cloudy; E. wind	25·9	Cloudy; N.E. wind	27·9	Very cloudy; E. wind	...	......
,, 20	...	......	20†	Very cloudy; snowing; E. wind	27·9	Very cloudy; snowing; E. wind	20†	Very cloudy; snowing; strong E. wind	...	......
,, 21	...	......	*	Very cloudy; snowing; mild S. wind	20†	Very cloudy; snowing; N. wind	20†	Very cloudy; snowing; N. wind	...	......
,, 22	...	......	*	Clear; N.E. wind	*	Clear; S.E. wind	*	Clear; S. wind	...	......
,, 23	...	......	*	Clear; E. wind	*	A few clouds; mild S. wind	20†	A few clouds; mild S. wind	...	......
,, 24	...	......	*	Cloudy; N.E. wind	*	Cloudy; E. wind	20†	Cloudy; E. wind	...	......
,, 25	...	......	13·9	A few clouds; E. wind	11·4	A few clouds; E. wind	13·4	A few clouds; mild S.W. wind	...	......

* In these cases the mercury receded into the bulb where it of course could not be read; but by estimate it is concluded that the prevailing cold was more than 18° below 0° of Fahrenheit's scale.
† These are approximate.

TEMPERATURE.

TABLE III—(Continued). Observations of Temperature of the Air.

AT SUKHAI N. C., DISTRICT KHORLU—(Continued).

Date	6 A.M.		9 A.M.		Noon		3 P.M.		6 P.M.	
	Temperature Fah.	Remarks	Temperature Fah.	Remarks	Temperature Fah.	Remarks	Temperature Fah.	Remarks	Temperature Fah.	Remarks
	Degrees		Degrees		Degrees		Degrees		Degrees	
1880 January 26	...	.....	4·9	A few clouds; S.W. wind	9·9	A few clouds; E. wind	21·9	Clear; S. wind	...	.....
" 27	...	.....	9·9	Clear; S. wind	21·9	A few clouds; mild S.W. wind	28·4	A few clouds; mild S. wind	...	.....
" 28	...	.....	14·4	A few clouds; S. wind	29·9	A few clouds; mild S. wind	35·9	Cloudy; mild S. wind	...	.....
" 29	...	.....	17·4	Very cloudy; E. wind	31·4	Cloudy; mild S.E. wind	30·4	Cloudy; S.E. wind	...	.....
" 30	...	.....	20·4	A few clouds; S.W. wind	31·9	A few clouds; S. wind	37·9	A few clouds; S. wind	...	.....
" 31	...	.....	21·9	Cloudy; S.W. wind	33·4	A few clouds; S. wind	38·9	A few clouds; S. wind	...	.....
February 1	...	.....	30·4	A few clouds; calm	43·4	A few clouds; strong W. wind	43·4	A few clouds; strong W. wind	...	.....
" 2	...	.....	21·4	Cloudy; E. wind	39·9	Cloudy; S. wind	42·4	A few clouds; E. wind	...	.....
" 3	...	.....	24·9	Very cloudy; mild N.E. wind	36·2	Very cloudy; mild E. wind	38·4	Very cloudy; S.W. wind	...	.....
" 4	...	.....	23·4	A few clouds; S.W. wind	40·4	A few clouds; S. wind	43·2	A few clouds; E. wind	...	.....
" 5	...	.....	25·4	Cloudy; S.E. wind	37·9	Cloudy; S. wind	43·9	A few clouds; S.E. wind	...	.....
" 6	...	.....	23·9	Very cloudy; E. wind	31·2	Cloudy; strong E. wind	33·2	A few clouds; strong E. wind	...	.....
" 7	...	.....	23·9	Cloudy; snowing; E. wind	29·7	A few clouds; S. wind	35·2	A few clouds; S.E. wind	...	.....
" 8	...	.....	17·9	Clear; S.E. wind	29·7	Clear; S.E. wind	41·4	A few clouds; mild S. wind	...	.....
" 9	...	.....	24·4	Very cloudy; E. wind	35·9	Very cloudy; mild S.W. wind	40·9	Very cloudy; calm	...	.....
" 10	...	.....	28·2	Cloudy; mild E. wind	40·4	Cloudy; S. wind	43·9	Cloudy; S. wind	...	.....

TABLE III.—(Continued). Observations of Temperature of the Air.

At Hoiduthara Village, District Khorlu.

Date	6 A.M. Temperature Fah.	6 A.M. Remarks	9 A.M. Temperature Fah.	9 A.M. Remarks	Noon Temperature Fah.	Noon Remarks	3 P.M. Temperature Fah.	3 P.M. Remarks	6 P.M. Temperature Fah.	6 P.M. Remarks
1880	Degrees		Degrees		Degrees		Degrees		Degrees	
March 2	...	......	23·9	Clear; E. wind	32·4	Clear; S.E. wind	36·9	A few clouds; E. wind	...	......
" 4	...	......	32·4	Very cloudy; mild S. wind	39·4	Very cloudy; mild S.E. wind	39·9	Very cloudy; S.E. wind	...	......
" 5	...	......	31·4	A few clouds; E. wind	45·7	Cloudy; duststorm from W.	39·9	Cloudy; storm continuing	...	......
" 6	...	......	24·9	Cloudy; E. wind	42·9	Cloudy; duststorm from W.	39·4	Cloudy; storm continuing	...	......
" 7	...	......	33·4	Clear; mild E. wind	34·9	A few clouds; strong E. wind	40·2	A few clouds; mild E. wind	...	......
" 8	...	......	27·9	Cloudy; E. wind	36·4	Very cloudy; strong N.E. wind	39·4	Very cloudy; strong N. wind	...	......
" 9	...	......	34·7	A few clouds; E. wind	41·9	A few clouds; E. wind	46·9	A few clouds; E. wind	...	......
" 10	...	......	43·2	A few clouds; mild E. wind	49·9	A few clouds; mild E. wind	57·4	A few clouds; mild E. wind	...	......
" 11	...	......	43·4	Cloudy; N.E. wind	55·9	Cloudy; N.E. wind	61·9	Cloudy; mild E. wind	...	......
" 12	...	......	40·7	A few clouds; E. wind	50·2	A few clouds; E. wind	59·4	A few clouds; E. wind	...	......

At Yembi, District Khorlu.

Date	6 A.M. Temperature Fah.	6 A.M. Remarks	9 A.M. Temperature Fah.	9 A.M. Remarks	Noon Temperature Fah.	Noon Remarks	3 P.M. Temperature Fah.	3 P.M. Remarks	6 P.M. Temperature Fah.	6 P.M. Remarks
April 3	...	......	48·9	Cloudy; mild S.E. wind	56·9	Cloudy; duststorm from N.	46·4	Very cloudy; storm continuing	...	......
" 4	32·9	Cloudy; N.E. wind	45·4	Very cloudy; E. wind	52·9	Cloudy; S. wind	55·4	Cloudy; S. wind	43·9	Cloudy; S. wind
" 5	22·9	Very cloudy; S. wind	41·9	Very cloudy; S. wind	52·9	Cloudy; S. wind	58·9	Cloudy; duststorm from N.	46·9	Cloudy; storm continuing
" 6	24·9	Cloudy; E. wind	45·9	Cloudy; E. wind	56·4	Cloudy; E. wind	63·4	Cloudy; E. wind	49·4	Cloudy; strong N. wind
" 7	34·9	Very cloudy; strong N. wind	44·9	Very cloudy; strong N. wind	48·9	Very cloudy; N. wind	42·9	Very cloudy; strong N. wind	32·7	Very cloudy; duststorm from N.

TEMPERATURE.

TABLE III—(Continued). Observations of Temperature of the Air.
AT YEMBI, DISTRICT KHORLU—(Continued).

Date		6 A.M. Temperature Fah.	6 A.M. Remarks	9 A.M. Temperature Fah.	9 A.M. Remarks	Noon Temperature Fah.	Noon Remarks	3 P.M. Temperature Fah.	3 P.M. Remarks	6 P.M. Temperature Fah.	6 P.M. Remarks
1880 April	8	Degrees 24·4	Cloudy; strong S. wind; fall of snow on surrounding hills last night	Degrees 36·9	Cloudy; strong S. wind	Degrees 45·4	Cloudy; strong W. wind	Degrees 36·9	Very cloudy; hailstorm; strong W. wind	Degrees 32·9	Very cloudy; strong N. wind
"	9	16·9	Cloudy; N.E. wind	29·4	Cloudy; strong S.W. wind	34·4	Cloudy; strong W. wind	39·9	Cloudy; strong W. wind	32·9	Cloudy; strong W. wind
"	10	19·9	A few clouds; mild E. wind	33·4	Cloudy; S. wind	39·4	A few clouds; strong W. wind	44·2	Cloudy; strong W. wind	39·9	Cloudy; strong W. wind
May	23	34·9	Clear; W. wind	52·9	Clear; mild W. wind	67·9	A few clouds; mild W. wind	66·9	Cloudy; strong W. wind	58·9	Cloudy; strong W. wind
"	24	31·9	A few clouds; S.E. wind	51·9	A few clouds; S.W. wind	70·7	Cloudy; S.W. wind	69·9	Cloudy; N. wind	64·4	Cloudy; N. wind
"	25	33·9	A few clouds; N.E. wind	56·2	Cloudy; S.E. wind	72·9	Cloudy; N.E. wind	74·9	Cloudy; strong N.E. wind	57·9	Cloudy; strong N.E. wind
"	26	49·9	Very cloudy; duststorm from N.E.	57·9	Very cloudy; storm continuing	56·9	Very cloudy; storm continuing	56·9	Very cloudy; storm continuing	47·9	Very cloudy; storm continuing
"	27	42·9	Very cloudy; S.E. wind; rain last night	50·9	Very cloudy; S.E. wind	61·9	Very cloudy; S.E. wind	56·9	Very cloudy; thunderstorm at distance	46·9	Very cloudy; S. wind; slight rain
"	28	37·2	A few clouds; N.E. wind; fall of snow last night on surrounding hills	52·9	A few clouds; N.E. wind	62·4	A few clouds; S.W. wind	66·9	A few clouds; strong N.E. wind	58·2	Cloudy; strong N.E. wind
"	29	38·9	A few clouds; mild E. wind	60·9	A few clouds; mild E. wind	70·9	A few clouds; strong N.E. wind	71·9	Cloudy; strong N.E. wind	62·9	Cloudy; strong N.E. wind
"	30	47·9	Very cloudy; strong N.E. wind	56·9	Very cloudy; strong N.E. wind	59·4	Very cloudy; duststorm from N.E.	54·2	Very cloudy; storm continuing	49·9	Very cloudy; storm continuing
"	31	42·9	Very cloudy; mild E. wind; rain last night	60·9	Cloudy; calm	54·4	Very cloudy; strong N.E. wind; hailstorm	60·2	Cloudy; storm from N.E.	54·9	Cloudy; storm continuing

EXPLORATIONS BY A——K IN GREAT TIBET AND MONGOLIA.

TABLE III—(Continued). *Observations of Temperature of the Air.*

AT YEMBI, DISTRICT KHORLU—(Continued).

Date		6 A.M.		9 A.M.		Noon		3 P.M.		6 P.M.	
		Temperature Fah.	Remarks	Temperature Fah.	Remarks	Temperature Fah.	Remarks	Temperature Fah.	Remarks	Temperature Fah.	Remarks
		Degrees		Degrees		Degrees		Degrees		Degrees	
1880 June	1	45·9	Clear; mild E. wind	57·9	Clear; mild E. wind	64·9	A few clouds; mild N. wind	73·7	Cloudy; strong N.E. wind	64·9	Cloudy; strong N.E. wind
"	2	50·9	Cloudy; N. wind	63·9	Cloudy; N. wind	71·9	Cloudy; strong N.E. wind	68·9	A few clouds; duststorm from N.E.	59·9	A few clouds; storm continuing
"	3	50·2	Cloudy; E. wind	62·9	Cloudy; strong N.E. wind	68·4	Cloudy; strong N.E. wind	62·7	Very cloudy; duststorm from N.E.	59·9	Very cloudy; storm continuing
"	4	42·9	A few clouds; mild N.W. wind	65·2	A few clouds; mild S.W. wind	70·4	A few clouds; duststorm from N.E.	69·7	A few clouds; storm continuing	59·2	Cloudy; storm continuing

March, 1884.

POPULATION.

TABLE IV. *Population &c. of Places within strips about 2 miles wide on either side of and along the routes traversed, and distances measured across each District or Patti.*

Place	District or Patti and distance in it traversed in miles	Forts	Gombas	Tents	Houses	Population Lay	Population Lámas & Dúbas
Lhása		1	10	...	...	17000	2000
Dabchilinga		...	...	...	2	10	...
Dabchi		1	...	...	...	300	...
Chiángro		...	...	...	12	70	...
Sára Gomba		...	1	...	1000	100	5500
Parisíga vil.	Lhasa, 10	...	...	...	5	30	...
Huñgusíga „		...	...	...	4	25	...
Kecháng „		...	...	...	5	30	...
Khutho Gomba		...	1	...	10	2	20
Gákánáka Cheñkháng		...	1	...	5	30	15
Lingbu Jong		1	...	...	10	60	5
Totals	...	3	13	...	1053	17657	7540
Baya vil.		...	...	...	5	30	...
Nálenda Gomba		...	1	...	...	10	100
Langta „		...	1	...	...	5	50
Debungsíga vil.	Phembu, 25	...	...	...	20	120	...
Village		...	...	...	5	30	...
Lundub Jong		1	...	...	50	300	...
Gomba		...	1	...	50	10	100
Village		...	...	...	5	30	...
Totals	...	1	3	...	135	535	250
Tálung Gomba	Talung, 10	...	1	...	300	300	300
Phondu Jong		1	...	...	50	300	...
Village	Phondu, 7	...	...	...	2	10	...
Chiomo Lhákháng		...	1	...	50	150	5
Totals	...	1	1	...	102	460	5
Láni Tarjum	Reting, 12	...	...	50	...	200	...
Dam	Dam, 16	...	1	200	3	800	...
Nomad Camps	Shangshung, 50	...	...	500	...	2000	...
Máne Khorchen		...	1	...	2	2	2
Shiabden Gomba	Nagchukha, 45	...	1	50	100	400	100
Nomad Camps		...	...	3000	...	5500	...
Totals	...	...	2	3050	102	5902	102

EXPLORATIONS BY A——K IN GREAT TIBET AND MONGOLIA.

Table IV—(Continued).

Place	District or Patti and distance in it traversed in miles	Forts	Gombas	Tents	Houses	Population Lay	Population Lāmas & Dábas
Nomad Camps	Jama, 11	...	...	1500	...	3000	...
Nomad Camps	Áta, 13	...	...	500	...	1000	...
Nomad Camps	Yagra, 44	...	...	1000	...	2000	...
Uninhabited tract	240	...	...	...	...	...	...
Amthum N.C. } Naichi „ } Tháglaga „ } Shiárthoge „ }		...	...	10	...	60	...
Golmo „	Thaichinar, 170	...	...	50	...	125	25
Hurthothále		...	...	20	...	50	10
Thugthe N.C.		...	...	50	...	125	25
Thágthe „		...	...	50	...	125	25
Dála „		...	...	4	...	10	2
Chúgu „		...	...	2	...	5	1
Dhánáhotho N.C.		...	...	2	...	5	1
Thingkali		...	...	100	10	250	50
Hárori N.C.		...	...	2	...	5	1
Dabásuthu „		...	...	4	...	10	2
Totals	...	...	...	294	10	770	142
Sukhai N.C. } Hoiduthára vil. }		...	...	100	2	250	50
Horga vil.		...	...	...	5	2	...
Bhága Chaidam	Khorlu, 305	...	...	50	...	125	25
Igi „		...	...	100	...	250	50
Urel		...	...	3	...	5	1
Yembi		...	...	300	...	750	150
Totals	...	...	...	553	7	1382	276
Saitu	Saitu, 72	1	...	...	2000	12000	...
Jún	Jun, 30	...	...	50	1	130	30
Gakcharnamaga N.C.		...	...	30	...	75	15
Bárong Chaidam	Barong, 30	...	...	50	10	170	30
Hádho vil.		...	...	1	...	3	...
Totals	...	...	...	81	10	248	45

POPULATION.

TABLE IV—(Continued).

Place	District or Patti and distance in it traversed in miles	Forts	Gombas	Tents	Houses	Population Lay	Lámas & Dábas
Uninhabited tract	105	...	...	...	...	...	...
Niamcho	NIAMCHO, 56	...	...	100	50	600	...
Dhingo vil.		...	...	...	10	40	...
Village		...	...	...	15	60	...
Tindhu vil.		...	...	...	10	40	...
Kanzo Gomba		...	1	...	50	100	50
2 Villages		...	...	...	20	80	...
Thiso vil.		...	...	...	30	120	...
Khutho vil.		...	...	...	20	80	...
Láso vil.		...	...	...	15	60	...
Thuden Gomba		...	1	...	30	10	30
Laindha vil.		...	...	...	50	200	...
Thándha ,, ...		...	,,	...	40	160	...
Dwinda ,, ...		...	...	...	50	200	...
Rángna ,, ...		...	...	...	15	60	..
Dhokor ,, ...		...	...	...	30	120	...
Jindha ,, ...		...	...	...	30	120	...
Bari ,, ...		...	...	...	10	40	...
Denda ,, ...	DARGE, 260	...	...	...	30	120	...
Bhonchi Gomba		...	1	...	50	10	100
Thombudha vil.		...	...	...	20	80	...
Rákna Gomba		...	1	...	20	5	40
Kegu ,, ,, ...		...	1	...	300	30	300
Kegudo		...	...	...	200	600	...
Táng Gomba		...	1	...	30	5	60
Bhenche ,, ...		...	1	40	30	90	50
Gomba		...	1	5	5	20	10
Khánsar vil.		...	...	...	25	100	...
Village		...	...	...	5	15	...
Shiongo Gomba		...	1	...	30	10	50
2 Villages		...	...	...	30	120	...
Siti vil.		...	...	...	10	40	...
Gomba		...	1	...	15	5	30
Donthok Gomba		...	1	...	50	10	100
Dogung vil.		...	...	...	10	40	...
Sháo vil.		...	...	...	5	20	...
Carried over ...	...	...	11	45	1290	2810	820

EXPLORATIONS BY A——K IN GREAT TIBET AND MONGOLIA.

Table IV—(Continued).

Place	District or Patti and distance in it traversed in miles	Forts	Gombas	Tents	Houses	Population Lay	Lámas & Dábas
Brought forward ...	...	...	11	45	1290	2810	820
Donti vil.		...	...	...	5	20	...
Dwinthang Gomba		...	1	...	100	20	200
2 Villages		...	...	...	20	80	...
Síla vil.		...	...	...	30	120	...
Dhingo Gomba		...	1	...	30	10	60
Rárang vil.		...	...	...	20	80	...
Chiti Gomba		...	1	...	35	10	70
Chingo „		...	1	...	50	10	100
Dolma Lhákháng		...	1	...	30	120	5
Losino vil.	Darge, 260	...	...	...	30	120	...
Káphu Gomba		...	1	...	25	5	50
Bága vil.		...	...	...	10	40	...
Rára „		...	...	...	5	20	...
Nágli Gomba		...	1	...	30	10	60
Chiri vil.		...	...	...	15	60	...
Gainjo Gomba		...	1	...	60	10	120
Jongu „		...	1	...	50	10	100
Village		...	...	...	7	28	...
Jokchen Gomba...		...	1	100	200	400	300
Yulung vil.		...	...	50	16	260	...
Village		...	...	...	10	40	...
Totals ...	...	...	21	195	2068	4283	1885
Lágarkhándo vil.		...	...	...	2	20	...
Durkug „		...	...	...	50	200	...
Dáge Gomba		...	1	...	300	50	1000
Ringo vil.		...	...	...	40	160	...
2 Villages	Rongbacha, 45	...	...	...	12	48	...
Bhiar Gomba		...	1	...	50	10	100
Nena „		...	1	...	35	10	70
Village		...	...	...	5	20	...
Kánzego Gomba		...	1	...	2500	2500	2000
4 Villages		...	...	...	40	160	...
Totals ...	...	...	4	...	3034	3178	3170
Khánsar vil.	Dau, 35	...	...	...	10	40	...
Jior Gomba		...	1	...	30	5	60
Carried over ...	...	...	1	...	40	45	60

POPULATION.

TABLE IV—(Continued).

PLACE	District or Patti and distance in it traversed in miles	Forts	Gombas	Tents	Houses	POPULATION	
						Lay	Lámas & Dábas
Brought forward ...	...	...	1	...	40	45	60
3 Villages		...	...	...	40	160	...
Dau		...	...	...	30	150	...
3 Villages	DAU, 35	...	...	...	15	60	...
Dwinda vil.		...	...	...	25	100	...
3 Villages		...	...	...	20	80	...
Gori vil.		...	...	...	15	60	...
Totals ...	...	...	1	...	185	655	60
Village		...	...	...	10	40	...
Dángo Gomba	DANGO, 25	...	1	...	1000	50	2000
Báthog vil.		...	...	...	15	60	...
Totals ...	...	...	1	...	1025	150	2000
10 Villages		...	...	...	90	360	...
Yáthok vil.		...	...	...	25	100	...
Dathok ,, ...		...	...	...	10	40	...
3 Villages	TAU, 40	...	...	...	30	120	...
Nichong Gomba		...	1	...	600	130	800
5 Villages		...	...	...	65	260	...
Giáro vil.		...	...	...	10	40	...
Totals ...	...	...	1	...	830	1050	800
2 Villages		...	...	...	20	80	...
Khánsar vil.		...	...	...	15	60	...
Gomba		...	1	...	10	5	10
7 Villages		...	...	...	40	160	...
Sháo vil.		...	...	...	15	60	...
3 Villages		...	...	20	20	140	...
Tombadu vil.		...	...	...	10	40	...
Chithog Giachug	MINIA, 100	...	...	...	25	100	...
Dárchendo or Táchiálo ...		...	4	...	1200	11600	400
Cháchukha Giachug		...	...	...	3	12	...
Village		...	...	...	10	40	...
Thicho vil.		...	...	...	15	60	...
6 Villages		...	...	...	30	120	...
Ánya Giachug		...	...	...	30	120	...
Carried over ...	...	...	5	20	1443	12597	410

Table IV—(Continued).

Place	District or Patti and distance in it traversed in miles	Forts	Gombas	Tents	Houses	Population Lay	Lámas & Dábas
Brought forward	...	...	5	20	1443	12597	410
4 Villages	...	...	...	...	25	100	...
Thondo Chiorten	...	...	1	...	8	32	...
7 Villages	...	...	...	...	45	180	...
Golokthok Giachug	Minia, 100	...	...	...	20	80	...
Golokthok vil.	...	...	...	...	20	80	...
2 Villages	...	...	...	...	5	20	...
Kashi Gomba	...	...	1	...	30	10	60
Totals	...	...	7	20	1596	13099	470
Urong Dongu Giachug	...	...	...	...	15	60	...
Village	...	...	...	...	2	8	...
Zíra vil.	...	...	...	...	3	12	...
Village	...	...	...	...	3	12	...
Urongshi vil.	...	...	...	...	10	40	...
2 Villages	Nagchukha, 30	...	...	...	6	24	...
Kharingbo Giachug	...	...	...	...	15	60	...
Village	...	...	...	...	5	20	...
Nagchukha	...	...	...	...	150	600	...
Village	...	...	...	...	10	40	...
Margen Dongu Giachug	...	...	...	...	5	20	...
Totals	...	...	...	...	224	896	...
2 Giachugs	...	...	...	...	8	30	...
Gelok Gomba	...	...	1	...	25	10	50
Golokthok vil.	...	...	...	...	15	60	...
3 Villages	...	...	...	...	12	50	...
Támaráthong Giachug	...	...	...	10	7	60	...
Giachug	...	...	...	10	2	40	...
Hapchukha Giachug	...	...	...	...	10	40	...
Nomad Camps	Lithang, 85	...	...	100	...	300	...
Giachug	...	...	...	...	1	4	...
Lithang (small city)	...	...	1	50	2500	2500	2500
Rito	...	...	1	...	5	5	15
Giachug	...	...	...	...	1	4	...
Jiambothok Giachug	...	...	...	...	4	16	...
Giachug	...	...	...	...	1	4	...
Gáralárcha Giachug	...	...	...	...	3	12	...
Carried over	...	...	3	170	2594	3135	2565

POPULATION.

TABLE IV—(Continued).

PLACE	District or Patti and distance in it traversed in miles	Forts	Gombas	Tents	Houses	POPULATION	
						Lay	Lámas & Dábas
Brought forward ...	...	...	3	170	2594	3135	2565
2 Villages		...	...	...	10	40	...
Ráno vil.		...	...	...	10	40	...
Máne Ringbo	LITHANG, 85	...	...	15	...	45	...
Village		...	...	...	10	40	...
Naida Giachug		...	...	...	10	40	...
Ráthi ,,		...	...	...	5	20	...
Totals ...	...	...	3	185	2639	3360	2565
Táshu Giachug		...	...	...	15	60	...
Nomad Camps		...	...	50	...	150	...
Pángthámo Giachug		...	...	...	5	20	...
Village		...	...	...	2	8	...
Báthang (Chíoti Gomba)		...	1	...	2000	3000	1000
Village	BATHANG, 55	...	...	...	10	40	...
Gomba		...	1	...	15	5	30
5 Villages		...	...	...	35	140	...
Village		...	...	...	10	40	...
Dubána vil.		...	...	...	30	120	...
2 Villages		...	...	...	20	80	...
Totals ...	...	...	2	50	2142	3663	1030
Konzukha Giachug		...	...	...	15	60	...
5 Villages		...	...	...	25	100	...
Giachug		...	...	...	6	24	...
Lhákháng		...	1	...	5	15	5
Village		...	...	...	10	40	...
Lhamdun vil.		...	1	...	20	80	10
3 Villages		...	...	...	30	120	...
Giachug		...	...	...	10	40	...
Phula vil.	MAKHAM, 55	...	...	...	20	80	...
2 Villages		...	...	...	10	40	...
Gárthok or Mákham		...	1	...	700	1000	400
2 Villages		...	...	...	10	40	...
Láo vil.		...	...	...	20	80	...
Gomba		...	1	...	10	4	20
3 Villages		...	...	...	10	40	...
Samba Dukha		...	...	...	5	20	...
Carried over ...	...	...	4	...	906	1783	435

EXPLORATIONS BY A――K IN GREAT TIBET AND MONGOLIA.

TABLE IV—(Continued).

PLACE	District or Patti and distance in it traversed in miles	Forts	Gombas	Tents	Houses	POPULATION	
						Lay	Lámas & Dábas
Brought forward ...	...	...	4	...	906	1783	435
2 Villages		...	...	...	15	60	...
Jio vil.		...	...	...	15	60	...
Jio Gomba	Makham, 55	...	1	...	15	5	30
2 Villages		...	...	...	4	8	...
Cha Chiorten		...	1	...	30	120	2
Gomba		...	1	...	10	4	30
Totals ...	...	...	7	...	995	2040	497
Dáyul vil.	Dayul, 30	...	...	...	15	60	...
Dáyul Gomba		...	1	...	100	100	100
Totals ...	...	...	1	...	115	160	100
Koli vil.		...	...	...	2	8	...
Village		...	...	...	6	24	...
Jior vil.		...	...	...	25	100	...
Jior Gomba		...	1	...	10	2	20
Gomba		...	1	...	5	2	10
Village		...	...	...	15	60	...
Yu vil.	Nuchu Giu, 60	...	...	...	12	48	...
Gomba		...	1	...	15	5	30
Hákha vil.		...	...	...	15	60	...
Ji vil.		...	...	...	15	60	...
2 Villages		...	...	...	3	12	...
No-yu vil.		...	...	...	20	80	...
Niakho ,, ...		...	...	...	15	60	...
Totals ...	...	...	3	...	158	521	60
Rika vil.		...	...	...	6	24	...
3 Villages		...	...	...	10	40	...
Dowa Gomba		...	1	...	25	5	50
3 Villages		...	...	...	20	80	...
Gáwa vil.	Zayul, 162	...	...	...	15	60	...
Chikung ,, ...		...	...	...	4	16	...
Dabla ,, ...		...	...	...	10	40	...
Village		...	...	...	2	8	...
Lhákháng		...	1	...	5	20	1
Carried over ...	...	...	2	...	97	293	51

POPULATION.

TABLE IV—(Continued).

Place	District or Patti and distance in it traversed in miles	Forts	Gombas	Tents	Houses	Population Lay	Population Lámas & Dábas
Brought forward ...	...	...	2	...	97	293	51
2 Villages		...	...	...	4	8	...
Shíkha		...	...	...	25	100	...
Ríma vil.		...	...	...	40	160	...
Village		...	...	...	10	40	...
Duning vil.		...	...	...	15	60	...
Singu „		...	...	...	7	28	...
Sáma „		...	...	...	7	28	...
Dungtang vil.		...	...	...	3	12	...
Salár „		...	...	...	1	4	...
Bonathang „		...	...	...	3	12	...
Thaling „		...	...	...	10	40	...
Tími „		...	...	...	1	4	...
Di „	Zayul, 162	...	...	...	7	28	...
Chiángsi Gomba		...	1	...	7	2	14
Thoyu vil.		...	...	...	3	15	...
Tithong „		...	...	...	3	15	...
Jungu Gomba		...	1	...	8	2	16
Murgu „		...	1	...	10	4	20
2 Villages		...	...	...	3	15	...
Sonling vil.		...	...	...	15	75	...
Isámedh „		...	...	...	1	5	...
Rangyul „		...	...	...	5	25	...
Isátodh „		...	...	...	1	5	...
Modung „		...	...	...	5	25	...
Sugu „		...	...	...	8	40	...
Lasi „		...	...	...	3	15	...
Áta „		...	...	...	7	35	...
Totals ...	...	...	5	...	309	1095	101
Camp		...	...	4	10	12	...
Lhágu vil.		...	...	...	20	80	...
Village	Nagong, 40	...	...	...	10	40	...
Khánsar vil.		...	...	...	1	4	...
Village		...	...	...	5	20	...
Carried over ...	...	...	...	4	46	156	...

TABLE IV—(Continued).

Place	District or Patti and distance in it traversed in miles	Forts	Gombas	Tents	Houses	Population Lay	Lámas & Dábas
Brought forward	...	...	...	4	46	156	...
Nágongjhio		...	1	...	10	40	2
Shiuden Gomba		...	1	...	150	150	100
Village	NAGONG, 40	...	...	...	10	40	...
Ránya vil.		...	...	...	10	40	...
Rahu „		...	...	...	8	32	...
Nankhazod		...	1	...	24	2	1
Totals	...	...	3	4	258	460	103
Goñkha vil.		...	...	...	5	20	...
Village		...	...	...	5	20	...
Dongsar vil.		...	...	...	40	160	...
Au-takpa Gomba		...	1	...	40	10	80
4 Villages	DAINSI, 30	...	...	...	20	80	...
Dángo Gomba		...	1	...	30	10	60
Diu vil.		...	...	...	8	32	...
Village		...	...	...	10	40	...
Buñg-yu vil.		...	...	...	8	32	...
Village		...	...	...	5	20	...
Totals	...	...	2	...	171	424	140
Camp		...	...	5	...	15	...
Tapsing vil.		...	...	...	5	20	...
6 Villages		...	...	...	35	140	...
Baimbu Gomba		...	1	...	15	5	30
4 Villages	PASHU, 50	...	...	...	20	80	...
Rángo		...	...	...	10	40	...
2 Villages		...	...	...	10	40	...
Niopha Gomba		...	1	...	10	5	20
Totals	...	...	2	5	105	345	50
Jiáphug Gomba		...	1	...	60	10	120
Ong „		...	1	...	20	5	40
4 Villages	LHOJONG, 25	...	...	...	20	80	...
Chukpodesa vil.		...	...	...	1	4	...
Lho Jong		1	1	...	150	200	200
7 Villages		...	...	...	30	120	...
Totals	...	1	3	...	281	419	360

POPULATION.

TABLE IV—(Continued).

Place	District or Patti and distance in it traversed in miles	Forts	Gombas	Tents	Houses	Population Lay	Population Lámas & Dábas
Jithog Gomba		...	1	...	200	40	400
3 Villages		...	...	...	15	60	...
2 Gombas	Jithog, 30	...	2	...	30	5	60
Shiobádo vil.		...	1	...	250	800	100
3 Villages		...	...	...	15	60	...
Totals	...	...	4	...	510	965	560
Gomba		...	1	...	10	3	20
Camp		...	...	20	...	80	...
Bari Giachug		...	...	...	4	16	...
Camp		...	...	10	...	40	...
Lháche Gomba		...	1	...	10	5	20
Village		...	...	...	5	20	...
Pemba Gomba	Pemba, 65	...	1	...	100	50	150
5 Villages		...	...	...	25	100	...
Chiákro Gomba		...	1	...	30	10	60
Bárgo "		...	1	...	15	5	30
Urgentámdha Giachug		...	1	...	15	60	5
Village		...	...	...	5	15	...
Totals	...	...	6	30	219	404	285
Namgialgon Giachug		...	1	...	10	40	5
Gomba		...	1	...	25	10	50
2 Villages		...	...	...	10	40	...
Nuldokár Giachug		...	...	...	10	40	...
Arig Gomba		...	1	...	20	5	40
Ji vil.		...	...	...	4	16	...
Áládo Giachug	Arig, 65	...	...	...	7	28	...
Álágák "		...	...	...	2	8	...
Áláchiago "		...	...	...	5	20	...
Camp		...	...	25	...	75	...
Village		...	...	...	5	20	...
Áládochug Giachug		...	...	...	6	24	...
Totals	...	...	3	25	104	326	95
Camp	Lharugo, 55	...	...	15	...	45	...
Cháchukha Giachug		...	...	...	5	20	...
Carried over	...	...	...	15	5	65	...

EXPLORATIONS BY A——K IN GREAT TIBET AND MONGOLIA.

TABLE IV—(Continued).

Place	District or Patti and distance in it traversed in miles	Forts	Gombas	Tents	Houses	Population Lay	Lámas & Dábas
Brought forward	...	...	...	15	5	65	...
Lhárugo Giachug		...	1	...	60	220	20
Archa „	Lharugo, 55	...	1	...	12	30	20
Gole „		...	...	...	3	20	...
Totals	...	...	2	15	80	335	40
Donthog Giachug		...	...	...	7	28	...
Gomba		...	1	...	20	5	40
Village		...	...	...	5	20	...
Laru Giachug		...	1	...	25	50	50
Giámda vil.	Kongbo, 75	...	...	...	300	1500	...
Village		...	...	...	5	25	...
Sángsar Gomba		...	1	...	20	5	40
Gam Giachug		...	...	...	10	50	...
Nimáring Giachug		...	...	...	5	25	...
Totals	...	...	3	...	397	1708	130
Chomoráwa Giachug		...	...	...	10	50	...
Village		...	...	...	5	20	...
Jingcho Gomba		...	1	...	60	50	100
3 Villages		...	...	...	15	60	...
Kánadeba vil.		...	...	...	2	20	...
Hoka Jong		1	...	...	250	600	...
Yáchu vil.		...	...	...	1	5	...
Khátha „		...	...	...	5	25	...
2 Villages		...	...	...	10	40	...
Shíkhár Jong		1	...	...	35	200	...
Zángri Khammedh	Lhokha, 147	...	1	...	20	5	40
Zángri Jong		1	...	...	30	180	...
Daisithí Gomba		...	1	...	40	10	80
Village		...	...	...	5	20	...
Hon-Ngari Thanjang Gomba		...	1	...	200	200	200
Chetáng		1	1	...	1000	4200	800
Niáko Dukha		...	...	...	1	5	...
Chyasa Lhákháng		...	1	...	10	5	20
Gerpa Duga		...	...	...	1	5	...
Dhomda vil.		...	...	...	10	50	...
Dushio „		...	...	...	2	10	...
Carried over	...	4	6	...	1712	5760	1240

POPULATION.

TABLE IV—(Continued).

PLACE	District or Patti and distance in it traversed in miles	Forts	Gombas	Tents	Houses	POPULATION	
						Lay	Lámas & Dábas
Brought forward ...	...	4	6	...	1712	5760	1240
Chinduchoka Gomba		...	...	...	10	65	...
Jiambáling Chiorten		...	1	...	40	10	80
Jera Gomba		...	1	...	150	100	200
Chitishio Jong		1	...	...	1000	5000	...
Dorje-dág Gomba		...	1	...	100	20	200
Taishioñ vil.		...	...	...	5	30	...
Chishio ,, ...		...	...	...	6	36	...
Rá-medh Gomba	LHOKHA, 147	...	1	...	100	20	200
Nianga Lhákháng		...	1	...	5	30	1
Gong-kha Chiorten		...	1	...	200	40	400
Gong-kha Jong		1	1	...	600	2400	100
Lhásang vil.		...	...	...	5	30	...
Kína ,, ...		...	...	...	5	30	...
Jiang-thang vil.		...	...	...	10	60	...
Khambabarji ,, ...		...	...	...	20	120	...
Totals ...	...	6	13	...	3968	13751	2421

April, 1884.

EXPLORATIONS BY A——K IN GREAT TIBET AND MONGOLIA.

TABLE V. *Abstract of Table IV. Population &c., in each District or Patti, within strips about 2 miles wide on either side of and along the routes traversed.*

District	Distance traversed in miles	Forts	Gombas	Tents	Houses	Population Lay	Lámas & Dábas	Average per square mile
Lhása	10	3	13	...	1053	17657	7540	629·9
Phembu	25	1	3	...	135	535	250	7·9
Tálung	10	...	1	...	300	300	300	15·0
Phondu	7	1	1	...	102	460	5	16·6
Reting	12	...	...	50	...	200	...	4·2
Dam	16	...	1	100	3	800	...	12·5
Shangshung	50	...	...	500	...	2000	...	10·0
Nagchukha	45	...	2	3050	102	5902	102	33·4
Jáma	11	...	...	1500	...	3000	...	68·2
Áta	13	...	...	500	...	1000	...	19·2
Yágra	44	...	...	1000	...	2000	...	11·4
Uninhabited tract ...	240	...	...	...	...	...	...	...
Thaichinar...	170	...	...	294	10	770	142	1·3
Khorlu	305	...	...	553	7	1382	276	1·4
Saitu	72	1	...	...	2000	12000	...	41·7
Jún	30	...	...	50	1	130	30	1·3
Bárong	30	...	...	81	10	248	45	2·4
Uninhabited tract ...	105	...	...	...	...	...	...	...
Niamcho	56	...	...	100	50	600	...	2·7
Darge	260	...	21	195	2068	4283	1885	5·9
Rongbácha...	45	...	4	...	3034	3178	3170	35·3
Dan	35	...	1	...	185	655	60	5·1
Dángo	25	...	1	...	1025	150	2000	21·5
Tau	40	...	1	...	830	1050	800	11·6
Minia	100	...	7	20	1596	13099	470	33·9
Nagchukha	30	...	...	...	224	896	...	7·5
Lithang	85	...	3	85	2238	3360	2565	17·4
Báthang	55	...	2	50	2142	3663	1030	21·3
Mákham	55	...	7	...	995	2040	497	11·5
Dáyul	30	...	1	...	115	160	100	2·2
Nuchu Giu	60	...	3	...	158	521	60	2·4
Zayul	162	...	5	...	309	1095	87	1·8
Nagong	40	...	3	4	258	460	103	3·5
Dainsi	30	...	2	...	171	424	140	4·7
Pashu	50	...	2	5	105	345	50	2·0
Lho Jong	25	1	3	...	281	419	360	7·8
Jithog	30	...	4	...	510	965	560	12·7
Pemba	65	...	6	30	219	404	285	2·7
Arig	65	...	3	25	104	326	95	1·6
Lhárugo	55	...	2	15	80	335	40	1·7
Kongbo	75	...	3	...	397	1708	130	6·1
Lhokha	147	6	13	...	3968	13751	2421	27·5
Grand Totals and general average population per square mile.	2815*	13	118	8307	25186	102271	25612	12·9*

* The distance exclusive of uninhabited tracts is 2,470 miles *for which* the average population is 12·9 per square mile within the 4 mile strip.

April, 1884.

VOCABULARY.

Vocabulary of certain words, affixes &c., occurring in the Report.

ABBREVIATIONS.—(*A*) signifies Arabic; (*C*), Chinese; (*H*), Hindi; (*M*), Mongolian; (*P*), Persian; (*S*), Sanskrit; (*T*), Tibetan; (*Tur*), Turki; (*U*), Urdu.

The spelling adopted in the vernacular words is phonetic, and is rendered by the help of vowel sounds as used in the Government Lists.

Where there is a double spelling in this List, the first one, *viz.*, that given without the parenthesis is the same as adopted in the Account; the second one, *viz.*, that within the parenthesis is the correct orthography.

Abra (*T*).	A rat without tail.
Álá (*T*).	Good, excellent; as in Álado, Álágák.
Ambán (*C*).	A governor.
Amur Bhaino (*M*).	Literally "are you in health"? Amur = health and Bhaino = is or are. Mongolian way of salutation.
Arki (*M*).	A kind of spirit distilled from sour milk called Cheka.
Ba or Pa (*T*).	Pertaining to, belonging to; as in Nangba, Chiba, Gúba, Tarjum Pa.
Baimbu or Chiba (Chhiba) (*T*).	One of the two sects into which the Buddhists of Tibet are divided. (See Nangba in this list).
Bam (*T*).	A disease in which red blotches appear on the legs.
Bazár (Bázár) (*P*).	A market.
Beli (*M*).	A chief or ruler higher in rank than a Besi.
Besi (*M*).	A chief or ruler in rank above Jhása.
Bhága (*M*).	Small; as in Bhága Chaidam.
Bhoj (*S*).	A kind of birch.
Bodh Kai (*T*).	One of the three dialects spoken in Tibet; the other two are Doag Kai and Kham Kai.
Bul (*T*).	A kind of soda used in washing, in boiling tea to extract its essence and for other purposes.
Bulág (*M*).	A spring of water; as in Dugbulág.
Cha (Chha) (*T*).	Salt; as in Cha Chu.
Chádámo (*T*).	This side; as in Dungbura Chádámo. (See Nádámo in this list).
Chága (*M*).	An oasis on the borders of a desert.
Chaidam (*M*).	A place of trade or market; as in Bhága Chaidam.
Cháka (Chhákha) (*T*).	A salt mine; as in Chiákta Cháka.
Chángma (*T*).	A species of the willow.
Chángpo or Sángpo* (*T*).	A large river; as in Migi Chángpo.
Chánja (Chhánja) Paulung (*T*).	An old Tibetan silver coin equal in value to about six annas of Indian money.
Che or Chai (*T*).	Above ground; as in Giángche, Chiokche, Chai or Poto La.
Che (Chhe) or Chen (Chhen) (*T*).	Chief, large; as in Chujachen, Rámoche.
Cheka (Chheka) (*M*).	Mare milk rendered acid by the addition of sour milk.
Chen (Chhen) (*M*).	A Mongolian weight equal to about 2 dr. avoir.
Chenkháng (*T*).	Chen = a demon who lives in the air, and kháng = a house. A temple dedicated to Chen.
Chhak (*M*).	A forest tree in Mongolia.
Chhang (*T*).	A description of beer made from a kind of barley called Ne.
Chi† (Chhi) (*T*).	A horse belonging to a great man; as in Chi Pon.
Chi (Chhi) Pon (*T*).	Master of a stable.
Chiák (*T*).	Iron; as in Chiákjamchori.
Chiákla (*T*).	A respectable Tibetan family resident in Dárchendo, who have subordinate jurisdiction over the original inhabitants.
Chiákpo (Chhiákpo) (*T*).	Broken; as in Chiákpori.
Chiánku (*T*).	A wolf.
Chigeb (*T*).	A chief officer who exercises magisterial power as well as collects revenue.
Chhingba (*T*).	A kind of coarse woollen cloth used for making tents. (See Phingba).
Chiomo or Jemo (*T*).	Goddess; as in Chiomo Lhákháng, Jemo-Lha Ri.
Chionga Chiopa (Chhiopa) (*T*).	Chionga = fifteen. Chiopa = to worship, also an earthen figure triangular in form. Chionga Chiopa is a festival observed by Tibetans on the day of the full moon in the first month of their year or about the middle of February.

---

* Sángpo is also the name of the river Nari Chu, and in fact *any large* river may be called Sángpo.
† A horse belonging to a common man is called Ta.

EXPLORATIONS BY A——K IN GREAT TIBET AND MONGOLIA.

Vocabulary—(Continued).

Chiorten (Chhiorten) (*T*).	...	A kind of temple within which images, religious books and other objects of veneration are placed.
Chipi (Chhipi) (*T*).	...	A small quadruped.
Cho (*T*).	...	A deer.
Cho (Chho) (*T*).	...	A lake; as in Namcho, Cho Onbo.
Choga (*Tur*).	...	A loose garment or long overcoat reaching to the feet.
Choi (*T*).	...	A grass which yields yellow color.
Chongju Saiwang (*T*).	...	A festival among Tibetans celebrated a month after the Chionga Chiopa or New Year festival.
Chu (Chhu) (*T*).	...	A stream, a river, or water; as in Di Chu.
Chuchan (Chhuchhan) (*T*).	...	A hot spring; as in Dam Chuchan.
Dába (*T*).	...	A monk, a scholar, a disciple. (See note to the word Gisi in this list).
Dág (*T*).	...	A rock; as in Dág Kárpo.
Dai Pon (*T*).	...	A high military officer.
Dáloi (*C*).	...	Properly chief officer. A commandant of Chinese soldiers who also exercises magisterial authority.
Dam (*T*).	...	A swamp; as in Lingdam.
Dau (*T*).	...	A kind of grain, called kotu (kútu), and phápar or phápra in India.
Demo* (*T*).	...	A brown bear.
Deodar (*S*).	...	A species of the pine.
Dhoto (*T*).	...	A place to which corpses are removed to be cut into pieces and thrown to kites and crows.
Di (*T*).	...	Literally mixed. Confluent streams; as in Di Chu.
Do (*T*).	...	Pair. Junction of two rivers; as in Dárchendo, Kegudo.
Doag Kai (*T*).	...	One of the three dialects spoken in Tibet. (See Bodh Kai and Kham Kai in this list).
Dong (*T*).	...	A wild yák.
Dong or Dongu (*T*).	...	A village; as in Margen Dongu, Urong Dongu.
Dorje Phámo (*T*).	...	The name of a goddess.
Dug (*M*).	...	A Mongolian weight equal to about 1 qr. 4 lbs. avoir.
Dukha (*T*).	...	Du = a boat, and kha = mouth, source. Dukha = a ferry; as in Samba Dukha.
Dungbura (*T*).	...	Dung = shell, and Bura = blown; as in Dungbura Chádámo.
Dunkur† (*T*).	...	A noble, a landlord.
Gang (*T*).	...	Rock, also ice; as in Rinchengang, Áta Gang Lá.
Gar Pon (*T*).	...	The chief of a caravan.
Giachug (*T*).	...	A rest-house for Chinese officials.
Giakháng (*T*).	...	A stage-house for Chinese officers.
Gialbu (*T*).	...	A prince, a chief.
Giáng (*T*).	...	High, *i.e.*, that which can be seen from a distance; as in Giángche.
Gisi or Gibsi‡ (*T*).	...	Literally learned. A degree next above that of Gilong.
Giu (*T*).	...	Neighbourhood, vicinity; as in Nuchu Giu.
Goa (*T*).	...	A chamois.
Gol (*M*).	...	A river; as in Naichi Gol.
Gomba or Gon (*T*).	...	A monastery. Gonchen = a large monastery.
Gur (*H*).	...	A coarse kind of sugar made into cakes or balls of different sizes by boiling cane juice.
Hap (*T*).	...	A mouthful; as in Hapchukha.
Hára (*M*).	...	Black; as in Hára-Núr.
Harmo (*M*).	...	A forest tree and its fruit.
Házo (*T*).	...	A fox.
Hu Hu (*C*).	...	The Mahomedans of China.
Humbu or Ombu (*T & M*).	...	Tamarisk.
Igi (*M*).	...	Large; as in Igi Chaidam.
Jam or Jám (*T*).	...	A bridge; as in Giokjam, Jám Pon.
Jám Pon (*T*).	...	A custodian of bridges in a district.
Jáng (Jiáng) (*T*).	...	Northern; as in Jáng Tálung.
Jhása (*M*).	...	A chief or ruler.
Jhio (*T*).	...	A lord; as in Jhio Sakia Muni, Gárto-jhio.

* There are two kinds of the brown bear in Tibet, one called Chhiugde and the other Mide.

† The chief noble families in Tibet are:—Sandu Photáng, During, Seta, Bhandi Shia, Raga Shia, Lhalu, Yutok and Poti Kháñsa.

‡ The degrees in descending order are those of Láma, Khanpo, Umze, Gisi, Gilong, Gichu, and Dába which last is also a general term applicable to all the inmates of a Gomba. A Gegu is an officer who has the management of a Gomba and who also exercises magisterial power over the inmates except the Láma.

VOCABULARY.

Vocabulary—(Continued).

Jing (M).	A Mongolian weight equal to about 1¼ lbs. avoir.
Jobo or Jopho (T).	The male of cross breed between a bull and a female yák or between a male yák and a cow.
Jomo (T).	The female of cross breed between a bull and a female yák or between a male yák and a cow.
Jong (T).	A fort.
Kacha (H).	Made or built of mud or sun-dried bricks.
Káfila (A).	A caravan.
Kai (T).	A language, dialect.
Káli (H).	The name of a goddess of the Hindus.
Kankar (H).	A kind of limestone. Gravel.
Kar or Kárpo (T).	White; as in Dongkar, Dág Kárpo.
Kauli (C).	A kind of grain.
Kha (T).	Source, mouth, also snow; as in Nagchukha.
Kham Kai (T).	One of the three dialects spoken in Tibet. (See Bodh Kai and Doag Kai in this list).
Kháng or Khán (T).	A house; as in Romkháng, Chenkháng, Khánsar.
Khátág (T).	A thin cloth made of silk or from the bark of a tree.
Khor or Khorlo (T).	Literally a circle. A cylinder used by Tibetans while repeating their prayers.
Khorchen (T).	A large Khor or Khorlo. A temple having a Khorchen or large Khorlo.
Khua (M).	The bank of a river; as in Maurusen Khua.
Khuthul (M).	A pass.
Ki (T).	Source; as in Ki Chu.
Kiáng (T).	A wild ass.
Kiáring Kuring (T).	Irregular; as in Cho Kiáring Kuring.
Kodo* (T).	A small grain known as Mandwa in India.
Koko or Khokho (M).	Blue; as in Khokhosíli, Khokho-Núr.
Kulath (H).	A kind of pulse.
Kurs?	An ingot of silver = about 156 rupees, Indian currency. (See Tamíma in this list).
Kutung (T).	A hollow monument of metal, in shape like a chiorten, raised over the body of a Láma after his death.
Lá (T).	A pass, a hill; as in Nub Gang Lá.
Láma (T).	A high priest or religious teacher in Tibet.
Lámathologa (M).	Round like Láma's head; thologa = head.
Lambardár (U).	The owner or headman of a village or villages who is responsible to Government for payment of revenue.
Len (M).	A Mongolian weight equal to about 1 oz. 5 dr. avoir.
Lhá (T).	A god; as in Lhákháng.
Lhákháng (T).	Lhá = a god, and kháng = a house. A temple.
Lhása (T).	Lhá = a god, and Sa = land. Name of the capital of Tibet.
Lho (T).	South; as in Lhoyul, Lhokha.
Li (Lí) (C).	A measure of length equal to about 390 yards.
Ling (T).	A continent, an island, a division; as in Darjeeling.
Línga (T).	A garden; as in Dabchilinga.
Lung (T).	A valley; as in Khamlung, Tálung.
Ma or Mar (T).	Red; as in Ma Chu, Chu Mar.
Mandwa (H).	A kind of grain.
Máne† Ringbo (T).	Máne = consecrated stone heaps or stone walls. Ringbo = long.
Mantra (S).	A sacred formula.
Masúr (H).	A kind of pulse.
Matar (H).	Pea.
Medh (T).	Lower; as in Pomedh. (See Todh in this list).
Mide (T).	One of the two kinds of the brown bear. (See note under Demo in this list).
Mo (T).	Female, woman. Denotes female sex; as in Lhámo, Phámo.
Molam Chemo (Chhemo) (T).	Molam = prayer, and Chemo = great. The month of asking blessings, i.e., the first month of the Tibetan year.
Muni (S).	A holy man, a saint; as in Jhio Sakia Muni.
Na (T).	A wild goat.
Nádámo (M).	The other side, opposed to Chádámo; as in Dungbura Nádámo.
Nag (T).	Black; as in Nag Chu, Rinag.
Nála (H).	A stream, a rivulet, a watercourse.

---

* A small grain of this very name, but quite different from Mandwa, is raised in India.
† A Khorlo is sometimes called Máne.

EXPLORATIONS BY A——K IN GREAT TIBET AND MONGOLIA.

Vocabulary—(Continued).

Nam (T).	... ...	The sky; as in Namcho.*
Namaga (M).	... ...	A swamp; as in Chákángnamaga.
Namda or Namad (P).	...	A kind of coarse woollen cloth, such as is used in making saddle-pads. Felt.
Náng (T).	... ...	Within the limits of; as in Pena Náng Chu, Chamchunáng.
Nangba† (T).	... ...	One of the two sects of the Buddhists of Tibet.
Nankhazod (T).	... ...	Nankha = heaven, and zod = storehouse. Name of a cave temple.
Ne (T).	... ...	A kind of barley.
Nhambu (T).	... ...	A kind of woollen cloth.
Nhen (T).	... ...	A wild rocky mountain sheep. The Ovis Poli?
Ning (T).	... ...	Heart; as in Cho Ning.
Nub (T).	... ...	West; as in Nub Gang Lá.
Núr (M).	... ...	A lake; as in Hára-Núr, Tengri-Núr.
Obo (M).	... ...	A place of worship where a number of flags or poles with strips of cloth attached are erected.
Onbo (T).	... ...	Blue; as in Cho Onbo.
Paka (H).	... ...	Made or built of burnt bricks or stones.
Padam?	... ...	A kind of fir tree. Pencil cedar?
Palden-Lhámo (T).	...	The name of a goddess.
Patti (H).	... ...	A division.
Pekang (T).	... ...	A kind of mustard.
Phingba (M).	... ...	A kind of coarse woollen cloth used for making tents. (See Chhingba).
Phug (T).	... ...	A cave; as in Riphug.
Pon (T).	... ...	A master; as in Jám Pon.
Pyjama (P).	... ...	Literally a dress for the lower limbs. Trousers, drawers.
Rabdun (T).	... ...	Rab = a ford, and dun = seven; as in Di Chu Rabdun.
Rája (S).	... ...	A king.
Rákshas (S).	... ...	A demon.
Ram (T).	... ...	Indigo; also a kind of grass which yields blue color.
Ri (T).	... ...	A peak, a hill; as in Rinag, Jemo-Lha Ri.
Rigong (T).	... ...	A rabbit.
Ringboche (T).	... ...	A title of dignity with which the Lámas and Gialbus and sometimes gentlemen of ordinary rank are addressed and spoken of.
Rito (T).	... ...	A place of retirement for religious contemplation.
Romkháng (T).	... ...	A cemetery. Ro = a dead body, and kháng = a house.
Rong (T).	... ...	A ravine, a defile, also a warm country; as in Rongbácha, Urong Dongu.
Sakia‡ (T).	... ...	Or Jhio Sakia Muni is the Shakya Muni of India.
Sándo (T).	... ...	A disease among animals in Tibet.
Sang (T).	... ...	Incense; as in Lhásang.
Sange Kuthong (T).	...	Sange = Bodh or Buddha, Ku = image, and thong = 1,000. A sacred place near Saitu.
Sar (T).	... ...	New; as in Khánsar, Dongsar.
Sardár (P).	... ...	A chief or a headman.
Sarson (H).	... ...	A kind of mustard.
Sattu (H).	... ...	Parched grain ground into flour and made into paste.
Shán (T).	... ...	A tree.
Shián-u (T).	... ...	The civil and magisterial officer of a district.
Shiár (T).	... ...	East; as in Shiár Gang Lá.
Shibdag (T).	... ...	The protecting god. Properly the beloved god or the god who is honored and loved in preference to other gods.
Shingcha (T).	... ...	Root of a plant exported to China for coloring silk; also said to be used as medicine in China.
Shio (T).	... ...	On ground; as in Bhánágshio.
Shugshing (T).	... ...	Shug or Shugu = paper, and shing = tree, wood. The bark of a plant used for making paper.
Síga (T).	... ...	A village held as a grant; as in Parisíga.
Taichun (T).	... ...	A kind of pulse.
Tamíma (T).	... ...	An ingot of silver equal to about 156 rupees, Indian currency: the same as Kurs.
Tanka§ (T).	... ...	The name given to Tibetan silver coins.

---

* The Mongolians call it Thíngkari (Tengri) Núr.

† The other sect is called Chiba or Baimbu. Sub-divisions of the Nangba sect are Ningma, Sakia, Gúba and Gilukpa.

‡ Also a sub-division of the Nangba sect of the Buddhists of Tibet. This sub-division takes its name from a large monastery west of Lhása.

§ Compare Tanga Safed of Turkestan equal in value to about four annas, Indian currency. Also the Bengal 'Taka'.

VOCABULARY.

Vocabulary—(Continued).

Tánthu (*C*).	...	Men with white turbans.
Tarjum (*T*).	...	A staging place where officials halt and change horses.
Taru (*T*).	...	A bush and its fruit.
Ten (*M*).	...	A Mongolian weight equal to about 3 cwt. avoir.
Tengri (Thingkari) (*M*).	...	The sky; as in Tengri-Núr.*
Thábu (*M*).	...	Five; as in Thábu Chaidam.
Thain (*C*).	...	Literally the sky. A Chinese officer.
Thang (*T*).	...	A plain; as in Báthang, Lithang.
Thok or Thog (*T*).	...	Roof; as in Donthok.
Todh (*T*).	...	Upper, opposed to Medh; as in Potodh.
Tola (*H*).	...	An Indian weight equal to 180 grains.
Ú (*T*).	...	The middle; as in Ú Cháng.
Uláng (*M*).	...	Red; as in Ulángmiris.
Urd (*H*).	...	A kind of pulse.
Whang (*C*).	...	A chief or ruler higher in rank than Beli.
Yi (*T*).	...	A wild cat.
Yul (*T*).	...	Place, province, country; as in Zayul, Lhoyul.
Zamíndár (*P*).	...	A landholder.

* The Tibetans call it Namcho. (See Nam in this list).

J. B. N. HENNESSEY,

April, 1884. *Offg. Dy. Surveyor General,*

In charge Trigonometrical Surveys.

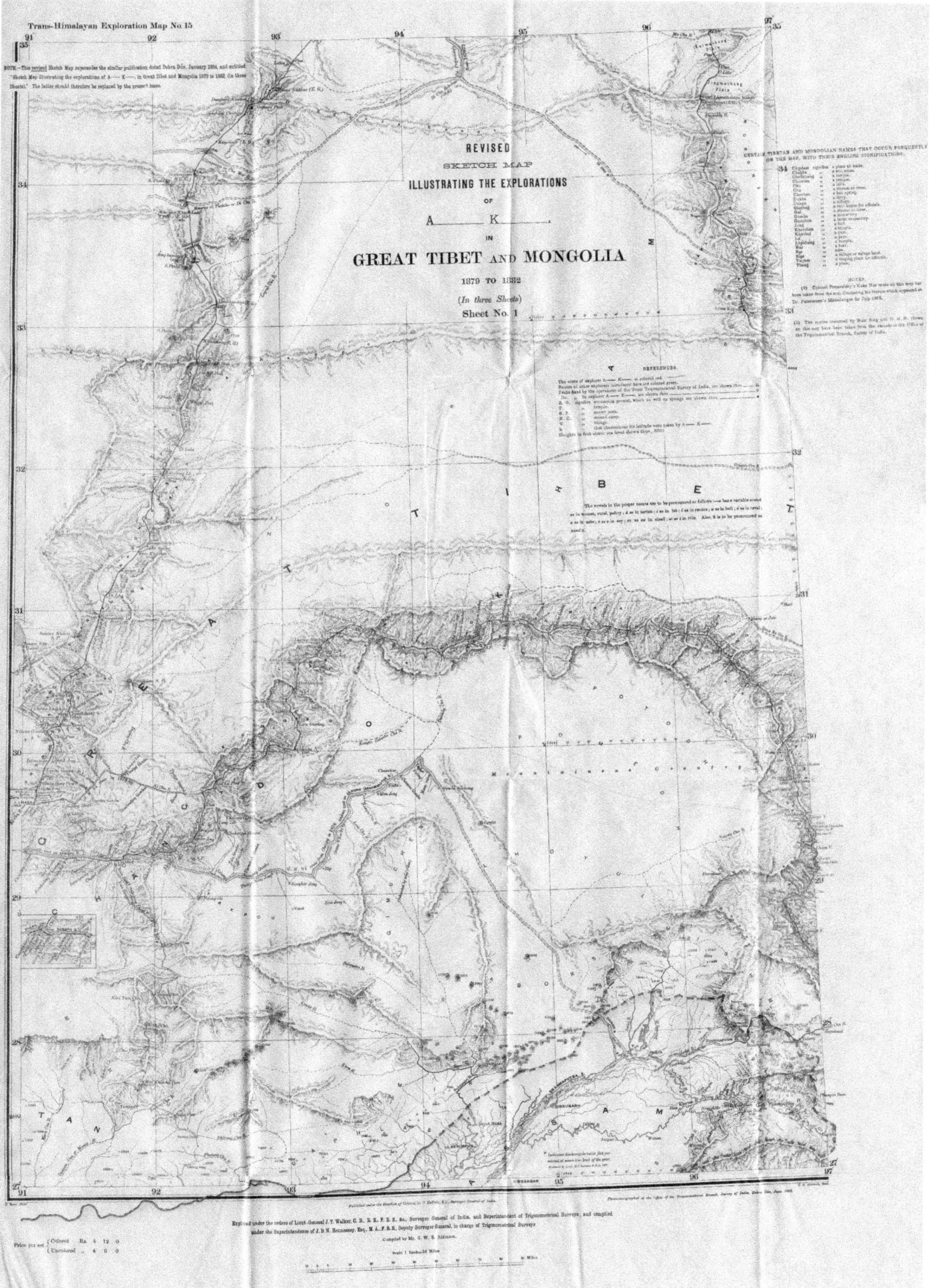

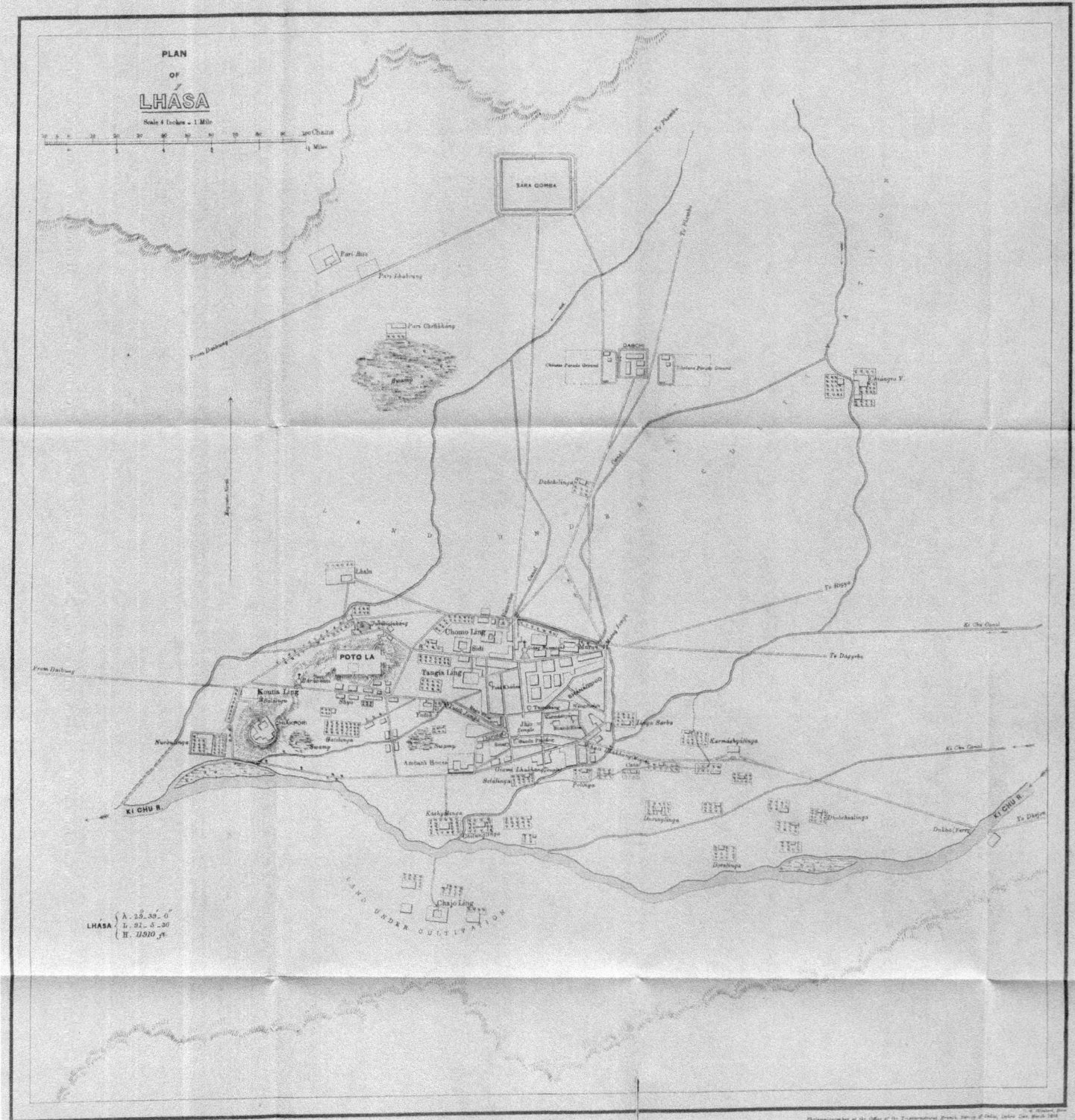

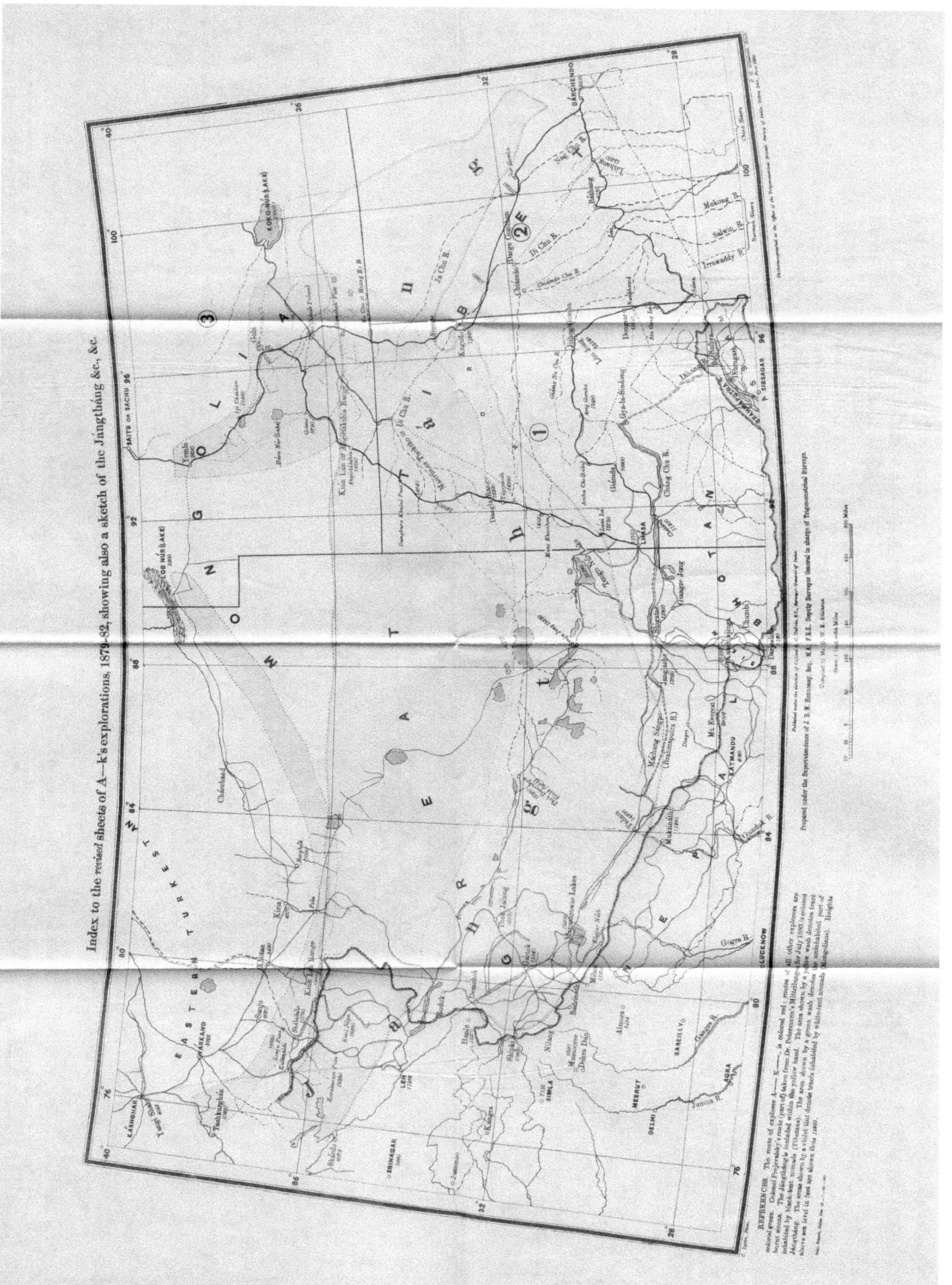

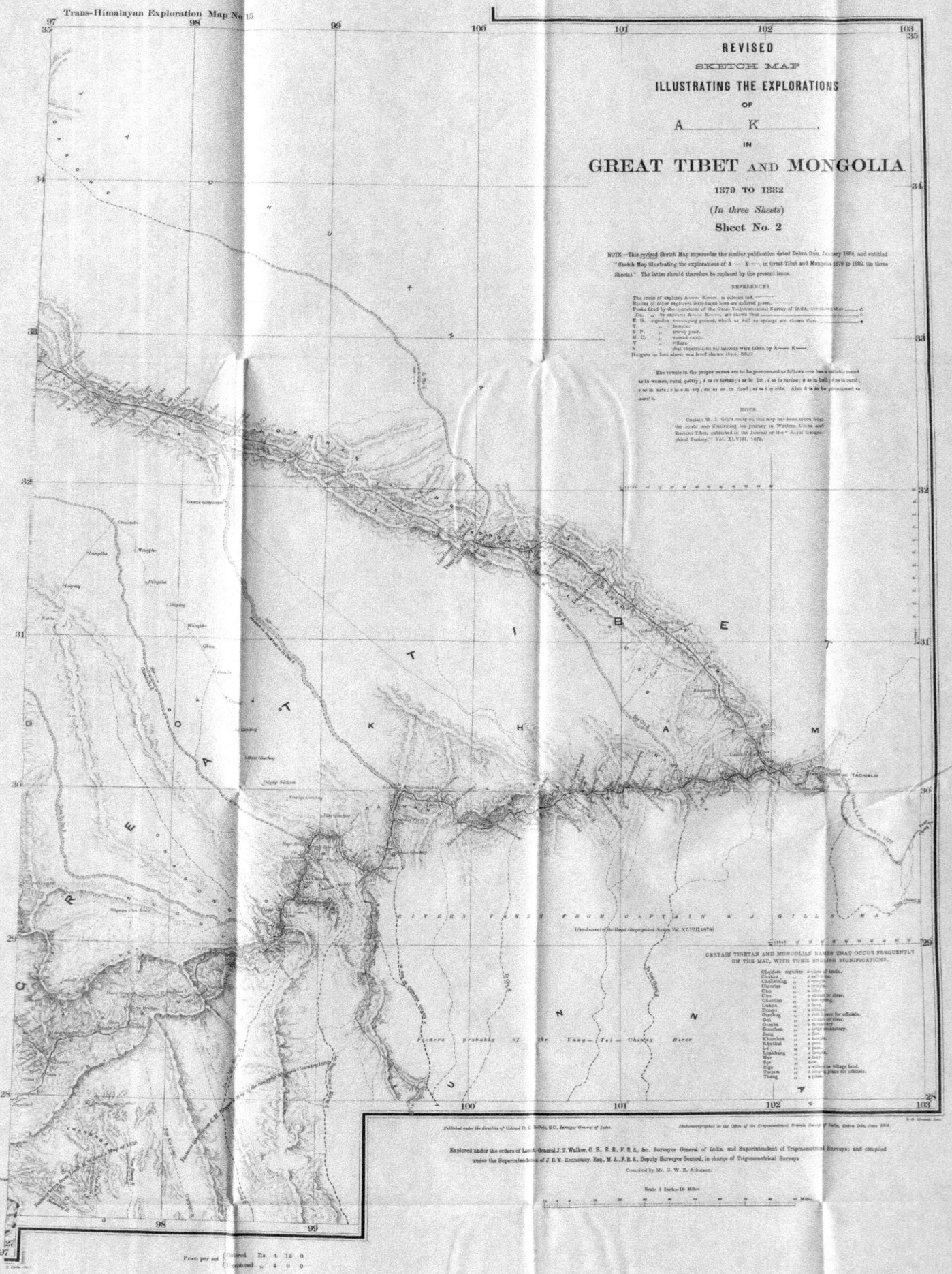

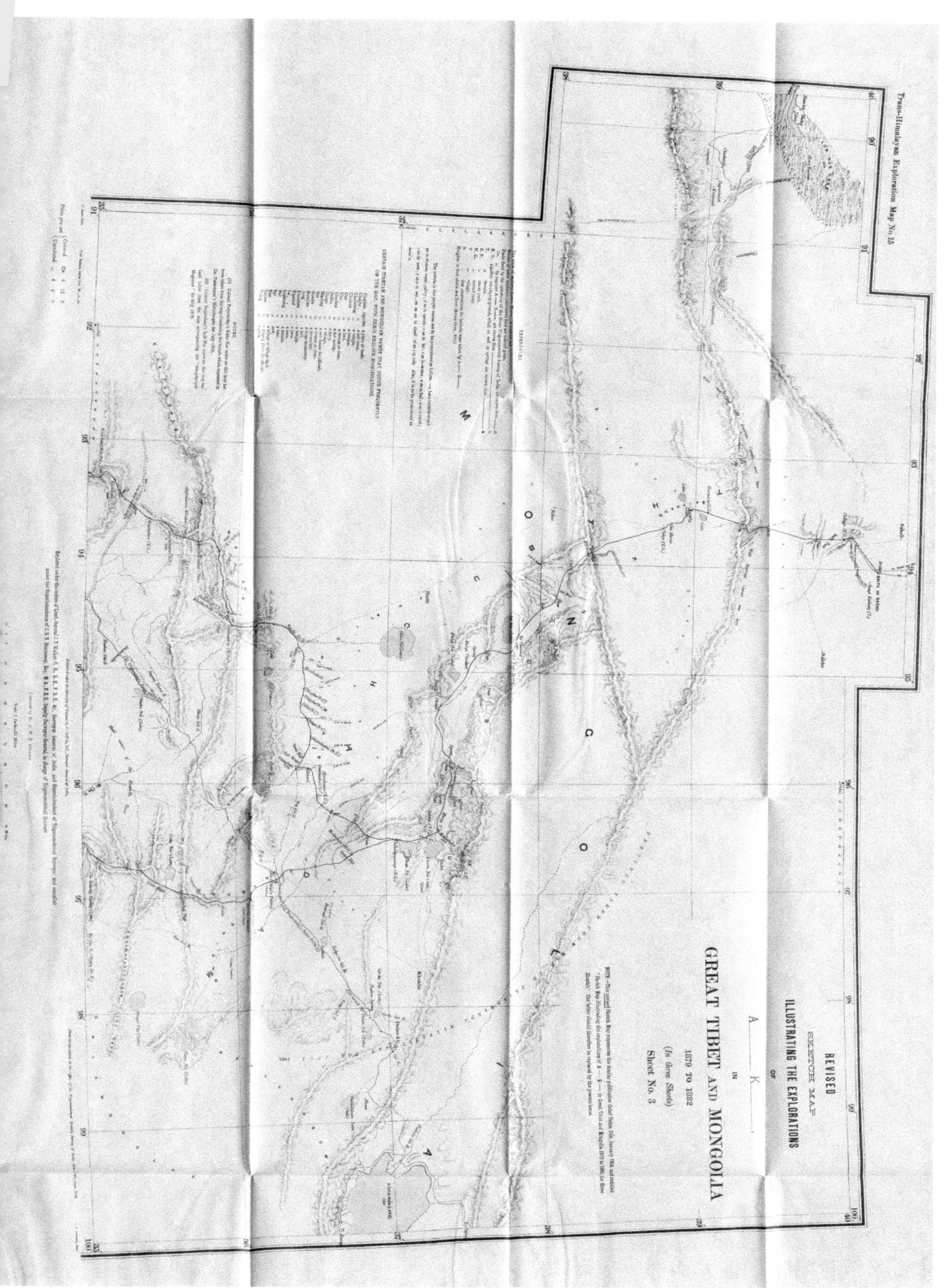